Friendship
and Moral Education

Rethinking Childhood

Joe L. Kincheloe and Janice A. Jipson
General Editors

Vol. 7

PETER LANG
New York • Washington, D.C./Baltimore • Boston
Bern • Frankfurt am Main • Berlin • Vienna • Paris

Ronald F. Reed
and Tony W. Johnson

Friendship
and Moral Education

Twin Pillars of Philosophy
for Children

PETER LANG
New York • Washington, D.C./Baltimore • Boston
Bern • Frankfurt am Main • Berlin • Vienna • Paris

Library of Congress Cataloging-in-Publication Data

Reed, Ronald F.
Friendship and moral education: twin pillars of philosophy for children /
Ronald F. Reed and Tony W. Johnson.
p. cm. — (Rethinking childhood; vol. 7)
Includes bibliographical references and index.
1. Children and philosophy. 2. Philosophy—Study and teaching
(Elementary)—United States. 3. Education—Philosophy.
I. Johnson, Tony W. II. Title. III. Series.
B105.C45R44   108'.3—dc21   98-38610
ISBN 0-8204-3776-X
ISSN 1086-7155

Die Deutsche Bibliothek-CIP-Einheitsaufnahme

Reed, Ronald F.:
Friendship and moral education: twin pillars
of philosophy for children / Ronald F. Reed and Tony W. Johnson.
-New York; Washington, D.C./Baltimore; Boston; Bern;
Frankfurt am Main; Berlin; Vienna; Paris: Lang.
(Rethinking childhood; Vol. 7)
ISBN 0-8204-3776-X

Cover design by Andy Ruggirello

The paper in this book meets the guidelines for permanence and durability
of the Committee on Production Guidelines for Book Longevity
of the Council of Library Resources.

© 1999 Peter Lang Publishing, Inc., New York

Printed in the United States of America

Table of Contents

Preface

Friendship and Moral Education: Twin Pillars of Philosophy for Children represents an attempt to introduce Philosophy for Children to educators and philosophers, while, at the same, teasing out two important components of Philosophy for Children: friendship and morality.

The work is not meant to be complete or definitive. Rather, it is hoped that it will serve as a lens through which readers might get a glimpse of the depth and breadth of the field. Given that glimpse, the reader might use the information presented in the two appendices as instruments leading to a broader understanding of Philosophy for Children.

The authors would like to thank Matthew Lipman, Ann Margaret Sharp, Margaret Oscanyan, Monica Wyfells, Laurence Splitter, and Helmut Schreier for their help and advice.

Christie Murr was responsible for the word processing and was always accurate, on time, and helpful.

Texas Wesleyan Univrsity administrators and fauclty were once again supportive. Appointed as Bebensee University Scholar by President Jake Schrum, I had freedom and time which made the writing of this book possible.

Finally, the authors thank their wives, Fran Johnson and Ann Reed. The book is dedicated to them.

Memorial Preface for Ronald F. Reed

Ronald F. Reed, the primary author of *Friendship and Moral Education: Twin Pillars of Philosophy for Children*, died suddenly and unexpectedly of a heart attack on August 23, 1998. Ron's accomplishments were many in his all too brief 52 years, but, as this work clearly demonstrates, he was just beginning to achieve his potential as a seminal thinker in both education and philosophy.

Ron and I conceptualized this work as a team, but he is responsible for roughly three quarters of it. Though he did not live to see the published copy of this work, Ron was happy and pleased with it. Largely due to his efforts, *Friendship and Moral Education: Twin Pillars of Philosophy for Children* is, in my opinion, the most significant history and analysis of the international movement known as Philosophy for Children published to date. Philosophy for Children is often touted as an outstanding critical thinking skills program, but, as the title suggests and as Ron argues convincingly in the manuscript, it is much, much more than this.

One theme discussed in the book is the languishing of Philosophy for Children in the United States while, simultaneously, its popularity and significance expanded throughout the world. Speaking for Ron as well as myself, it is our hope that this work will contribute to the continued worldwide advancement of this unique blend of education and philosophy and, simultaneously, serve as a stimulus for a vigorous revival of Philosophy for Children in the United States. I can think of no greater legacy for my friend, colleague, and primary author of this work.

Tony W. Johnson

Chapter 1

Philosophy for Children: An Introduction

Philosophy for Children began in the late 1960s, when Matthew Lipman, who at the time was a professor of philosophy at Columbia University, became upset with some fundamental problems. Put into the contemporary language of education, Lipman was upset with a cognitive and an affective problem. The former related to a perceived diminution, supported by declining scores on standardized tests, of American children's ability to reason and to solve problems. The latter problem, a more diffuse and equally upsetting one, was concerned with how children felt about schooling and about the academic endeavor. Stated simply, the longer children were in school, the less they seemed to like and to value it.

At first, Lipman toyed with the idea of writing a story that individual children might chance upon in a library or bookstore and which would model a cooperative community of inquiry with children (almost like an intellectual version of the Peanuts comic strip) and would, in effect, invite children into the fictional world, giving them a place where they would practice and hone the art and craft of thinking.[1]

Over the course of the next few years (1970–1974) as Lipman tested his novel, now known as *Harry Stottlemeier's Discovery*, in schools around the Columbia campus, that idea was modified and expanded. The quality of happenstance—the individual child stumbling over the volume on a library shelf—was jettisoned. In its place, especially as Lipman left Columbia in 1972 and moved to Montclair State College in New Jersey, and with Dr. Ann Margaret Sharp, formed the Institute for the Advancement of Philosophy for Children (I.A.P.C.), came the notion that *Harry Stottlemeier's Discovery* would be the first element in a conscious process of reforming and restructuring the educational enterprise.

Between 1973 and 1988, six more programs were constructed by Lipman and his associates at I.A.P.C. *Elfie,* for grades K through 2, concentrates on the making of distinctions, connections, and comparisons within the context of a variety of broad philosophical issues. Two programs were constructed for grades 3 and 4. *Pixie* concentrates on analogical reasoning skills and philosophy of language, and *Kio and Gus* emphasizes practice in a variety of reasoning skills that prepare children to investigate nature. *Lisa* (for grades 7 and 8) focuses on ethical inquiry, *Suki* (for grades 9 and 10) on aesthetics inquiry, and *Mark* (for grades 11 and 12) on social and political inquiry.

At this point, Philosophy for Children is being taught in some five thousand schools in the United States. The program has been translated into eighteen languages, and there are Philosophy for Children Centers throughout the United States and in Chile, Costa Rica, Brazil, Mexico, Nigeria, Spain, Portugal, Guatemala, Iceland, Denmark, Canada, Austria, Australia, and Taiwan. Experimental research in the United States and in many of the countries cited above has demonstrated that children exposed to philosophy by well-prepared teachers gain significantly in reasoning, reading comprehension, and mathematical performance.

There has been, then, a quiet—if explosions can be quiet—explosion in Philosophy for Children over the course of two decades. Philosophy for Children is no longer the creation of one person. It has been changed, expanded, restructured, and transformed as it has passed through different hands and different cultures. Philosophy for Children, today, may be a family of practices and practitioners, but as in the case with many large families, individual members may not even be recognizable to others. The rest of this chapter will be devoted to examining Philosophy for Children practice as it emerged during the period 1974–1987. In a later chapter, we will look at Philosophy for Children, 1988 to the present.

It is important to think carefully about *Harry Stottlemeir's Discovery.* Like a first child, it tells much about the parent's intentions, and it tells much about both what Philosophy for Children is and what it was meant to be.

Harry is a ninety-six page novel written for twelve-year-olds. It details the adventures, intellectual and otherwise, of a group of children who inquire into a host of philosophical and logical issues—issues like the nature of fairness, the mind-body problem, personal identity, logical relationships, sentence conversion, and so on. In effect, it "contains" the issues and problems that typically appear in a freshman introduction to philosophy course, along with a smattering of formal and informal logic.

The assumption behind *Harry* is that philosophy is a significant pedagogical tool, and that if one could find a way to introduce (or to reintroduce) philosophy into the curriculum one would be on the way to significant educational reform.

What Lipman noticed—and what it may be assumed educators in countries like France, Spain, and Denmark, where philosophy is part of the school's curriculum noticed—is that there is a similarity in terms of structure and content between the questions young children, especially very young children, ask and those that are asked by mature philosophers. The idea then is to make this similarity work, to provide an instrument whereby the child's interest in the typical problems of philosophy could be tapped. And that, the compendium of philosophical issues along with a built-in (built into the novel) model of children cooperatively inquiring about those issues, a model that could be emulated by real-life children, is what *Harry Stottlemeier's Discovery* represents.

That which differentiates *Harry* (we will let *Harry* stand for the I.A.P.C. way, circa 1974–1987, of doing Philosophy for Children) from the novels presented in Germany and Spain include the following: (1) *Harry* is aimed at a younger audience than European schooling addresses. In Germany and Spain, philosophy is packed into secondary school curriculum, with adolescents typically getting their first exposure to the tradition around the age of fourteen or so. Even at its inception, Philosophy for Children began to achieve some success and once it was in a position to begin testing standard Piagetian claims regarding young children's ability to reason abstractly, the curriculum was quickly extended to the youngest of the school-age population so that by 1987, even kindergartners were being exposed to philosophy.

(2) *Harry* attempts to provide an avenue whereby children can be connected to the traditional problems of philosophy, but it does this in a decidedly ahistorical way. Where school-age philosophy on the continent involves learning about the systems of, for example, Kant and Hegel, and seeing how those two philosophers react to the Cartesian program that is known as Modernism, children in Philosophy for Children are not introduced to the great names and systems of the tradition. Rather, the attempt is made to put them in a position where

they act as philosophers instead of learning about philosophers. The attempt is to get them to do philosophy. In the course of that doing, some of them may act as David Hume did, while others might take a less empirical, more rationalistic stance. The history of philosophy is frequently replicated in a Philosophy for Children classroom, but that replication in many ways is accidental to the inquiry. Perhaps more precisely, that replication emerges from the process of inquiry in the same way that Hume's response to the problem of other minds emerged from his inquiry.

(3) *Harry* is an explicit attack on standard philosophical jargon and terminology. The continental assumption, and it may be pointed out, the assumption behind most traditional college philosophy courses and philosophy texts in the United States, is that in order to do philosophy one must first have mastered a rather extensive and esoteric vocabulary. Lipman assumed that it was possible to take the typical problems of philosophy, divest them of their forbidding terminology, and embed them in a story—*Harry Stottlemeier's Discovery*—where they could be discovered by attentive readers and students.

So, Philosophy for Children—and keep in mind we are looking at Philosophy for Children, circa 1974–1987, in what might be called an "homogenous" state, a state where there was far more agreement than there is today—begins with a philosophically rich text. That text contains a series of gems, a series of interesting, important philosophical problems. It does not follow that teachers should be in the business of leading the children to discover now this gem, and now that one. What is important to remember is that *Harry*, this coherent whole, this narrative, is an exercise in philosophy. The task then, once one begins with this narrative, is how to unpack it and enable it to yield what it contains.

Ultimately, Philosophy for Children is about that which is typically the most private of events, that is, thinking, and most explicitly the improvement and enhancement of the child's ability to think. Since that which is "private" is inaccessible to direct contact, one has to find indirect means to reach it. This happens most obviously at the beginning of a typical Philosophy for Children session. Each child, or perhaps each couple or trio of children, has a copy of *Harry*. The children, in the best of all educational worlds, are sitting in a circle where they can see each other. The session begins with a child reading a paragraph of *Harry* aloud. The next child picks up where the previous child has finished, continuing to read aloud. The process continues around the circle until a chapter—typically four or five pages—has been read. The reading, and depending on the skill level of the readers, it may be a rather long and, at times, labored reading, allows individual children to personalize the text by bringing their inflections and their emphasis to individual paragraphs. It allows their (private) thoughts to determine what will be stressed and what will receive most attention. At the same time, however, the community is looking at one, shared text and hearing, and sharing, a series of different verbal interpretations of the text. The reading, if it goes well, if it is more than a simple preamble to the talk which comes next, serves as a bridge between the public and private. It brings the child out of herself/himself, gives the child something to do, that is, read a text so that the child does not have, as it were, to make thought out of whole cloth, but is respectful of, indeed dependent on, that which is most personal to the child, that which the child determines to be worth stressing in the reading.

When the reading is complete, the teacher asks a deceptively simple question or family of questions. That question or questions, combined with the existence of the text, provides a ready way to place Philosophy for Children within the political-educational spectrum that has developed in the United States. Where the radical teacher on the far left might be said to rely exclusively on student interest (one thinks here of Neil Postman and Charles Weingartner's classic educational text of the 1960s, *Teaching as a Subversive Activity*), while her/his more conservative colleague on the far right might be said to ignore interest and focus on a pre-existing curriculum that all students must know regardless of their feelings about it, Philosophy for Children, steers a middle ground. The question asked by the Philosophy for Children teacher relies on interest in the text. The teacher says, in effect, "What did you find interesting in the chapter we have just read? What do you want to talk about? What do you find curious, problematic, and so on about the chapter?" The discovery of interest is necessary for the process to continue, but, it should be pointed out, even though the questions that the children have about the text may be very free-form, unpredicted and unpredictable, bizarre, or tangentially related to the text, the discovery that is being attempted is *about* or *into* the text. One starts with the text (in this case, *Harry*), and it is the text that provides a coherent whole, a meaningful starting point from which students may develop their own interests.

Before we go too much further into our fictional lesson, it may be helpful to remind ourselves that "interest," though it is a term bandied about in educational circles, is a highly complex, rich, multi-layered word. In *Democracy and Education,* John Dewey toyed with some of those layers and discovered three significant meanings of interest, all of which, according to Dewey, should be taken into consideration by educators as they go about the task of working with their students.[2] Interest may be conceived of as a mere liking or simple statement of preference. Thus when I say I am more interested in baseball than ballet, I am telling you that I like baseball better than ballet and, all things being equal, I would prefer attending a game rather than a performance. Dewey also points out that interest may be thought of as a quality existing in an object or subject matter. So, just as one may ascribe hardness to this desk and glossiness to that magazine cover, one may say of certain other objects or subject matters that they are inherently interesting. Thus, one may say that art history is interesting while accounting is dull. When one says this one is doing more than simply stating a preference. One is attempting to describe the subject matter. Finally, according to Dewey, when one talks of interest, one may be talking about the connection or relationship that ties or binds a person with an object or subject matter. To say, for example, that Mary has a legal interest in this piece of property is to suggest that she is related to the property in ways in which those of us who do not have a legal interest in it are not related to the piece of property.

To repeat, when the Philosophy for Children teacher asks the deceptively simple question: "What do you find interesting about *Harry*?", not only is she/he defining Philosophy for Children's place in the political-educational spectrum, she/he is asking a rich and evocative question, a question which practice has shown generates all sorts of possibilities.

Now, let us continue on with our fictional lesson. A reading has been completed, and the teacher asks what the children find interesting in the chapter. The next step is to record the children's responses. Let us suppose that the children have ten questions about the chapter. Let us further suppose that the questions fall into more or less natural categories. Some questions are about the logical rules ("if you take a true all-sentence and reverse it, it will become false") that are discovered in chapter one. Others are what one might call more philosophical, that is, what does it mean to discover a logical rule or, stated another way, are logical rules discovered or invented? Others are clearly psychological, namely, why was Harry so embarrassed in class, and why did he trust Lisa and not someone else to help him out of his difficulty? Still others are about the author's intentions—why did Matthew Lipman write this story? Do the names of the characters mean anything? Is it significant that part of Harry Stottlemeier's name sounds a lot like Aristotle?

At this point, a decision has to be made. Which question or group of questions should we deal with now, in this class? In this chapter we do not have to make that decision, but we can point to some of the factors that weigh on the decision, that generate the decision, or that could be taken into account in order to make the decision most productive.

Sometimes, one question forces itself on the community. The list of questions is read and, almost by unspoken consensus, it becomes clear that this question and not some other is the one with which to begin. Other times it seems natural to start with the first question, while in other cases the gestalt that emerges when soliciting questions determines that the last question asked will be the first question with which we deal. Sometimes the class may vote and let majority rule decide the issue. Still in other cases, it may happen that the teacher takes a somewhat more directive role and suggests to the class, since all of the questions are of interest to at least some of the members of the community, that it may prove helpful to start with this question and not some other. The reasons that may support this suggestion (and note, we are talking about a suggestion and not a command) include the following: (1) the amount of time remaining in the class period. Philosophy for Children, unlike, say a Madeline Hunter-like program, does not demand "closure" for individual lessons. People involved in Philosophy for Children quickly come to the realization that thought and the process of inquiry proceed according to its own dynamic and one cannot, without damage, fit it into neat, prepackaged parcels. Still, the experienced Philosophy for Children teacher will realize that certain discussions, development of questions, exercises, and so on are better suited to some time periods than others. If, for example, there are fifteen minutes remaining in the classroom period, the teacher may suggest that the class deal with a question it can handle during that time frame rather than a more ambitious one. She/he may suggest the development of a textual question ("Who did what to whom?") rather than a more open-ended one.

(2) The teacher's knowledge of previous classes and previous discussions. In one sense, each class, each discussion is unique. Only a dull teacher would think that previous experiences with other groups

should generate or determine what is done with this group. Still, teachers who *have* experience with Philosophy for Children with other groups can learn things that are transferable from one group to the other. For example, she/he may find that starting with one question or one type of question at a certain time in the community's development may typically yield the highest payoff. On the basis of that experience, she/he may suggest (and not command) a starting point to the class.

(3) The teacher's knowledge of the present class and its recent history. Philosophy for Children classes go through the same sorts of growth spurts and pains as do other groups. Sometimes, for example, as the community matures, it tends to focus on one sort of problem. It may, continuing the example, constantly deal with ethical problems and ignore problems of formal logic. When that happens, the teacher may find it appropriate to suggest starting with a problem of logic—assuming that such a question has been raised as one of those of interest to some member of the community. The teacher, borrowing a term from Neil Postman, has a "thermostatic" function. Her/his task is to monitor the discussions that takes place and make sure they become neither too hot nor too cold. Stated another way, it is possible to go overboard on one type of issue, and ignore others. When this happens the teacher can counterbalance things by suggesting this point and not some other.

(4) The teacher's knowledge of the novel, the teacher's manual, and the history of philosophy. *Harry* and all of the novels in the traditional (Lipman) corpus come along with two things—a manual filled with discussion plans and exercises that are meant to open up each chapter and facilitate discussion of the issues contained in each chapter, and some training, both graduate and undergraduate, in the history of philosophy and the pedagogy of Philosophy for Children. When, after reading a chapter, one solicits questions from the class, when one asks, then, what they find interesting and what they would like to talk about in the chapter, one is setting an agenda. Typically, in the case of *Harry,* the chapter's agenda, assuming that the class meets twice a week, fifty minutes per session, will be played out over a five to six week period. It should be remembered, however, that even when the agenda is saved, on butcher-block paper or in students' notebooks, it frequently happens that the agenda develops and changes as the community begins discussing things. In the messy real world of classroom discussions, issues of interest frequently become pushed aside or pushed

so far down the agenda that they never get discussed. This is not a glaring problem for many of the issues in *Harry*. If agenda item A in chapter one is overlooked, it will recur in chapter three and nine and fourteen. There is still ample opportunity to deal with it. Other items, however, are different. For instance, many of the logical rules are introduced and discussed in single chapters. Thus, if the class does not talk about symmetrical relationships at this point in *Harry*, it will not get another opportunity. Moreover, to the extent that one logical operation is essential to the next, if the class does not talk about the former it will not be able to discuss the latter. Now, to make judgments like that the teacher has to be very knowledgeable about the text, the novel, and the tradition. Given that knowledge, the teacher should make some suggestions about the starting point of the agenda.

Imagine for a moment a person almost totally unfamiliar with Philosophy for Children. The person's only exposure to the subject has come in the first part of this chapter. There she/he has been told something about Matthew Lipman and Philosophy for Children. Our observer knows that given the "homogeneous" tradition (1974–1987), one begins with a philosophic text expressly written for the purpose of generating discussions, the class reads aloud from a chapter from the text, the teacher gathers questions of interest from the class about the text which generates an agenda for discussion, and then some decision-making procedure is utilized to determine where to start. At this point, then, things are fairly straightforward. Now, however, our observer may begin to experience some difficulties, especially if she/he is the sort of person who likes to have nice, precise directions, because the next thing that occurs is that the community "simply" talks about the question. In order to help our observer, to help her/him deal with the perceived "vagueness" of this step, we will do two things: look at different ways or different models of understanding what Philosophy for Children talk is, and remind ourselves of the nature of thinking that is presupposed by the traditional Philosophy for Children materials (*Harry*, especially) and that emerges from talk with students in a Philosophy for Children setting.

Those with a conventional background in philosophy (an undergraduate course in philosophy) tend to look at Philosophy for Children and suppose that things are fairly straightforward, that is, teachers have been admonished to emulate the character and style of Socrates and what they are trying to do is to engage their students in a "Socratic" dialogue.

Rosalyn Sherman Lessing was not the first to notice that there is a problem with the admonition to teach Socratically, but she is one of the clearest critics of that admonition.[3] Simply put, a negative definition of Socratic teaching, which is defined as "not lecturing," will be of little pedagogical use to the prospective teacher. In a similar vein, to suggest that one exhausts the definition of Socratic teaching by means of a stipulation that the Socratic teacher asks questions is to ignore the fact that Socrates asked many different sorts of questions for many different sorts of reasons. If one is to be in a position to emulate the behavior of Socrates, especially as it relates to questioning, one must first have a feel for the variety of contexts in which those questions were posed.

To become sensitive to those contexts is to learn, quickly and forcefully, that there is more than one "Socrates" to imitate. The callow youth one meets in the *Paramenides* asks questions that cause Socrates a good deal of discomfort not to mention throwing suspicion on the entire Theory of the Forms. On the other hand, the mature Socrates we encounter in the *Meno* uses questions to lead the slave boy to a series of "correct" answers that, not coincidentally, lends support to a Platonic doctrine of the recollection of knowledge.

The problem, then, is that discovery in Plato will differ from dialogue to dialogue and that if we are to choose among the discoveries, if we are to figure which one to imitate, we must have some criteria in place to make that choice. Presumably, those criteria will be related to the educative worth of the conversation. If that is the case, however, the use of Socrates as a model will be merely heuristic, and we would be as well served by simply listing those criteria. The same, of course, might be said of any existing models that are recommended—that is, in order to recommend them, we must have some criteria in mind.

The difficulty alluded to here was not lost on teacher education in Philosophy for Children during the period in question (1974–1987). It was recognized that at the heart of Philosophy for Children practice was something incredibly vague and hard to define. At the heart of the practice was an admonition, variously stated as, "talk with children," "engage them in dialogue or conversation or in a philosophical discussion," or, most open-ended, "do philosophy with children." Those commands had some cognitive context, but it was not easy to put it into words or reduce it to a neat formula. Instead, "philosophic talk" was modelled over and over again in the education of the prospective Philosophy for Children teacher. At institutions like Montclair State

College's Institute for the Advancement of Philosophy for Children and, from 1979, Texas Wesleyan's Analytic Teaching Center, teachers were immersed in Philosophy for Children practice. I.A.P.C. ran residential workshops, where teachers would meet for three week periods in the summer and read and discuss, say, *Harry Stottlemeier's Discovery* and one or two of the other Lipman novels. The sessions, typically lasting ten hours a day and running six days a week, showed teachers what worked and what did not work, what were the pitfalls and what were the benefits of the talk that was being recommended. Those sessions, led by Lipman and Sharp, and later by people trained by Lipman and Sharp, made virtually no mention of theory and or pedagogy. The belief, and it was pragmatic both in the ordinary sense and the philosophic sense, was that we would learn by doing, and that theoretical and pedagogical questions would be answered by practice.[4]

Still, prior to practice, prospective teachers demanded some sort of theoretical underpinning to the practice. That was provided in large part by four dominant images that Lipman propounded in training sessions during this period. The images were not meant to substitute for practice but were meant to give the teacher a sort of rough glimpse that practice with adults, and later with children, would refine.

The first image, borrowed from psychology, suggested that every discussion and every inquiry had its own specific "gestalt." It had a pattern or texture and was leading in a specific direction. The task of the facilitator of the discussion (the teacher) was to help the community discover the "gestalt" implicit in the discussion and then to encourage the students to follow the inquiry where it led.

Another image, closely aligned with the preceding, was that the teacher "facing" the discussion was like a sculptor staring at a block of marble, trying to find the statue hidden in the marble. Just as different blocks of marble would yield different statues, so too different discussions would yield different disclosures. The teacher-sculptor's task was to discover that which was hidden.

A third image was that of the teacher as a sort of conductor of a large and varied orchestra. The conductor is faced with a number of different instruments, each with its own strengths, weaknesses, and limitations. In addition she/he has a score, a piece of music that is to be played. Her/his task is to get the orchestra members to work together so that they can make the music that is represented by the markings on the page.

Finally, the teacher was seen as the captain of a sailing ship. Straight-ahead was the port, but the wind was blowing against the ship. The ship must "tack" now to the left, and now to the right in order to get to the port. The teacher in a Philosophy for Children discussion was like that captain, "nudging" the conversation, now to the left, and now to the right in order to bring it to the port that was its conclusion.[5]

There are a few things that permeate the four images and that tell a good deal about Philosophy for Children practice. The first is that each image (the psychologist, the sculptor, the conductor, the ship's captain), in varying degrees, presents a model that blends craft with art. Each field has its own canons, techniques, and each, at times, uses its own algorithmic decision-making procedures. One can, and at times one must, "do" psychology, sculpture, music, and sailing in a mechanical fashion. There are times when it is reasonable to simply follow the rules.

There are times, however, when a slavish following of the rules would be antithetical to good decision-making, when one must be more artful than craftlike. Paraphrasing G.E. Moore's famous saying, one should proceed by a step-by-step procedure until one is forced to leap. Then one should jump.

To recapitulate, each image suggests a complex model of the Philosophy for Children teacher. The teacher's practice will be informed by knowledge of the rules of her/his craft, but it will not be completely determined by the rules. Stated another way, complete knowledge of the rules (whatever they may be) will not enable an observer to predict with complete accuracy the teacher's behavior. The images are all antireductionist in the sense that while they all recognize the importance of mechanics, they refuse to equate leading a Philosophy for Children discussion with those mechanics.

The other thing that is worth noting is that while the student's interest determines what is originally talked about, there is more involved in a Philosophy for Children discussion than the more-or-less random following of interest. Just as, to deal with one of the images, the conductor has to be cognizant of the score and get the musicians to follow it, the teacher has to bring the students back to the discussion. That means, of course, that the teacher will have to monitor comments for relevance and, when necessary, gently bring the students back to the topic at hand.

There is one final thing to do in this chapter and that is to remind ourselves of the complexity of thinking that is presupposed by *Harry*.

Philosophy for Children is often mistakenly called a "thinking-skills" program. Especially when people become aware of the formal logic component of *Harry*, they assume that by teaching children some rules of reasoning, the assumption is being made that thinking is being reduced to a set of skills, like bicycle riding or needlepoint, that can be improved by drill and repetition. A quick glance at *Harry* and at the manual *(Philosophical Inquiry)* that accompanies *Harry* should be sufficient to show that that assumption is not justified. In *Harry*, every time that a logical rule is learned it comes with a caveat attached, almost like the warning on a package of cigarettes. Consider, for example, this exchange that occurs early on in *Harry*:

> "I mean," said Harry, "your father said, 'All engineers are good in math,' right? But that's one of those sentences which can't be turned around. So it doesn't follow that all people who're good in math are engineers. And I'm sure that's so. I'm sure that there are lots of doctors who're good in math, and airplane pilots who're good in math, and all sorts of other people who aren't engineers who're good in math. So it doesn't follow that just because you're good in math, you have to be an engineer!"
>
> Tony said, "That's right!" Even if its true that *all* engineers are good in math, it doesn't follow that only engineers are good in math." He stood up, gave Harry a snappy salute, and raced off home.
>
> Harry decided to try the monkey bars a while before going home. He had a feeling that Tony's father wouldn't be too much impressed with Tony's new argument. But at least he'd gotten Tony to see that the idea had some use. With that thought Harry put the matter out of his mind, and tried a new trick on the jungle gym.[6]

Consider also that Lisa, the character who may be most directly responsible for the development of the formal logic in *Harry*, is perhaps the least analytical, the least methodological, the most intuitive character in the book. Indeed, by the end of the book, Lisa has serious doubts about any attempt to reduce thinking to a set of mechanical skills.

The point, then, that becomes clear when one looks at the traditional corpus (Lipman's novels) along with the manuals that accompany them, and when one recalls the style and the extent of education in Philosophy for Children 1974–1987, is that thinking itself is complex. Anticipating the current fascination with multiple intelligences, Lipman recognized the fact that there was no such thing as intelligence defined as a single quality of mind which could be enhanced by a single methodology. Thinking, from the inception of Philosophy for

Children was conceived of as having cognitive, affective, visual, mechanical, intuitive, aesthetic, ethical, and logical characteristics. To enhance thinking, in effect, was to attempt to deal with *all* of those qualities.

Complex problems, in this case the enhancement of thinking, do not always generate complex solutions. In this case, however, they did. What was required was a philosophically rich text that could be discussed in philosophically rich and provocative ways. The next two chapters will deal with some of the philosophy behind Philosophy for Children.

Before, however, moving into that chapter, it may prove helpful to correct possible misrepresentations.

We have been talking of an historical period (1974–87) which we have labeled "homogeneous." That label has been affixed to the period in order to distinguish it from that which would come later. The period, of course, is more complex than the label suggests. Even though there was less diversity in material and practice during this period than the subsequent one, Philosophy for Children has never been monolithic, and has always reflected, especially during this time period, the work of Ann Margaret Sharp, Frederick Oscanyan, and Gareth Matthews.

Matthew Lipman, justly, is identified with Philosophy for Children. He is the author of all the novels within the traditional corpus (1974–87) and, to a large extent, Philosophy for Children is his idea. Still, it would be a mistake to ignore the contributions of two of Lipman's co-authors and/or co-editors—Ann Margaret Sharp and the late Frederick Oscanyan—along with those of Gareth Matthews.

Sharp met Lipman in 1973 after he moved from Columbia and took up residency at Montclair State College. Lipman's interest were in philosophy, specifically aesthetics, and were grounded in both a continental and a British-American tradition. Sharp, at the time, was a brand-new assistant professor of education with interests in philosophy of education, South American history and culture, and the writings of Frederick Nietzsche and Simone Weil. She brought all of that, along with her understanding of the practical needs of schools and teachers, to the development of Philosophy for Children. Her hand is most apparent in the teachers' manuals which accompany Lipman's novels and in the teacher education sessions which emerged as Montclair State College evolved its master's program. Sharp was and is a skilled, sensitive teacher and she is responsible, in large part, for creating a curriculum which is understandable and accessible to school people. Finally, as the period came to a close, Sharp spearheaded a number of initiatives which would see Philosophy for Children transported (and transmuted) around the world. Her skills as teacher were and are matched by her skills as proselytizer.

The late Frederick Oscanyan was a nice counterpart to both Lipman and Sharp. Formal, Aristotelian logic is frequently said to be the backbone of the Philosophy for Children curriculum. If that statement is true, Oscanyan may be said to be the backbone of the backbone. Trained as a logician, but with the pedagogical skills of a good logic teacher (the terms "logician" and "logic teacher" are not synonymous), Oscanyan was instrumental in the development of the formal logic that permeates *Harry Stottlemeier's Discovery* and *Philosophical Inquiry*, the teacher's manual which accompanies *Harry*. In addition, an early article on the logic of *Harry Stottlemeier*, published in the journal *Teaching Philosophy*, was instrumental in bring Philosophy for Children to a wider educational and philosophical community.

Gareth Matthews's role in Philosophy for Children was and is harder to define. Never directly involved in the creation of curricula or teaching materials, Matthews's historical role has been to point out the sometimes hidden philosophical abilities of children, and present ways in which those abilities could be nurtured by adults trained in philosophy, using the traditional texts of children's literature. Matthews's regular columns on children's literature in the journal *Thinking* over the past sixteen or so years have been models of gentle and reasoned persuasion.

Notes

1. Matthew Lipman, "On Writing a Philosophical Novel" in Ann Margaret Sharp and Ronald F. Reed (eds.), *Studies in Philosophy for Children* (Philadelphia: Temple University Press, 1992), p. 7.

2. John Dewey, *Democracy and Education* (1917: reprint, New York: Macmillan, 1966), pp. 124–138.

3. Rosalyn Sherman Lessing, "Is It Possible to Teach Socratically?" in William Hare and John P. Portelli (eds.), *Philosophy of Education: Introductory Readings.* (Alberta, Canada: Detselig Enterprises, 1988), pp. 243–59.

4. During the period 1979–1990, the authors attended and/or ran over thirty I.A.P.C. workshops.

5. The four metaphors are derived from workshop practice.

6. Matthew Lipman, *Harry Stottlemeier's Discovery* (Montclair, New Jersey: I.A.P.C., 1985), p. 8.

Chapter 2

The Pragmatic Context
of Philosophy for Children

In this chapter, we will examine a part of the philosophic tradition which, it is hoped, will shed light on the practice of Philosophy for Children. The careful reader, of course, will notice that no definition of philosophy has been proffered at this point. The reason for that is an assumption on the part of the writers that definitions extracted and cut off from the tradition that generate them easily degenerate into trivial and miseducative slogans. Stated bluntly, the slogans become substitutes for thought. In this chapter, we will examine the pragmatic tradition and attempt to generate a thoughtful understanding of philosophy in the pragmatic mold and one which is applicable to the practice of Philosophy for Children. After doing that, we will turn to Plato and Socrates.

In the early days of Philosophy for Children, the charge was frequently made that there was a parochialism about Philosophy for Children, that is, it stemmed from a specific philosophical tradition and, consequently, exhibited all the prejudices and blindness of that tradition. Marxist critiques, for example, saw Lockean waters "run" through a pragmatic filter which led to Philosophy for Children being used as an educational instrument by the dominant class to support its continual oppression of the less propertied.[1]

Charges like that have not completely diminished, although now, more likely than not, they tend to come from feminist critics who see Philosophy for Children as replicating, to some extent, a male-dominated philosophical tradition. What Matthew Lipman has been able to show through the continued and expanded practice of Philosophy for Children is that even if the texts (novels and teachers' manuals that accompany the texts) do exhibit the biases alluded to, the classroom discussion, led by an educated and sensitive Philosophy for Children teacher, counteracts whatever biases may be inherent to the texts. Thus, for example, if the language or the situations depicted in *Harry Stottlemeier's Discovery* hint at the sexism that runs through the Western tradition of philosophy, the community of inquiry, that most fundamental of Philosophy for Children creations, is the most appropriate place to deal effectively with that sexism. Lipman need not claim, nor should he claim, that Philosophy for Children is a sort of generic philosophy. All he need claim is that while seven novels and their accompanying manuals, along with texts such as *Philosophy in the Classroom* and *Thinking in Education*, do, in some sense, "emanate" from a specific tradition or series of specific traditions, the practice of Philosophy for Children is such that it engenders frequent reflection on its own presumptions. That reflection, built into the very nature of the community of inquiry, serves as a safeguard against the wallowing in bias alluded to by critics of Philosophy for Children.

Now, let us try to translate the original into what may be called its educational equivalents. Here the argument was that as *educational* instrument or innovation, it was context-dependent in the way, *pace* John Dewey, all educational instruments and innovations are context-dependent. An instrument of reform in Situation I may be inapplicable in Situation II and may be irrelevant to Situation III. What has occurred in practice, however, is that the model of community of inquiry has emerged, clearly, as transcontextual, and perhaps more surprisingly, although the corpus of Philosophy for Children continues to expand, the seven novels that Lipman created along with their corresponding manuals, have shown a remarkable resilience. Even that most American of Philosophy for Children novels, *Harry Stottlemeier's Discovery*, which has as one of its main themes the distinctively American custom of standing while saluting the flag, is used with success throughout the world.

One has reason to believe then, as philosophy and as educational program, that Philosophy for Children exhibits, if not universality, then at least widespread utility. Assuming that Philosophy for Children practice has established the truth of the preceding, it may be helpful, in terms of our *understanding* to think less, again, at this point, as to what Philosophy for Children yields and more about from whence it comes, that is, to examine the tradition which engenders the widespread utility to which Philosophy for Children is heir. Once one begins that task, however, one begins to see how myopic a charge of parochialism really is. A cursory reading of the seven novels and their corresponding manuals would find Lipman utilizing extensively the Pre-Socratics, the Sophists, the Socrates of the early dialogues of Plato, Aristotle, the Augustine of *Concerning the Teacher*, Descartes, Spinoza, Nietzsche, the pragmatists, Austin, Wittgenstein, Foucault, Derrida, and Habermas. Stated another way, the Philosophy for Children corpus can be viewed as a replaying, though not in chronological order, of the history of Western Philosophy. Stated still another way, it can be viewed as a tracing of the emergence of modernism and its culmination in postmodernism.

Very simply, there is an eclecticism and a philosophical richness to Lipman's work that makes it difficult to say he is working within one and only one tradition. Just as Dewey, for example, acknowledges the Hegelian deposits in his philosophy, Lipman might as easily acknowledge a Cartesian one. Having said that, however, the scholar still can use various traditions as instruments for understanding the individual philosopher's works.

Throughout the rest of this chapter, we will use the pragmatic tradition, most notably the work of John Dewey, especially as it is found in "My Pedagogic Creed," *Democracy and Education*, and *Experience and Education*, and that of William James in both his popular writing (*Talks to Teachers*) and his more technical writing (*Principles of Psychology*) as ways of attempting to shed light on Philosophy for Children and its relationship to the educational environment. Then for reasons which we hope will become apparent, we will cut back a few millennia to Socrates and the development of the dialogue as a teaching instrument.

John Dewey was a prolific scholar throughout his life. He published scores of books and pamphlets, hundreds of articles for scholarly and popular journals and magazines, and gave innumerable speeches and lectures—public as well as academic—on topics ranging from Hegelian metaphysics to women's suffrage. Indeed, it is not an exaggeration to suggest that from 1900 to 1940, Dewey published more each year than many small college faculties produced during all those years. Unfortunately, Dewey did not always write well. As Chief Justice Oliver Wendell Holmes remarked: "Dewey writes as the creator would write, if he were intent on explaining all of his creation but was hopelessly inarticulate." Dewey's words are often misunderstood, but more frequently Dewey is not read.

It is relatively easy, then, given the extent of Dewey's writing and the general shoddiness of scholarship about John Dewey, to create a "Dewey" who could support virtually any educational position. To avoid this, as much as possible, we will try to stay as close as we can to the text and to keep our focus as narrow as possible.

In "My Pedagogic Creed," the masterful pamphlet that Dewey had published in 1917, he gives a formal definition of education that, it can be argued, he spent *Democracy and Education* and *Experience and Education* refining, expanding, and justifying. The definition was "education must be conceived as a continual reconstruction of experience; that the process and the goal of education are one and the same thing."[2] The refinement, expansion, and justification suggested that the person to be educated was thrust into what William James called a "whirring, buzzing" confusion, and that her/his task was to make sense of things and to see how things hang together or fail to hang together. Education, at heart, was seen as a process of sense-making or meaning-discovery (or invention). This process was ongoing. To the extent that the individual was growing and functioning effectively in her/his environment, to that extent the individual was being educated.

That means, of course, that education is not the sole responsibility of the school and that school age is not equivalent with the age of education. For Dewey, the informal environment (the neighborhood, the home, the church) is typically the most potent educative environment and the preschool child, the very young child, is typically the most proficient learner. If the school is to become an effective educative environment, the school must look to the potency of the informal environment and the proficiency of the preschool learner.

In regards to the latter, Dewey sees two characteristics of very young children that make them such effective learners and that may serve as things to which the educators of older children may aspire. The first characteristic is dependence and it denotes a power rather than a weakness; it involves interdependence. There is always a danger that increased independence will decrease the social capacity of an individual. In making him more self-reliant, it may make him more self-sufficient; it may lead to aloofness and indifference. It often makes an individual so insensitive in his relations to others as to develop an illusion of being really able to stand and act alone—an unnamed form of insanity which is responsible for a large part of the remediable suffering of this world.[3]

The second characteristic that the very young possess that make them such efficient learners is what Dewey calls "plasticity."

This is something quite different from the plasticity of putty or wax. It is not a capacity to take on change of form in accord with external pressure. It lies near the pliable elasticity by which some persons take on the color of their surrounding while retaining their own bent. But it is something deeper than this. It is essentially the ability to learn from experience; the power to retain from one experience something which is of avail in coping with the difficulties of a latter situation. This means power to modify actions on the basis of the results of prior experiences, the power to *develop dispositions*. Without it, the acquisition of habits is impossible.[4]

The wise teacher recognizes that she/he is neither dealing with a blank slate nor with an imperfect adult (an adult-in-waiting). The wise teacher recognizes the fact that she/he is in the presence of an able scholar, a scholar with a history of significant educational success—for example, the very young unpack and learn how to manipulate concepts as complex as "Mommy" and "Daddy" before they are even proficient in the use of the language in which those terms are embedded. The wise teacher uses the child's scholarly characteristics as instruments for continuing and expanding the educative process.

In regard to the informal environment, Dewey explicitly states that it has a "built-in" reality. One does not, as all too often happens in the classroom, doubt the reality of the neighborhood or the home (one may, of course, question the worth of each, but the reality is perceived as given). The urban neighborhood, for example, is an environment that requires intelligence, if only of the most instrumental sort. If the individual cannot figure out ways to deal with the problems presented by that environment, she/he, quite literally can suffer fatal emotional and/or physical harm. Education in the informal environment, again quite literally, is a matter of life and death, and the wise teacher will find some way to make connections between the problems children experience in school and that which is problematic in the informal environment. Using Dewey's language, if the school is to be felt as real and, not coincidentally, have an educative impact, it must exist on a continuum with the informal environment.

At the same time, the wise teacher recognizes the fact that education does not take place in a historical or cultural vacuum. Children are born into specific cultures at definite times in history. The conservative educator may rail about the child's responsibility to learn a pre-set curriculum while her/his more liberal counterpart stresses the child's right to inquire into what interests her/him. Dewey steers a sort of middle course and suggests that the child has a right to "a cultural inheritance" or, as referred to in other places, the "funded capital of civilization." There is a body of knowledge and accrued meanings, a series of significant events, actions, inventions, discoveries, and so on to which the child is rightful heir. There are a series of events, call it the child's "cultural inheritance" that define a given culture and that are, in effect, that culture's way of dealing with its collective experience. Again, the child has the right to know what is significant in a culture and how she/he might use it to reconstruct her/his experience.

Part and parcel of cultures (contemporary, postindustrial cultures) are the disciplines. In a postindustrial age, the sciences and the arts, are more than repositories of arcane fact and are something other than the province of a priestlike class. They are the prime avenues of sense-making that contemporary cultures have devised. As such, children have a right to be connected to the disciplines in such a way that they can use the disciplines to make sense of their own experiences.

It does not take a great deal of reflection to see that Dewey is a good deal more complex than the caricature that is frequently alluded to in many educational circles. Even the most cursory reading of "My Pedagogic Creed" shows that Dewey is not trying to minimize the role of the teacher and that, in fact, Dewey is not in favor of a child-centered curriculum. Rather, Dewey is saying that the teacher must have an enormous amount of knowledge. She/he must have expertise not only in the child, the class of children, but also in the significance of a culture, especially as they are filtered through contemporary disciplines. Then, recalling one of the notions of interest mentioned in the previous chapter—interest as being that which is between subject matter and person, that which is a vital link between the two—the teacher must find some way of forging and/or discovering the connection between the student and the curriculum. Certainly Dewey is in favor of a child-related curriculum, but that connection, as we have tried to show, is enormously complex.

Before leaving Dewey, it may prove helpful to look at another slogan typically attributed to John Dewey—"Education for Democracy." In a democratic society, like the American one of the twentieth century, it is clear that the members of the electorate must be able to sift through all kinds of complex matters, to pick and choose, to analyze and evaluate, and, perhaps most importantly, to vote intelligently. Certainly, one has reason to believe that Dewey was in favor of educating for the demands a democratic society imposes on its citizenry. Still, there is a sense in which it can be argued that Dewey stands the slogan on its head and is, at least as concerned with democratizing for education as he is for educating for democracy.

In *Democracy and Education*, Dewey poses a question. What is it, he asks, that differentiates a community from a mere aggregate? What is it, in effect, that differentiates the family from a mere collection of people gathered together in an elevator? Dewey comes up with two characteristics that communities qua communities share. These characteristics will be used to suggest improvements in the community that is the classroom:

> Now in any social group whatever, even in a gang of thieves, we find some interest held in common, and we find a certain amount of interaction and cooperative intercourse with other groups. From these two traits we derive our standard. How numerous and varied are the interests which are consciously shared? How full and free is the interplay with other forms of association? If we apply these considerations to, say, a criminal band, we find that the ties which consciously hold the members together are few in number, reducible almost to a common interest in plunder; and that they are of such a nature as to isolate the group from other groups with respect to give and take of the values of life. Hence, the education such a society gives is partial and distorted. If we take, on the other hand, the kind of family life which illustrates the standard, we find that there are material, intellectual, aesthetic interests in which all participate and that the progress of one member has worth for the experience of other members—it is readily communicable—and that the family is not an isolated whole, but enters intimately into relationships with business groups, with schools, with all the agencies of culture, as well as with other similar groups, and that it plays a due part in the political organization and in return receives support from it. In short, there are many interests consciously communicated and shared; and there are varied and free points of contact with other modes of association.[5]

Dewey stipulates that a community with a great degree of likemindedness (the former characteristic) and the most fluid and various intercourse (the latter characteristic) is "democratic." Note, this is a stipulation, and Dewey is defining terms in somewhat an odd way. One can see this most clearly when one examines the paradigmatic example of a democracy that Dewey offers—the traditional nuclear family circa 1917. That family, if one needs reminding, was not an exemplar of majoritarian decision-making. Decisions, for the most part, were made by the father, implemented by the mother, and, in effect, followed by the children. What that family did possess, as the quotation shows, was an enormous amount of likemindedness and fluid and flexible commerce with other communities. The traditional nuclear family was democratic in Dewey's stipulative sense.

At this point a question becomes apparent: How might one construe the relationship of democracy to education given the stipulation? Here

Dewey is fairly straightforward. Just as one may educate for democracy, one might democratize for education. What a democracy does (keep in mind the notion of the family as a paradigm) is to give the individual a starting point, a set of shared beliefs, hopes, values and aspirations. In a family, the individual is not a windowless monad and the individual does not have to use a method of Cartesian doubt to burrow down to a bedrock of incontestable first principles. These principles are shared. They are what differentiates this family from others, and, in a very concrete sense, are "given." This does not mean, however, that the given is taken as "sacred." The child starts with a set of beliefs which enables him/her to begin an intellectual journey of sorts. As the child meets and interacts with other communities, as this second characteristic of community life comes into play, the child is forced to think about and to examine that which is given. Stated in a negative way:

> Lack of the free and equitable intercourse which springs from a variety of shared interests makes intellectual stimulation unbalanced. Diversity of stimulation means novelty, and novelty means challenge to thought. The more activity is restricted to a few definite lines—as it is when there are rigid class lines preventing adequate interplay of experiences—the more action tends to become routine on the part of the class at a disadvantage, and capricious, aimless, and exploitive on the part of the class having the materially fortunate position.[6]

Democracies, given Dewey's stipulative definition, are important educationally precisely because they provide an environment in which children are required, by their very presence in the community, to think and act in a thoughtful manner. The wise teacher democratizes her/his classroom (and advocates the democratization of the larger community) for pedagogical as well as ethical and political reasons.

John Dewey looms as a giant over Philosophy for Children practice, but there is another pragmatist, William James, whose work sheds an enormous amount of light on Philosophy for Children. In the following, we will focus on James' understanding of the problem of other minds, and the nature of experience. Historically, there has been a dispute among Jamesian scholars (and here one includes philosophers, educators, litterateurs, and so on) as to which of the Jameses—the popular James whose work is best exhibited in, say, *Talks to Teachers* and *Essays on Faith and Morals*, or the technical James of *The Principles of Psychology* and *Radical Empiricism*—is most worthy of attention. The vast majority of philosophers find the popular works, if not a downright embarrassment, then far less worthy of serious attention than the technical works. The claim, in effect, is that the notoriously vague and often muddled James is at his worst when trying to communicate with a general audience. On the other hand, again as one might expect, the vast majority of nonphilosophers find James' weaving together of popular culture, optimism, respect for and interest in atypical behavior, moral exhortation, and literary reference and criticism, far more interesting and evocative than the technical James. Recently, Jamesian scholars have begun to rethink the dualism and have suggested that the way to unpack James is to use the strands (popular vs. technical) of James's writing as hermeneutic, that is, the popular serves as commentary and extension of the technical, and the technical serves the same purpose for the popular.

If one takes that suggestion to heart, perhaps the best place to start is not only with the most popular of James' writing, namely, *Talks to Teachers* but also with that article, *On a Certain Blindness in Human Beings*, which may serve as a paradigm for James' popular writing. There one finds James reminding teachers that the blindness in human beings is precisely one *about* (other) human beings.

> Our judgements concerning the worth of things, big or little, depend on the feeling the things arouse in us. When we judge a thing to be precious in consequence of the idea we frame of it, this is only because the idea is itself associated already with a feeling. If we were radically feelingless, and if ideas were the only things our minds could entertain, we should lose all our likes and dislikes at a stroke, and be unable to point to any one situation or experience in life more valuable or significant than any other. Now the blindness in human beings, of which this discourse will treat, is the blindness with which we are all afflicted in regard to feelings of creatures and people different from ourselves.[7]

Just as, using one of James' more memorable examples, your fox terrier must be befuddled by the hours you spend staring at the book you hold in your hand, precisely because she/he does not share your concern, for example, your desire to discover the informant's true identity, she/he will not be able to understand the significance of your activity. Put in its context—he is talking with teachers—James is giving some very good, some very humane advice: Don't assume that you know what your students are thinking. Don't think you can know what they are thinking unless you also know what they are feeling. Be quick to evaluate and, hence, dismiss the worth of your students' mental activity and you may find yourself in precisely the position of James' fox terrier. The pedagogy is powerful when viewed, simply, as propaedeutic to teacher education. But look what happens when "Blindness" is augmented by a technical piece or two. Look at what happens when it is interpreted through what might be called the Berkelean strand of James' radical empiricism, his description of the epistemic quality of that experience, and how that epistemic quality relates to the problem of other minds. James equates experience with reality and just as it is a mistake to claim that the *esse* of an idea is not equivalent with its *percipi*, so too, for the radical empiricist, there is no noumena lurking unperceived beyond the phenomena. Experience does not wait on reality, dutifully patient to receive the imprint of the real. The qualities experienced are the qualities of the real. As experience is significant, laden with meaning, vital, so too is reality. Experience constitutes reality and, if an institution, such as the school, is guilty of denuding experience of its richness, it is guilty of a similar "ontological" crime regarding reality. In regards to the epistemic quality of experience, James busies himself, as radical empiricist must, with eradicating the dualism between "thought" and "thing."

> Experience, I believe, has no inner duplicity; and the separation of it into consciousness and content comes, not by way of subtraction, but by way of addition—the addition, to a given concrete piece of it, of other sets of experience, in connection with which severally its use or function may be of two different kinds. The paint will serve here as an illustration. In a pot in a paintshop, along with other paints, it serves in its entirety as so much saleable matter. Spread on a canvas, with other paints around it, it represents on the contrary, a feature in a picture and performs a spiritual function. Just so, I maintain, does a given undivided portion of experience, taken in one context of associates, play the part of a knower, of a state of mind, of 'consciousness'; while in a different context the same undivided bit of experience plays the part of a thing known, of an objective 'content'. In a word, in one group it figures as a thought, in another group as a thing.[8]

James is justly remembered for his replacement of an associationist theory of inert ideas with a dynamic, fluid "stream of consciousness," and the above passage points out how dynamic and how fluid that stream really is. The stream of consciousness—and we would do well to keep in mind that the stream of consciousness, given the equivalence alluded to previously, could just as easily be called the stream of reality—is constantly changing, is recreating itself and its elements. Using the language of the philosophic tradition that James inherits, knower "flows" into thing know and later becomes knower again; thought becomes object becomes thought becomes object. Imagination flows into "reality" and, later, ebbs out. And on and on. The point to keep in mind is that James rejects the dualism that yields a world filled with material stuff mysteriously attached to a world consisting of mental stuff. For James, there is, *simpliciter*, experience and the various situations in which it finds itself. Viewed in one way (assuming counterfactually that one could get out of the stream and occupy the position on shore where God would rest), one could see the X that is now knower metamorphize into the Y that is known. Viewed in other way, the stream washes away traditional ontological distinctions. There are no ontological distinctions among thinker and thought and thing. There are (theoretical) constructs that people use in order to deal with and talk about their experiences.

Needless to say, this is a significantly radical view of the world. It is, of course, a view which demands exploration and justification which is beyond the purview of this chapter and which, it may be argued, has been supplied amply and well within the pragmatic tradition. Still, one can begin to see how James would construct such explorations and justifications by looking at how he deals with the traditional problems of other minds and, specifically, within the stream, of distinguishing one's own mind from someone else's.

> What I do feel simply when a later moment of my experience succeeds an earlier one is that though there are two moments, the transition from one to the other is continuous. Continuity here is a definite sort of experience: just as definite as is the discontinuity experience which I find it impossible to avoid when I seek to make the transition from an experience of my own to one of yours. In this latter case I have to get on and off again, to pass from a thing lived to a thing conceived, and the break is positively experienced and noted. Though the functions exerted by my experience and by yours may be the same (*e.g.*, the same objects known and the same purposes followed), yet the sameness has in this case to be ascertained expressly (and often with difficulty and uncertainty) after the break has been felt, whereas in passing from one of my own moments to another the sameness of object and interest is unbroken, and both the earlier and the later experiences are of things directly lived.[9]

The world that James and other radical empiricists inhabit is a world characterized by conjunctival and disjunctival relations. As I attend to my own experience, as that which is me flows from experience to experience, what is also experienced is a sense of continuity, that in some sense the latter is a yield of the former. When, however, I go public, when I try to understand your experience, what is experienced, what is just as forthright and as blatant as the feeling of succession when I attend to my own experience, is a feeling of disjunction, a feeling of discontinuity. Entering another person's stream of consciousness is possible. We are not the isolated consciousness of the modernist, windowless monad, bumping but never truly interacting with one another. Still, James is enough of a modernist to suggest that the interaction among persons and the relations among persons is always characterized by a feeling of otherness, that is, X's intimacy with Y, X's knowledge of Y, X's ability to teach Y is always experienced as and characterized by a feeling of otherness.

At this point, one might stop and contrast the richness and complexity of James's epistemology and metaphysics with what must be, if practice is indicative of theory, the epistemology and metaphysics that engendered at least some educational systems. A survey of the undergirdings of such systems might yield the following: There are two worlds. A world of pure mental stuff and a world of material stuff. Teaching involves, in large part, attempting to achieve "correspondence" between the mental and the material. A person is educated, in part, to the extent that he/she sees things as they really are. There are things that are worth knowing and, hence, have a place in the curriculum and other things which are trivial, and, hence, have no place in the curriculum. Educators, even prior to meeting students, know the contents of those two categories and their task, a la Mortimer Adler and the Paideia Group, is to bring students to know what they should know. In other words, students have real interests (even if they are not aware of those interests) in knowing what they "should" know, in coming to know what educators think they should know. Educators can and should develop those interests in directions to which they already point.

Given this view—and as much as one hopes that it is a caricature, one is afraid that it is not—education is a mechanistic, inherently authoritarian affair. One person, that is, the educated, figures out which ideas are worth learning. The task then consists in presenting those ideas in such a way that students will come to know them and, if not see their significance, at least be able to recall them when asked to do so. The students' task is to acquiesce.

Now, we are in a position to make explicit some ways in which an understanding of the pragmatic tradition facilitates an understanding of Philosophy for Children practice. Note, we are not making a claim regarding generative or causative issues—we are not suggesting that, say, Matthew Lipman read the passages previously cited, took them to heart, and built Philosophy for Children on pragmatic foundations.

Of course, the process was not that simple. Indeed, given Lipman's own testimony, the chances are fairly strong that he was not all that familiar, for example, with "My Pedagogic Creed" before and during the writing of *Harry Stottlemeier's Discovery*. Rather, we are making a claim about our own understanding—to make sense of Philosophy for Children, it is helpful to recall some facts and refresh our understanding of the pragmatic tradition. We are using pragmatism as a sort of reading lamp, fully aware of the fact that other traditions (Early Greek or Modern Continental, for example) could also shed significant light on our subject. To make things as explicit as possible, we will simply compile a list: (1) Philosophy for Children, and it will not hurt to keep in mind that we are dealing with Philosophy for Children, circa 1974–1987, is quite mindful of the idea that education involves connecting a child with, at least, some part of his/her cultural inheritance. It is, after all, *Philosophy* for Children and what Philosophy for Children is about is creating an environment in which children can become philosophers and deal with the problems, questions and ideas that have occupied philosophers since the time of the Pre-Socratics. The novel may be viewed as a "container" of that tradition. A better image, however, might be a lens through which the tradition might be viewed.

(2) Philosophy for Children does not denigrate or minimize the importance of information and/or knowledge of facts, but what it does do, quite thoroughly, is to shift the model of the classroom from one of mere information-transmission to one of sense-making, meaning discovery, and so on. Using Dewey's language, education is reconstruction of experience and facts have instrumental value to the extent that they contribute to that reconstruction.

(3) Philosophy for Children assumes that the child who comes to class (the five-year-old on her/his first day, the fifteen-year-old back from winter vacation) is an efficient learner. The educative task is to take the power the child displays so ably outside of school (in the informal environment) and put it to work in school.

(4) Philosophy for Children takes seriously the claim that the child's interest, in any of the senses alluded to by Dewey, plays a vital role in the building and running of the curriculum. This does not mean that the teacher panders to or wallows in interest. Education always is a process of conversion, it always involves taking the interests at hand and converting or changing or nurturing them. Still, in order to convert, in order to change, one must first know what the interest is.

(5) Philosophy for Children sees the disciplines as instruments cultures have devised for reconstructing experience. If one looks at the traditional corpus, one can see Lipman using the novels in order to connect children with the instrumental value of the disciplines. *Mark* is about social science, *Lisa* is about ethical inquiry, and *Suki* is about aesthetics. The novels encourage children to, among other things, scientifically, ethically, and aesthetically make sense of their own experience.

(6) Philosophy for Children stresses the importance of community as an essential part of the educative process. Children do not learn in groups in Philosophy for Children because it is too expensive to educate them individually but because, with Dewey, it is believed that likemindedness and diversity are essential goads to intelligent thought and action.

(7) Philosophy for Children is holistic. It refuses to reduce the child down to any simple characteristic. It sees the child as a somewhat mysterious conglomeration of thought and feeling, cognition and affect. To teach a child is to teach the (whole) conglomeration at once.

(8) Philosophy for Children underscores the complexity of experience. Where traditional education assumes a relatively static world with fixed boundaries, Philosophy for Children, with William James, suggests a more fluid environment, an environment more difficult to describe or capture, an environment more needful of hermeneutics than description.

Notes

1. This claim is derived from workshop practice during the early 1980s.

2. John Dewey, "My Pedagogic Creed" in John J. McDermott (ed.), *The Philosophy of John Dewey* (Chicago: University of Chicago Press, 1981), p. 450.

3. John Dewey, *Democracy and Education* (1917: reprint, New York: Macmillan, 1966), p. 44.

4. *Ibid.*, p. 44.

5. *Ibid.*, p. 83.

6. *Ibid.*, p. 84.

7. William James, "On A Certain Blindness in Human Beings" in John J. McDermott (ed.), *The Writings of William James* (Chicago: University of Chicago Press, 1977), p. 629.

8. *Ibid.*, p. 172.

9. *Ibid.*, p. 198.

Chapter 3

The Socratic Context
of Philosophy for Children

When educational reformers want to criticize the drill and recitation that too often characterizes the contemporary classroom, they frequently contrast it with a Socratic way of teaching. They counsel teachers to be "Socratic," to be like Socrates. If by that they mean something like stop talking so much, stop lecturing so much, listen to your students, question them, they are probably giving some good advice, but it is hard to see the advice as constituting a genuine alternative to a more traditional way of doing things. Also, it seems hard to see how simply talking less and questioning more will enable children to inherit what Dewey called the "funded capital of civilization"[1]—all of the "significata" (the great music, poetry, experiments) of a culture to which children are entitled and which the school must deliver. Surely, if the injunction to teach Socratically is to be educationally significant, it must mean something more than that. Of all the programs within the critical thinking movement, Philosophy for Children may be the one that has explored the injunction most deeply. To get to the exploration, some historical background is appropriate.

Philosophy begins in the West with a group of philosophers variously known as the natural philosophers or the pre-Socratics. Philosophers such as Thales, Anaximenes, Parmenides, Empedocles, and Heraclitus were all engaged in an attempt to discover the secrets of the natural world, to reduce the mass of phenomena to a few manageable principles, and to understand their natural environments. What held them together was a belief that one could reason one's way to the truth, that by looking at natural effects one could deduce their causes. What distinguished one from the other was that each reasoned their ways to different causes. For some the natural world was reducible to one immovable substance. For others, there were four basic elements (earth, air, fire, and water). Others saw five or six or even more basic causes.

This led a group of philosophers, the Sophists, to react against the program of the natural philosophers. Where the natural philosophers assumed that an educated person, a wise person, was one who knew the truth about things natural, the Sophists claimed that since "reason" generated so many different conclusions, there was something unreliable about reason itself. If, the Sophists suggested, reason was a reliable tool, it should always yield the same results. It did not; hence, the Sophists shifted inquiry away from an attempt to discover the truth about the natural world to an attempt to teach a useful skill.

The Sophists were the first professional teachers. They went around to the families of young boys—the history of western philosophy, in large part, at least until the twentieth century, is a history that virtually excludes women—and offered to teach those boys how to argue persuasively. The Sophists said, in effect: We don't care what your position is. We don't care whether you are telling the truth or not. We will teach you how to make your case and how to win arguments. This was an especially valuable skill because eventually those boys would, as heads of households, have to speak in the public forums that constituted Greek democracy. If they could not speak well, their families' fortune would suffer.

Into this mix—a mix that included a switch from the educated person as she or he who knew the truth about the natural world to the educated person as she or he who could argue persuasively regardless of the truth or falsity of the position—comes the character Socrates.

If one reads the dialogue *Apology* carefully, one will see that two of the accusations against Socrates suggested that he was both a natural philosopher and a Sophist at the same time. Certainly, since one was a reaction against the other, Socrates could not be both. But who was Socrates? What was his doctrine? Why was he so important? And most of all, what does it mean to emulate the character of Socrates?

Most of what we know about Socrates comes from three sources. Socrates did not write, indeed he mistrusted the written word, and so we must rely on the plays of Aristophanes and the dialogues of Xenophon and Plato. For our purposes, we will concentrate on those writings that are clearly the most important, both philosophically and historically—the writings of Socrates' student, Plato.

Most commentators divide Plato's writing into three major periods.[2] In the early dialogues, *Apology*, *Charmides*, and *Phaedo* for example, Plato gives a fairly accurate portrayal of Socrates. Plato was almost like a "fly on the wall" or a tape recorder, and one "hears" dialogue that may actually have taken place; this is the place to go find out what Socrates was about and what he was teaching. In the middle period, in dialogues like the *Republic*, Plato uses Socrates to espouse his (Plato's) own doctrine. That doctrine is called the Theory of the Forms, and the middle period is the place to go if one wants to see what the mature Plato thought. Toward the end of his career, Plato had some doubts about his theory; in later dialogues like *Parmenides*, *Theatetus*, and the *Sophist*, one sees Plato rethinking and, perhaps, rejecting the theory. At the same time, because Socrates was Plato's mouthpiece in the middle period, the character of Socrates now becomes a minor figure, a figure of ridicule and scorn, or drops out altogether. The later dialogues are not the place to go to get an accurate picture of the historical Socrates.

So who was Socrates and what did he espouse? The dialogue *Apology* is probably the best place to start. As mentioned previously, Socrates was on trial for his life. After rejecting a number of the more far-fetched accusations (accusations that suggested he was a natural philosopher and a Sophist)[3] Socrates wonders what the real charge against him is. He settles on the charge that he is guilty of corrupting the morals of the youth of Athens.[4]

The charge was brought against him because Socrates, in the company of his students, engaged those with a reputation for wisdom in a dialogue. Over the course of those dialogues, Socrates discovered, as did his students, along with the people who were questioned, that those with a reputation for wisdom did not always deserve it. Socrates was wiser than the "wisest" people because he knew his own limits; he knew that he did not know, while they mistakenly thought that they did. For Socrates, the educated person is precisely the person who knows his or her limitations, who knows that he or she does not know.

There are two points that are worthy of consideration. The first is that this person, whom many consider to be one of the two great teachers in the Western tradition (Jesus is the other), professed to have virtually no doctrine and said that what he knew was unimportant. Over and over again, in the *Apology*, the *Phaedrus*, and the *Charmides*, Socrates suggests that true wisdom is the property of the gods, and that what he has—human wisdom, this knowledge of his own limitations—is worth hardly anything at all.[5]

The second point is that Socrates puts an enormous amount of weight (some might call it faith) on the power of the dialogue, that back-and-forth linguistic motion between speakers, to uncover the truth. When Socrates discusses ideas with those with a reputation for wisdom, a truth always emerges from the dialogue—in the *Apology*, the truth is about some mistaken claims to knowledge. Socrates is different from the Sophists because he thinks there is a truth to be discerned. He is different from the natural philosophers because the method he uses—discourse, dialogue, conversation—is public and is open to scrutiny in a way that reasoning, as a purely mental activity, is not.

Plato, as one would expect from a student, took much from his teacher Socrates. For Plato, education is a matter of leading a person from mere belief to knowledge. In his classic Allegory of the Cave,[6] Plato suggests that we, as uneducated persons, are chained in a cave, seeing shadows on the wall and mistakenly believing that the shadows (and the cave itself) are real things. Education involves breaking those chains and leading a person from that cave into the bright sunshine. The good teacher does this through the dialectical process, leading the student as far as she or he is capable. The best students, those most philosophical, those best educated, will use the dialectical process to discover beauty, goodness, and justice. Plato is different from his teacher Socrates because the wisdom that Plato's students would discover is worth a good deal; that is, it involves knowledge of objective standards (the Forms) that will enable people to lead good, productive lives.

The early Socrates is an awfully hard master, but there are ways in which his behavior helps determine the ideals of teaching which emerge both in the literature and practice of Philosophy for Children. The first involves Socrates' attitude toward his own knowledge. Where banking-model proponents prize their own knowledge—what the teacher knows is to be deposited in the passive students' account[7]— Socrates says explicitly, "I am only too conscious that I have no claim to wisdom, great or small."[8] What motivates Socrates, what gives force and urgency to his questioning, is an awareness of this lack of knowledge. When he is being most "Socratic," when he is functioning in the early Platonic dialogues, Socrates is not so much trying to convince others—he is not being a Sophist—as he is trying to convince himself, to find reasons for belief, to find justification. Because Socrates does not know, he must inquire. And here, perhaps, is the fundamental characteristic of the skilled Philosophy for Children teacher—she or he inquires *with* children. To the extent that she or he already knows the answer or, more moderately, to the extent that she or he cannot conceive the possibility that what she or he believes could be wrong, to that extent she or he is not being Socratic, is not approaching one of the ideals of the Philosophy for Children teacher.

Alfred North Whitehead might call Socrates' situation one of scholarly ignorance[9]—that awareness of a problem that begins to point to a solution. In addition, however, there is a good deal more going on with Socrates. Over and over again, especially in the early dialogues, Socrates shows himself to be a master of the dialogical form. He listens carefully, has a grasp for the right question in much the same way that an artist has a grasp for the right brush stroke, can detect potential flaws in argument pattern, and has the ability to convey those flaws to the participants in the dialogue. Moreover, Socrates has the ability to keep a focus so that it is reasonable for us to say that this dialogue is *about* love and that one about friendship and this one about courage.

When Socrates talks with others, he is always talking for some purpose. He is not rigid, he does allow change of direction, but ultimately, it is clear that he has an idea of the topic and that he experiences the demands the topic places on him. The talk in the early dialogues may be laden with anecdotes and allegory, but those anecdotes and allegories are always, somehow, in service to the topic. Perhaps the clearest example of this is the way that the Allegory of the Cave serves to illuminate the relationship of the intelligible world to that of the sensory. The cave story almost line by line tells something significant about what Plato means by the two-world theory.

The task of the Philosophy for Children teacher, when she or he is told to emulate the character of Socrates, is to try to achieve a similar mastery of the dialogue with children—the teacher must be a skilled dialectician. She or he, without falling into a trap of rigidity, has to remember what the discussion is about and has to find ways in which the demands of the topic can be experienced by members of the community. Otherwise the dialogue runs the risk of degenerating into a series of unrelated monologues in which people express their opinions but in which no gestalt, no informing purpose, may emerge. There is a motto which is uttered frequently in Philosophy for Children training sessions: The teacher must be philosophically self-effacing and pedagogically strong. The first part of the statement relates to Socrates' attitude toward his own knowledge, while the second, it seems, points to the skill in talking with others that Socrates exhibited and to which the Philosophy for Children teacher must aspire.

Another thing that one notices when one looks at the early dialogues, at the historical ones, is how inconclusive they are. Although theories and hypotheses are rejected on the basis of counter-examples, perceived weaknesses, and so on, one is hard-pressed to say that the focus is appreciably narrowed. Indeed, it is a commonplace of the dialogue, that things seem more up in the air, more unsettled than they did when the participants got together. Poor Crito discerns this most forcefully when his simple plan to help Socrates escape turns into a wonderfully complex discussion of the rights and responsibilities of citizenship.[10]

When Philosophy for Children began to take roots in the southwest United States in the early 1980s, two of its chief competitors were Lee Canter's Assertive Discipline and Madeline Hunter's Mastery Teaching. Though each had different purpose, Canter's, as the name suggests, was about gaining control of the classroom whereas Hunter's was about instructional strategies-each viewed the unit of the lesson (or the school day) almost as if it was a traditional nineteenth century novel. There should be a clearly defined beginning, middle, and end, and, most importantly, that end should involve closure. Not only do we specify the problem, work to solve the problem, in fact, solve it, we make sure that students are aware of what it is that was done.

In a word, teachers who had been through the Canter and Hunter programs found Philosophy for Children "maddening." It seemed to them that rather than concluding, Philosophy for Children just ended. There was an untidiness, an almost glorification of loose ends that they found disturbing. The best way, if not the only one, of getting them to stop trying to impose a forced, artificial closure on the discussion was to get them to pay attention to Socrates.

Rather than viewing the Platonic dialogues as novels or short stories, it is helpful to think of them as a series of snapshots. Here is Socrates talking with his accusers about the nature of wisdom, and here, on his deathbed he talks with Phaedo regarding the immortality of the soul, and before that, a more vigorous Socrates, in the *Lysis*, talks about the nature of friendship. Beyond all of that, figuratively standing behind the dialogues is the historical character of Socrates—now focusing on this interest, now lighting on this as truth, resting for awhile, but then continuing on his way. Each dialogue has its own gestalt, but in a sense, it is more appropriate to view Socrates' life as a dialogue itself while the individual dialogues that Plato gives are moments frozen in time—snapshots, if you will.

The really good Philosophy for Children teacher is like Socrates. She or he, it is true, is constrained by the traditional bells and buzzers of the classroom day. She or he must make the Philosophy for Children lesson conform to the individual classroom period and, to that extent, she or he must be concerned with ground covered, and, with how much time is spent on reading, soliciting of interest, discussion, exercises, and so on; but ultimately she or he, along with the classroom community, must be concerned, like Socrates with following the inquiry where it leads. And that means, of course, into the next day, and the day after that, and the day after that.

There are other characteristics of Socrates that are crucial for understanding Philosophy for Children—and that play a marked rule in the evolution of Philosophy for Children in the 1980s and 1990s. The first is the utter seriousness with which Socrates pursues inquiry. He can be playful, humorous, and ironic, but there is a real urgency to what he is about. In the *Apology*, he says explicitly that he is on a religious mission.[11] The oracle at Delphi said that Socrates was the wisest of men. Socrates, aware of his own limitations, liked to disprove the oracle by questioning those with reputations for wisdom. In the course of that questioning, it became apparent to Socrates, to the person being questioned, and to the young Athenians who served as Socrates' students, that the person with a reputation did not know what he was talking about, but mistakenly believed that he did, while Socrates, at least, did not mistakenly believe that he knew what he did not. To that extent, he was wiser than them. When the oracle said Socrates was the wisest he:

> . . . has merely taken my name as an example, as if he would say to us, the wisest of you men is he who has realized, like Socrates, that in respect of wisdom he is really worthless. That is why I still go about seeking and searching in obedience to the divine command, if I think anyone is wise, whether citizen or stranger, and when I think that any person is not wise, I try to help the cause of God by proving that he is not. This occupation has kept me too busy to do much either in politics or in my own affairs. In fact, my service to God has reduced me to extreme poverty.[12]

The second characteristic of Socrates crucial for an understanding of Philosophy for Children, and perhaps one sees the fruits of this more in the middle period, is a doggedly persistent attempt to discover some truth, to get to the bottom of things. Even in the most leisurely of settings, say the banquet scene of the *Symposium*, Socrates and his friends are not merely expressing opinions. There is neither the flabbiness of thought one experiences in a coffee house or a bar-room nor the uncritical, uncensored statement of feeling one experi-ences in a brainstorming event. Instead, there is the sort of muscular-ity of thought, a rigor that occurs when one recognizes that there is the possibility of discerning the truth—if only we are willing to work hard enough, to think hard enough, to do our best. To the extent that Socrates is on a religious mission, the attempt to discern a truth (about friendship, about goodness, about the best possible state) has almost sacramental status. What one is about in a Philosophy for Children classroom, to the extent that one emulates the character of Socrates, has something to do with this relationship to truth. Perhaps, that is why, quite literally, characters in *Harry Stottlemeier's Discovery* cannot sit still at different points in Lipman's first novel. They feel that they are about to burst through, to escape the cave, to see a light, to discover something that is truly intelligible. When something like that happens in the classroom community of inquiry, it inspires the sort of awe that can be described as religious.

The third characteristic is that the activity of inquiry, for Socrates, is not merely important, it is somehow definitional. In a recent inter-view, the novelist, short story writer, and editor William Maxwell, who is in his nineties, spoke of old age as creating a barrier between him-self and the land in which stories are born—at a certain point of his life, because of the infirmities of age, he could no longer "hear" the nascent gurglings of stories.[13] It is chilling to think of it, but just as Beethoven, because of deafness, was deprived of the sound that de-fined him, Maxwell has become deprived of the stories that define him. When we do philosophy with children, we are not simply adopt-ing a new tool or strategy. A sort of definition or redefinition is taking place, a definition that involves who and what we are. Just as Socrates is defined by his relationship to inquiry, so is the classroom community.

The final characteristic, and the one which probably caused Socrates, himself, the most difficulty, was his ability to spot mistakes, faulty reasoning, and falsehoods and, most importantly, the ability to make those errors crystal clear to the participants in the dialogue. He did this in many ways but, perhaps most forcibly, by means of the power-ful counter-example. When Socrates posed a counter-example—All Xs have Y, but surely this is an X and most surely it does not have Y—it became both logically and psychologically impossible to hold that which previously had been claimed.

Since the Platonic dialogues are so concerned with the discovery of truth, participants must be ever vigilant regarding the possibility of error. They must consistently be reflecting on their own practice with an eye toward weeding out mistakes, with an eye toward self-correction. Socrates typically, but most explicitly by means of the counter-examples, exemplified this practice of self-reflection. In turn, the Philosophy for Children teacher, at her or his best, emulates this Socratic practice.

A summary is in order, but before doing that, let's remember what is being claimed here and what is not. We are not making specific historical claims, for example, that Lipman, or some other Philosophy for Children theorist, read, say, the *Laches*, and on a basis of that reading made specific suggestions regarding Philosophy for Children practice. Although things like that have certainly happened, the claim being made here is that *our* understanding of Socrates, and *our* returning to Plato's dialogues is helpful for our understanding of Philosophy for Children. Especially as things in Philosophy for Children became unsettled in ways that they were not during the period 1974–1987, it is helpful to have a touchstone. This is not to use Plato as an authority. Rather, it is to use him as he has always been used—as an intelligent guide through myriad contemporary philosophical and practical problems.

Now a brief summary of the ways in which an understanding of Socrates and Plato might inform Philosophy for Children practice:

(1) Socrates is neither Sophist nor natural philosopher—Socrates did not attempt to make the weaker argument appear to be stronger (that is the charge against the Sophists). He did not inquire into things "above the earth and below the heavens." He was always concerned with things that grew out of and defined human experience. The Philosophy for Children teacher, to the extent that she or he emulates Socrates, is sensitive to the structure of argumentation, avoids rhetoric that is convincing when the pattern of argumentation is not convincing, and always tries to build discussion from the interests of the community members.

(2) Socrates teaches by means of the dialectic. He engages his students in a teaching-learning experience called the "dialogue." A dialogue, in turn, involves a group of two or more people who are engaged in a discussion about a limited number of topics (usually one or two). The dialogue is purposeful—a resolution of some sort is sought. The task of the dialectician (the teacher) is to help with that resolu-

tion, to serve as a midwife, to aid in the process of birth (of meaning or truth) that is implicit to the dialogue. The Philosophy for Children teacher, emulating Socrates, tries to find the hidden gestalt of the dialogue, tries to expose the direction in which the dialogue is heading, and then, helps the classroom community, so the Philosophy for Children motto goes, "follow the inquiry wherever it leads."

(3) Socrates was, at once, a person who claimed to have no great wisdom while at the same time having an enormous amount of expertise. He really did not think highly of what he knew, or, for that matter, what other people knew. At the same time, he was adept at using a dialectical method to help people, if they would only listen, achieve the highest wisdom of which they were capable. In the *Apology*, the wisdom will be the knowledge that one does not know. In other dialogues, the *Republic*, for example, it might mean knowledge of the forms.

The Philosophy for Children teacher, emulating the character of Socrates, should be philosophically self-effacing but pedagogically strong. She or he might realize that what she or he knows, even if it appears in a curriculum guide, even if it is deemed essential by a state legislature, even if it is thought to be a defining characteristic of what some educated theorists deem "cultural literacy," pales in comparison with all that she or he does not know. In the face of all that she or he does not know, intellectual modesty appears the appropriate attitude. Starting from that attitude, the Philosophy for Children teacher must learn and master the skills of the sailing ship captain, of the orchestra leader. She or he must learn how to use the wind, the musical score, to achieve certain goals—arriving safely in port, performing beautifully a musical piece. She or he must learn how to help others follow the inquiry wherever it leads.

(4) Socrates exemplifies a belief in the power of the dialogue to discover truth and uncover meaning that borders on the religious. When one looks at the corpus of Platonic dialogues, Socrates, in almost an undiscriminating fashion, talks with the old and the young, with the expert and the novice, with the famous and the unknown, about matters of weight and importance. From the intimidating natural philosopher, Parmenides, to the unschooled slave in the *Meno*, Socrates enters the dialogue with the enthusiasm of one who firmly believes that something of significance will emerge. In a similar manner—and here, perhaps, is the defining belief of Philosophy for Children—the teacher believes that children can talk and think well about matters of the utmost significance, that the classroom, even the kin-

dergarten and first-grade ones, can be a place where such significant discourse can occur. The teacher believes, in effect, that young children have something important to contribute to philosophy and that philosophy has something important to contribute to them.

(5) Socrates lives philosophy. It is not something, one piece of clothing, that he dons for a brief period. If philosophy begins in wonder, in curiosity, then Socrates is always at the beginning of things. Philosophy is not something to be gotten over with so that one could get on to something else. For Socrates, this is the best thing that a person can do. Philosophy defines him and the fact that the dialogues are inconclusive only goes to show that there is always something more to wonder about.

One cannot mandate the sort of wonder that Socrates exhibits, but for the Philosophy for Children teacher, wonder is one of the cardinal educational virtues. She or he recognizes its worth, seeks it out, and nurtures it whenever possible. Wonder may not be quantifiable and, thus, may be overlooked in more traditional curriculum, but in Philosophy for Children it is the most necessary of conditions.

(6) Socrates is rigorous. What goes along with, what provides a very nice complement to the almost childlike quality of his curiosity is what William James would call "tough-mindedness" and what Ernest Hemingway called the ability to detect crap. Socrates, especially by means of the crucial counter-example, was constantly testing the theories of those around him for weakness. One of the now standard definitions of the critical thinker suggests that such a person is self-monitoring with an eye toward self-correction. The critical thinker may not discover the truth—that might be the province of the gods—but what the critical thinker is best at is recognizing and rooting out falsehood and mistakes. The Philosophy for Children teacher, emulating the character of Socrates, brings this quality of critical thought to the classroom community of inquiry. In both the primary and secondary literature on Philosophy for Children, the teacher is thought of as a sort of umpire—one who can bring the rules of a game (here, critical thinking) to a situation, and who can make sure that the rules are being followed.

We have used Socrates as a touchstone, as a way of looking at Philosophy for Children. One thing we have not done explicitly, although it can be argued that it is implicit in everything we have said, is to look at how what might be called Socrates' art is related to the perceived question of Philosophy for Children classroom practice.

The Philosophy for Children teacher is presented with a series of decisions that must be made. When do I let a child go on? When do I encourage him/her to get to the point? When do I squelch an anecdote? When do I nurture it? When do I bring children back to the original point? When do I allow a new path to emerge and, subsequently, control our discourse? All of these questions, and similar ones can be reduced to a simple one relating to the nature of the control the teacher exerts over the classroom discussion. The literature of Philosophy for Children since the early 1980s has yielded an "either-or" type answer to the question—either dialogue or conversation, but not both. A reference to Socrates and his art may go some way toward overcoming the dichotomy in the answer.

For example, the split between conversation and dialogue is seen in two companion articles by Laurence Splitter and San MacColl. Professor Splitter distinguishes dialogue from conversation by means of three necessary and "perhaps jointly sufficient" conditions. Dialogue is:

> (1) *essentially problematic*, *i.e.*, they (ideas or topics) are focused on some problem or issue for which there are at least two conflicting solutions or points of view.
> (2) Dialogical thinking is self-corrective or self-regulated thinking. Participants in dialogue are prepared both to challenge the thoughts of others, and to change their own minds in response to such challenge. This reflective aspect of thinking is characteristic of all modes of inquiry.
> (3) The characteristic—or perhaps we should say the environment in which the conversation occurs—is *egalitarian*, *i.e.*, the participants value themselves and one another equally for the purposes of the dialogue.[14]

Professor MacColl, on the other hand, argues that dialogues can be constraining precisely because they preclude the teacher from attending to important information—information that would, itself, contribute to the process of inquiry:

> It is the constraint of dialogue in a community for inquiry that leads to the neglect of non-verbal responses, pauses, expressions of emotion, and diversions from the logical course of the dialogue. They are all taken to be distractions from the dialogue, one way or another. I want to emphasize the significance of these features of conversation for a community of inquiry. With regard to the silences or the laughter and diversions, their force in directing—or stopping—a conversation is as legitimate as the force of logical steps. Anyone practicing community of inquiry takes them into account and no one could object to this.[15]

The point that MacColl makes in that first sentence is a crucial one. Practicing communities of inquiry, in fact, take into account that which, redundantly, counts. They and their teachers take into account the elegant logical move, the flawed bit of reasoning, and they applaud the former, while taking steps to correct the latter. But that is not all they do. Just as much, they and the teachers involved, take account of the variety of silences that occur in the course of a discussion. They note when the silence expresses confusion or hostility or, when the fates are kind, the impending emergence of a good idea. They take note of grimaces and sighs precisely because those grimaces and sighs might suggest, as much as a simple sentence, where the inquiry may or should go. The discussion is a function of a group of people thinking and feeling and acting together, and all of those things fuel the process of inquiry.

In a very real sense, both MacColl and Splitter are right if we can, as it were, just add a little sympathetic interpretation to their positions. Both, it would seem, are arguing that the teacher should attend to all relevant information. Splitter, in the specific article in question, is most concerned with focusing on that information that would be called linguistic or logical. MacColl, in her article, is more concerned with that information that could be called expressive or affective. To play with the metaphor, Splitter focuses on the notes while MacCall focuses on the rests. The music occurs when the notes and rests are put together.

But now the question reappears: How does a reliance on the character of Socrates help us, help the teachers, figure out what to do? How does a reliance on the character of Socrates help the teacher decide when to focus on the linguistic and when to focus on the affective? If one focused on the Platonic dialogues, one would find Socrates doing both, but it must be admitted, one would find him, almost invariably, coming down on the side of the linguistic. The Socrates of the dialogues is a creature of logic, more concerned with the validity and soundness of argumentation than with the feeling or intentions of arguers. But when we burrow a bit deeper into the character of the historic Socrates, it becomes clear that something more is going on, something that suggests that Socrates, himself, would argue that the reader not be misled by the written word:

> You know, Phaedeus, that's the strange thing about writing, which makes it
> truly analogous to painting. The painter's products stand before us as though

they were alive, but if you question them, they maintain a most majestic silence. It is the same with written words; they seem to talk to you as though they were intelligent, but if you ask them anything about what they say, from a desire to be instructed, they go on telling you just the same thing forever.[16]

The written dialogue, at best, is only a pale imitation of the spoken one. In the former, once the words are written they remain forever unresponsive. In the latter, when uttered, one can always go back to the speaker, as presumably Socrates did, and ask them what they mean. When one does this, one, of necessity, will have to interpret the words and the silence, the logic and the affect. While the historic Socrates does not answer all of the practical questions that the Philosophy for Children teacher has regarding the next step in the discussion process, he does point to the very complexity of the task we take upon ourselves when we attempt to do philosophy with children. An awareness of that complexity might be the most important asset the teacher has.

Notes

1. John Dewey, "My Pedagogic Creed" in Jo Ann Boydston (ed.), *John Dewey: The Early Works, 1895–1898, Vol. 5.* (Carbondale, Illinois: Southern Illinois University Press, 1972), p. 84.

2. Wayne P. Pomerlau, *Twelve Great Philosophers.* (New York: Ardsley House Publishers, 1997), p. 9.

3. Plato, *Socrates' Defense* in Edith Hamilton and Huntington Cairns (eds.), *The Collected Dialogues of Plato.* (New York: Pantheon Books, 1964), p. 5.

4. *Ibid.*, pp. 9–10.

5. *Ibid.*, p. 9.

6. Plato, the *Republic* in Edith Hamilton and Huntington Cairns (eds.), *The Collected Dialogues of Plato.* (New York: Pantheon Books, 1964), p. 7.

7. The imagery of course, is the late Paulo Freire's. Paulo Freire, *The Pedagogy of the Oppressed.* (New York: The Continuim Publishing Corporation, 1990) pp. 57–74.

8. Plato, *Socrates' Defense* in Edith Hamilton and Huntington Cairns (eds.), *The Collected Dialogues of Plato.* (New York: Pantheon Books, 1964), p. 7.

9. A. N. Whitehead, *The Aims of Education.* (New York: Free Press, 1976), p. 37.

10. Plato, "Crito" in Edith Hamilton and Huntington Cairns (eds.), *The Collected Dialogues of Plato.* (New York: Pantheon Books, 1964), pp. 27–39.

11. Plato, *Socrates' Defense* in Edith Hamilton and Huntington Cairns (eds.), *The Collected Dialogues of Plato.* (New York: Pantheon Books, 1964), p. 8.

12. *Ibid.*, p. 9.

13. "Interview With William Maxwell" in *New York Times Magazine.* March 9, 1997.

14. Laurence Splitter, "Dialogue, Thinking and The Search for Meaning" in Ronald F. Reed (ed.), *When We Talk.* (Fort Worth, Texas: Analytic Teaching Press, 1992), pp. 1–2.

15. San MacColl, "Conversation and Dialogue—Not Just What You Say But How You Say It" in Ronald F. Reed (ed.), *When We Talk.* (Fort Worth, Texas: Analytic Teaching Press, 1992), p. 79.

16. Plato, *Phaedrus* in Edith Hamilton and Huntington Cairns (eds.), *The Collected Dialogues of Plato.* (New York: Pantheon Books, 1964), p. 521.

Chapter 4

The Social Context
of Philosophy for Children

One is tempted, when trying to sketch the social and political context of Philosophy for Children, to point to the turmoil that was the United States in the late 1960s and early 1970s, that is, Vietnam, protests, the student movement, civil rights movement, Black separatism, feminism. It was a gaudy era, as silly as it was tragic, as serious as it was comic. Marlon Brando, in the classic youth-rebellion movie, *The Wild One*,[1] when questioned as to the purpose of his rebellion, answered "What do you got?" Rebellion was infectious; and, at the time, it seemed that revolution was in the air.

The American philosopher John Dewey (1859–1952) warned repeatedly against "either-or" splits, against staking out extreme positions and then forcing the reader to choose between them. The late 1960s and early 1970s were characteristically "either-or." Indeed, one of the great tag lines of the era was "either you are part of the solution, or you are part of the problem." It seemed that there was no middle ground.

In education, the book that best showed this either-or dichotomy was Neil Postman and Charles Weingartner's *Teaching as a Subversive Activity*. True to its name, the book assumed a thoroughly corrupt education system which required drastic overhaul. The teacher's task was subversive. To help the teacher achieve that task, Postman and Weingartner proposed a series of mandates, at once serious and fanciful, which included the declaration of a five-year moratorium on the use of all textbooks, a requirement that "'English' teachers 'teach' math, math teachers English, social studies teachers science, science teachers art,"[2] "the transfer of all elementary school teachers to high school and vice versa,"[3] and a limit of "three declarative sentences per class, and 15 interrogatives"[4] per teacher.

The point of those sixteen or so rules was to attack retaining walls (textbooks, expertise, teacher talk) so that a decaying edifice might fall of its own weight, thereby offering new teachers the opportunity to create a more pupil-friendly building. Rightly so, Postman and Weingartner, along with their myriad readers on university campuses and, especially within schools of education, viewed the work as revolutionary. Postman and Weingartner each were former high school teachers, knew the school system from the inside, and knew where and how to best use subversive force. Their purpose, explicitly, was political.

Today, stripped of the jargon of sixties radicalism, *Teaching as a Subversive Activity* seems more a book of gentle, good sense than a primer on revolution. It is a book on the side of the child, of using what today would be a holistic approach to education. Still, there are ways in which it is markedly different from Philosophy for Children. This difference, in turn, points to ways in which Philosophy for Children is different from much of the immediate context of its birth.

First, and in some ways foremost, is the character of the person who originated Philosophy for Children. Matthew Lipman was born in New Jersey in 1922, where he attended public schools, graduating from high school in 1940. His undergraduate study, which encompassed courses taken at Stanford University (California), Shrivenham America University (England) and Columbia University (New York), was interrupted by a three year military service with the United States Infantry during World War II. Lipman returned to Columbia in 1946 and received a B.S. in General Studies in 1948. During the next six years, he studied philosophy at Columbia University, the Sorbonne in Paris, and the University of Vienna. In 1954, he received his Ph.D. through the Department of Philosophy at Columbia University.

From 1953 to 1972, Lipman held a variety of teaching and administrative positions. He was instructor in philosophy at Brooklyn College (Spring 1953); lecturer in Philosophy and Contemporary Civilization, Columbia College, Columbia University (1954–1962); lecturer in Contemporary Civilization, Mannes College of Music, New York City (1955–1963); adjunct assistant and associate professor, School for General Studies, City College of New York (1953–1975); lecturer in Contemporary Civilization, College of Engineering, Columbia University (1961–1963); assistant, associate, and full professor of philosophy, College of Pharmaceutical Sciences, Columbia University (1954–1972); visiting professor of philosophy, Sarah Lawrence College (1964–1965); chairman, Philosophy Department, Evening Division, Baruch School, City College of New York (1960–1972): and chairman, Department of General Education, College of Pharmaceutical Sciences, Columbia University (1962–1972).

During that period of nearly twenty years, Lipman's main interests were in the area of aesthetics. Although he did produce a general introductory text in philosophy, *Discovering Philosophy*, the vast majority of his work was either in aesthetics or in areas closely related to aesthetics. During that time, he produced "The Relation of Critical Function and Critical Discussions to Art Inquiry," "The Physical Theory in Aesthetic Experience," "The Aesthetic Presence of the Body"; and reviews of *The Artist as Creator* by Melton C. Nahm, *Art, Form, and Civilization* by Ernest Mando, and Nelson Goodman's *Language of Art*. In addition, Lipman produced two books on aesthetics during this period: *What Happens In Art* and *Contemporary Aesthetics*.

By the time of the creation of Philosophy for Children (1969–1974) Lipman was a well established philosopher, along with being an academic who had successfully navigated the waters of tenure and administration. Rather than being a part of the student uprisings of the 1960s, in many ways, he was, if not the target, then the recipient of a good deal of that unrest. A professor in his late forties at the time, a veteran of World War II, he could, regardless of his political leanings, have been expected to view a good deal of the rhetoric of protest with some skepticism, if not with downright hostility. After all, when Mario Savio, leader of the Free Speech movement at Berkeley, uttered his famous "Don't trust anyone over thirty," he was not, it is to be assumed, excluding professors of philosophy from Columbia.

Lipman, himself, points to his own reaction to the student riots of 1968 as part of the genesis of Philosophy for Children:

> At the time, I was a professor of philosophy for Columbia University. No doubt the student riots of 1968 contributed to my uneasiness about what I was doing. As I watched the fumbling efforts of the university to reappraise itself, I couldn't help concluding that the problems of Columbia could not be solved within the framework of that institution. Teachers and students alike, we had all come out of the same matrix of elementary and secondary education. If we had been miseducated in those early grades, then very likely we had come to share many misconceptions that would enable us to botch our later schooling in happy collusion with one another.[5]

Lipman, here, places himself squarely in the middle of the dispute between administration and faculty. That middle, it will be remembered, is precisely the location that was denied by both radicals of the left and of the right during the 1960s. In effect, Lipman is making a twofold claim. The first part of the claim is that there should be some way that reason might mediate between or among competing claims, that is, if students and administrators—or extending things to include the ultimate disputants of 1960s campus debate, hawks and doves—sat down and reasoned together, their efforts would yield a workable solution to the problems at hand. The second part of the claim is as straightforward as the first: given the breakdown in elementary and secondary education to which both parties were heir, a reliance on reasoning at the university level is misplaced.

Those claims came from the professorate. Unlike Postman and Weingartner, Lipman was not a former school teacher trying to effect change in a familiar environment. Rather, he was a professor of philosophy and logic who was beginning to have severe doubts about the efficacy of logic to do that which traditionally it was thought, best of all, to do:

> In 1969, having taught introductory logic to college students for some years, I was beginning to have serious concerns about its value. I had entertained similar doubts while I was a graduate student, for I hadn't found the subject a congenial one. But when one has taught a course for several years, one comes to think of it as useful and meaningful, whatever one's earlier reservations. Yet, I found myself wondering what possible benefits my students were obtaining from studying the rules for determining the validity of syllogisms or from learning how to construct contrapositives. Did they actually reason any better as a result of studying logic? Were not their linguistic and psychological habits already so firmly established that *any* sort of practice or instruction in reasoning would come too late? [6]

To summarize, Lipman's immediate context, the context for the genesis of Philosophy for Children, was the university and not the public school. Within the university, Lipman was troubled by the seeming inefficiency of logic and philosophy as tools for improving the reasoning skills of young adults. In addition, it will not hurt to bring in two additional factors: First, Lipman was working in a subdiscipline which is typically viewed as soft or esoteric. If one is troubled regarding the impact of formal logic on reasoning skills, one must have serious reservations regarding the utility of, say, philosophy of art to do the same things. Secondly, he was working in professional, technical schools (schools of pharmacology, the Baruch School of Business, Mannes College of Music). Students and professors at liberal art universities may, at least, give lip service to the idea that, say, philosophy has intrinsic merit. Professors and students in professional schools tend to demand a more utilitarian justification.

In retrospect, then, it is easy to pull together this demand for practical results coupled with a belief in traditional ways of doing philosophy and see Lipman's response as the only logical one: prepare university students to reason well by reasoning with them (well) before they get to university. Even though the idea is novel, *in retrospect*, it has a feeling of inevitability to it. But that feeling is contradicted by the facts.

Philosophy, historically, has been thought to be the province of the mature. Plato started the discipline down that road in *The Republic*. Speaking of the "dialectic," the character Socrates says of young people:

> When they get their first taste of it, [they] treat argumentation as a form of sport solely for purposes of contradiction. When someone has proved them wrong, they copy his method to confute others, delighting like puppies in tugging and tearing at anyone who comes near them. And so, after a long course of proving others wrong and being proved wrong themselves, they rush to the conclusion that all they once believed is false; and the result is that in the eyes of the world they discredit, not themselves only, but the whole business of philosophy.[7]

To give the tools of philosophy to the young was seen as analogous to giving a very young child a loaded gun: she/he could do damage to herself/himself, to others, and to the instrument itself.

In addition to philosophers, there was, and is, a feeling among adults, in general, and parents in particular, that the task of the child was primarily one of obedience. Since, *pace* Jean Piaget, children were said to be incapable of abstract reasoning, the sort of reasoning that philosophy demands, children would be better served if they *did* the right thing; if they did as a responsible adult dictated, rather than attempt to reason their way to a correct plan of action.

The final prejudice against philosophy comes from the school system itself. In many ways, the late 1960s began what might be called a period of "overload" in the schools. The schools were, at once, being asked to tend to the traditional curriculum, keep children and teachers abreast of the information explosion that was being signaled by the advent of computer use related to schooling; and respond to the myriad social, political, and economic issues that faced the family in late-century America.

Lipman's own educational background was of little help. A product of public schooling in the 1930s, he had little knowledge of what the public school classroom was like in the late 1960s. Lipman's schooling was colored by the experience of the Depression and the foreshadowing of World War II and was grounded in a tradition of the arts and the humanities. It was a period of remarkable homogeneity, especially when compared with schooling in the late 1960s—a period when, given the challenge of Sputnik and the subsequent National Defense Education Act of 1958, education was shifting from a traditional arts curriculum to one more heavily connected with science and technology.

In addition, Lipman's background in educational theory was minimal. What he knew about it, he had gleaned from reading a copy of John Dewey's *Intelligence in the Modern World*, which he carried in his duffel bag during World War II.[8] That work gives glimpses of Dewey's educational philosophy but hardly has the breadth or depth of Dewey's *Democracy in Education* or even the slimmer *Experience and Education*.

It is not surprising, then, that the notion of educational reform, let alone revolution, was not at the forefront of Lipman's thinking at the time of the creation of Philosophy for Children. He originally conceived of a story or vignette that children might stumble on in a library, in much the same way that he had stumbled on *Intelligence in the Modern World*. That story would use philosophy as a goad to the study of logic. Writing about his initial thought, three decades later, Lipman said:

> . . . it occurred to me that children could be induced to study logic only by bribing them with philosophy. Youngsters and philosophy are natural allies, for both begin in wonder. Indeed, only philosophers and artists systematically and professionally engage in that perpetuation of wonder so characteristic of the everyday experience of the child. Why not borrow the ideas of the philosophical tradition, then, inserting then into the novel so that the children in the story could go beyond wonder and could reflect upon and meaningfully discuss the metaphysical, epistemological, aesthetic, and ethical aspects of their experience?[9]

What is telling about this quotation is the way in which Lipman saw the relationship of philosophy to logic. The former was seen as something to which children have a natural curiosity. Children wonder at the world in much the same ways that philosophers do. In fact, the questions that very young children trouble their parents with—"Where do things come from?", "Where do they go when they die?", "What makes me, me?", and when the child is a bit older, "What is fairness and why don't you treat me fairly?"—are precisely the questions that philosophers trouble themselves with.

Lipman, here, and one must assume that his meaning is accurate, took no stance, at the time of the creation of Philosophy for Children, regarding Plato's remarks about the ill effects of the "dialectic" on young people, or of parents' and educators' fears that philosophy might engender disobedience among young people. Rather, he made a rather straightforward statement about the convergence of philosophical activity with the activity of the child. He then proposed to make much of that convergence and use it to get children to swallow the medicine (logic) which would improve their reasoning abilities. If successful, the endeavor would, in the long run, contribute to an improvement in the quality of thought in the university.

So far, the attempt has been made to avoid any sweeping claims, any generalizations about America in the late 1960s. Rather, we have attempted to focus on the concrete situations in which the creator of Philosophy for Children found himself during that period, that is, a professional academic who was troubled by specific disabilities among his students and who sought specific ways of remedying those disabilities. Because Philosophy for Children has become so large and because it means so many different things to different people, it seemed appropriate to keep things narrow at the beginning. There are, however, things that are global and cannot be ignored when describing the context of the genesis of Philosophy for Children: the Cold War, and the civil rights movement. Each had roots in World War II and its aftermath. Each, in effect, grew up with Lipman.

At this point, the Cold War is receding in memory, already having a patina of age if not quaintness. Today's first graders grew up in a world that did not have what Ronald Reagan called an evil empire. For that generation, as it goes through school, the Cold War will become simply another artifact of history class: The Spanish-American War, the Dust Bowl, and the Cold War. But for people and programs like Philosophy for Children, the Cold War spun out metaphors that defined consciousness.

Here was Thomas Hobbes's state of nature played out on a global stage: two empires of rough equality, fighting for a limited number of goods, each poised, ready to annihilate the other, with the fate of each best characterized as in Hobbes's none-too-melodramatic prose as "solitary, poor, nasty, brutish, and short."[10] It was a state of (cold) warfare: a state in which one had every reason to believe that the other would kill one for what one had. Thus, caution and timidity, coupled with a seeming brashness, a sort of whistling in the dark mentality, were the order of the day. Jonathan Schell wrote a series of articles for the *New Yorker,* later published as *The Fate of The Earth,*[11] in which he showed how immune to reason the nuclear stand-off between the Soviet Union and the United States was and how aleatory the entire situation had become. According to Schell it was a function of chance that nuclear annihilation had not yet occurred. It was only a matter of time until luck would run out.

Schell's despair, however, came after three decades of nuclear stockpiling, after a third of a century of cold war. At the beginning, in the late 1940s through the 1950s and 1960s, it was thought that the battle could be won. In Admiral Hyman Rickover's words, and here perhaps, the dominant metaphor of the era, there was a race among the nations—we were engaged in a race with the Soviet Union—and victory would go to the fastest and to the strongest, to those who could endure, who could stay the course.[12]

It is hard to overstate the impact of both the literal (cold war) and the metaphorical (race among nations) on consciousness in general, and particularly on thought within universities. Regardless of one's politics, it was clear that something of monumental importance was at stake, that something significant could be gained or lost, and that history stood ready to judge the actors on the political stage.

Perhaps that is why the focus turned so quickly and even violently to educational questions. Since we were involved in a life-and-death struggle with the Soviet Union, we needed all of our resources at hand, functioning at full capacity. Yet when one looked at the youth of the day they seemed, at once, superficial, distracted, and not equal to the task.

This was the beginning of an identifiable youth culture in the United States, and Madison Avenue had recognized it and was now catering to it, supplying a steady stream of bad situation comedies, simplistic music, and gaudy movies, all of which would anesthetize teenagers so that any kind of vigorous thought would be as foreign to them as the streets of Nairobi. Again, the race would be lost unless something could be done with American youth, something that would help them achieve a seriousness of moral purpose along with the cognitive ability to ascertain and achieve morally worthy aims. The race would be lost unless American youth could match the seriousness of purpose of their Soviet counterparts.

The other factor that defined the era in which Philosophy for Children was born is the civil rights struggle and its nascent awareness of social injustice. If the Cold War is a memory, how even more ephemeral the climate in this country regarding race in the years immediately following World War II. Black men and women had served their country well in a largely segregated armed forces. They fought and many of them died in defense of the ideals—democracy, fair play, helping the powerless—that this country prides itself upon. They returned to a country in which they were not entitled to the rights for which they had just fought. Racism was not just condoned, it was mandated by law.

The experience of Jackie Robinson and the Brooklyn Dodgers gives a clear glimpse of the American society of this period.[13] The noble experiment involved breaking the color barrier that had precluded blacks from playing major league baseball during the twentieth century. The experiment, and at the time, it was considered an experiment which carried with it the real possibility of failure—involved not just finding a baseball player who excelled at the game, a player who could run and throw and hit. It involved finding a person of a certain age; a person who was mature and intelligent enough to understand the ramifications of the experiment; a person who could calculate the long-term benefits of submitting to the vile abuse that would be heaped upon him by bigoted players, managers, and fans; a person who could refrain from reacting to injustice for reason of justice.

The abuse and the indignity that Robinson suffered, the strength of his character, and the support of a few of his teammates (Pee Wee Reese, Carl Erskine, and Ralph Branca) has become, with good reason, the stuff of legend. For a year, 1947, Robinson may not have attempted to live up to the principles of the gospels—return good for evil—but he certainly did live up to those of the Platonic dialogues—do not return evil for evil. He had made a promise to Brooklyn's general manager, Branch Rickey, that for a year he would do nothing to jeopardize the experiment. He was thrown at by opposing pitchers, spiked by runners, and taunted at every turn. He kept his promise.

What receives less attention, however, is the status of the experiment in the years after 1947, in the years after the promise was kept. During the period 1948–1958, Robinson established a reputation for being a fierce competitor, a man sensitive to offense and attack, a man who was always willing to return physical and mental abuse with its like. That Jackie Robinson is certainly not the one portrayed in many of the stories and celebration that marked the fiftieth anniversary of the integration of major league baseball, but in many ways he is, if not a more compelling moral figure, then certainly a more complex one. That complexity, in turn, points to the complexity of the age.

The Jackie Robinson of 1948–1957, rather than being a saint, was simply a decent, intelligent man, who on a day-to-day basis, had a growing awareness, a visceral one, that he was involved in a situation that was, at once, unintelligible and unjust. The taunts, the racial epithets did not stop once the case was made, convincingly, that blacks and whites could play baseball together. Indeed to some extent, the success of the experiment created more problems, that is, it created the illusion, just as Brown versus the Board of Education created the illusion, that the significant problems had been solved. For example, the success of the Brooklyn Dodger experiment allowed teams like the New York Yankees and the Boston Red Sox, to refrain from hiring black ball players. In a curious logical move, Robinson's integration of baseball freed some owners from the pressure to integrate their own teams.

In a future chapter, we will talk about the dispute between modernism and postmodernism,[14] but here, it will not hurt to point to some of the changes that were being played out in the Jackie Robinson experiment. Modernism is typically said to begin with the Enlightenment—mainly the French Enlightenment, but also that movement as it occurred in England and the United States. It was a period characterized by an almost religious faith in the ability of reason to solve human problems, problems that previously had seemed unsolvable. Seventeenth-century precursors of modernism like the philosopher Descartes and the scientist Isaac Newton had provided a firm foundation for thought ("I think, therefore I am"), along with a methodology for discovering truth (the scientific method) that seemed reliable. It seemed that not only was it possible to solve all problems but that it would also be possible for an educated person to know everything worth knowing. Thus, the establishment of a truly audacious attempt—the construction of a complete encyclopedia.

Behind this belief in the ability of human reason to know and to do, was a belief about the nature of reality. The world, including human nature, was said to have a structure, and the theories that people constructed in, say, chemistry or biology were attempts to correspond with the way things really are. One sees this belief in a structure to which theories are meant to correspond in the classic American Enlightenment document, *The Declaration of Independence*, where people are said to be endowed by their creator with certain inalienable rights. Those rights may be hidden, they may be obscured, but reason, reasonable people, can uncover what is there. It is possible to create a more just society by following the dictates of right reason.

The 1947 Jackie Robinson experiment reads like pure modernism. Although it would be foolish to discount the economic forces that were at play—changing racial patterns in cities where major league baseball was played, the migration of southern blacks to those cities, and so on—there is a sense in which the experiment is a straightforward modern morality play: Black people have been denied the rights to which they are entitled. When people who have been denying those rights come to understand the error of their ways, they will change their behavior.

Those modern beliefs seemed at best problematic post-1947, at least in regard to the Robinson experiment. It did not seem, on the one hand, that some people could be led to the truth and, on the other, that a change in behavior would occur even if people come to understand the truth. Stated another way, there was a portion of American society that either would not see the injustice in racist policies, or was insufficiently bothered by that racism to do anything about it.

The attempt is not made to present history as purely linear, nor to put too much weight on an example from the world of sports. Surely, something very much like the Robinson experiment as modern morality play took place during the early days of the civil rights struggle of the 1960s. There is hardly a more modern document than Martin Luther King's "Letter from Birmingham Jail." Even when he is calling for civil disobedience, even when he recognizes, with the theologian Reinhold Niebuhr, that groups may not be as able as individuals to grasp moral truth, there is a belief in the ability of reason to solve human problems that is almost identical to that displayed in the Robinson experiment. Writing to his fellow clergymen, Dr. King said:

> You may well ask, 'Why direct action?' 'Why sit-ins, marches, etc.?' 'Isn't negotiation a better path?' You are exactly right in your call for negotiation. Indeed, this is the purpose of direct action. Nonviolent direct action seeks to create such a crisis and establish such creative tension that a community that has consistently refused to negotiate is forced to confront the issue. So the purpose of the direct action is to create a situation so crisis-packed that it will inevitably open the door to negotiation.[15]

Still, the point is that the principles of the 1965 letter—the faith in the efficacy of human reason once people were awakened by means of a crisis—were put to a severe test in the years following 1965 just as those same principles were put to a test in the years following the Robinson experiment. Both events, the civil rights struggle as played out post-1947 and post-1965, are significant parts of the context of Philosophy for Children. To understand Philosophy for Children involves recognizing an evolving understanding of the power and efficacy of reason itself. We will return to this issue in the modern-postmodern chapter.

Notes

1. The 1950s film was clearly a precursor of events in the 1960s.

2. Neil Postman and Charles Weingartner, *Teaching As a Subversive Activity.* (New York: Delta Books, 1969), p. 138.

3. *Ibid.*, p. 138.

4. *Ibid.*, p. 138.

5. Matthew Lipman, "On Writing a Philosophical Novel" in Ann Margaret Sharp and Ronald Reed (eds.), *Studies in Philosophy for Children: Harry Stottlemeier's Discovery.* (Philadelphia: Temple University Press, 1992), p. 3.

6. *Ibid.*, p. 3.

7. Plato, *Republic*, Book 7, trans. Francis Cornford. (New York: Oxford University Press, 1945), p. 261.

8. Matthew Lipman, "On Writing a Philosophical Novel" in Ann Margaret Sharp and Ronald Reed (eds.), *Studies in Philosophy for Children: Harry Stottlemeier's Discovery.* (Philadelphia: Temple University Press, 1992), p. 5.

9. *Ibid.*, p. 5.

10. Thomas Hobbes, *Leviathan.* (New York: Collier Books, 1971), p. 100.

11. Jonathan Schell, *The Fate of The Earth.* (New York: Knopf, 1982).

12. H.G. Rickover, *American Education: A National Failure.* (New York: E.P. Dutton & Co., 1963)

13. The Jackie Robinson analysis is derived from Roger Kahn, *The Boys of Summer.* (New York: Harper Row, 1972).

14. Modernism and Postmodernism have as many definitions as there are writers. Here, and in the following chapter, we will largely follow Richard Rorty's distinction between those terms as exposed in Richard Rorty, *Objectivity, Relativism, and Truth.* (New York: Cambridge University Press, 1991)

15. Martin Luther King, "Letter From Birmingham Jail" in Robert C. Lamm, *The Humanities in Western Culture.* (Chicago: Brown & Benchmark, 1996), p. 476.

Chapter 5

Modernism, Postmodernism, and Philosophy for Children

Think for a moment about Plato's two-world theory, especially as exemplified in the Allegory of the Cave. There are two worlds—the intelligible and the sensory. The process of education is one of leaving the sensory through the dialectic to arrive at the intelligible (the world of Forms). That other world, the intelligible one, is that which gives the world in which we find ourselves, whatever meaning, reality, or beauty that it has. This action, for example, is more courageous than that because it more closely resembles or partakes in the form of beauty which exists in the intelligible word. The task is to emerge from the cave, fashion an exit from the cave which, in turn, will illuminate the cave and all the things which exist there. Once one understands the Allegory of the Cave, once one gets a feeling for the two-world theory, it is obvious that the intelligible world has an enormous impact, a defining one, on the sensory one.

Now, taking some license with Plato, imagine a tri-world theory. First, there is the world of everyday experience. This is the world in which we live and breathe, hope and wonder, plan, and attempt to control. We push against our environment, we try to achieve things; the environment pushes back, it responds, and on the basis of that response, we continue on, or we try something else.

Above or beyond that world is another one—the world of the disciplines such as chemistry and history and psychology. Those disciplines are comprised of organized bodies of information, specific areas or domains, and agreed-upon ways of dealing with that information. The biologist looks at certain things (living ones) and discerns certain information about them through methods that a lay-person would call scientific or biological.

This world of the disciplines has an obvious, almost line-by-line connection with the world of everyday experience. We use, although not as effectively as we would like, the findings of the disciplines to make our way through the everyday world. We use those findings to predict, to control, and to understand. In many ways, the world of the disciplines has the same relationship to everyday experience as the intelligible world has to the sensory.

But what of this third world? Imagine a third world, a world in which reflection about the world of disciplines and the world of everyday experience takes place, a world in which the relationship of the disciplinary world to that of everyday experience is questioned. Call that shadowy place the world of the philosophy of the disciplines, a world in which the criteria, standards and assumptions of the disciplines are themselves questioned. While it is clear that disciplinary work has a strong relationship to everyday experience—the scientist discovers a vaccine, the artist presents a novel way of looking at things—it is not all that clear what the relationship is between the world we have called philosophy of the disciplines and the world of everyday experience.

Consider, for example, the enormous, at times almost violent, debate that has been waged on university campuses and within scholarly journals for the past two decades. During that period, it is not too much of an overstatement to say that the two sides in the debate—modernists and postmoderns—have acted in ways closely analogous to the Soviet Union and the United States during the Cold War. Modernists have presented themselves as champions of order, tradition and stability while picturing postmoderns as barbarians at the gate who would like nothing so much as to destroy the canons of Western civilization and replace them with drivel and fluff. Postmoderns argue that modernism is racist, sexist, and classest, an outdated attempt to maintain an oppressive social and political system. It is probably a good thing that neither side has access to nuclear weapons.

While all of this has been going on, however, the payoff in terms of everyday experience has been mixed. In some fields, like philosophy or art, there clearly has been influence. Given the rise of postmodernism, one simply does not do philosophy the way one did it forty years ago. The assumptions about truth, perspective, nature, and so on have, at least, been challenged, thereby forcing attempts at justification and explanation that were considered unnecessary in previous days. To the extent that philosophy (and art) have an impact on every-

day experience, to that extent the debate has had practical consequence. In other disciplines, however, disciplines such as chemistry or
geology, one is hard-pressed to see that there has been a debate or, if
such a debate has occurred, what the ramifications are for everyday
experience.

There is another problem with the modernism-postmodernism debate. It has something to do with dating and for our purposes we will
call it the historical one. Some theorists view the advent of
postmodernism as beginning with a reaction to the atrocities of World
War II. Here the claim is that Hitler is a sort of classical modern figure,
heir to the excesses of Enlightenment thought, reason decontextualized,
leading to the insanity of the Holocaust.

Other theorists date postmodernism from the time it entered specific disciplines or migrated to different countries. Thus postmodernism
begins in American philosophy in the 1970s largely due to the work
of French intellectuals being studied on American campuses during
that period. Still others view it as a recurring event. For example,
thinkers like Lyotard[1] define it as any period of revolutionary activity,
anytime when dominant paradigms are overthrown, and so thinkers
like Aristotle or Augustine or even Descartes himself can be thought
of as postmodern (revolutionary) thinkers.

In this chapter, we would like to avoid the acrimony of the debate.
We assume that the debate itself is enlightening, that it can and does
help illuminate basic philosophical, philosophy of education, and philosophy for children problems. Basically, our assumption is that the
debate and the consequent careful attention to problems can help us
answer philosophical questions like "What should I do?" and "What
should I believe?" or, relating it directly to Philosophy for Children
practice, "What sort of person am I trying to create when I do Philosophy for Children?" and "How do I go about doing that?"

In addition, in this chapter, we will also avoid the historical, not
because we think it is unimportant, but because we believe that conceptual questions have more of a direct impact on questions of practice. We will assume, for example, that Richard Rorty's understanding
of postmodernism is clear and to the point without assuming either
that postmodernism itself is good or viable or appealing. We will then
relate that understanding of postmodernism to Philosophy for Children practice. The argument will be that postmodernism (more precisely, the debate between modernism and postmodernism) engenders rethinking about such crucial issues as truth, objectivity, fairness,

and justice. Ultimately, the debate encourages thought about the nature of philosophy and what it means to be educated. This chapter will overlap but, to some extent formalize, things that were mentioned in chapter 4 on the social context of Philosophy for Children.

When one looks at the work of the French philosopher, Rene Descartes (1591–1650) one sees the seeds of modernism. In works like *Rules for the Direction of Understanding* (written in the 1620s but not published until 1701), *Discourse on Method* (1637), *Meditations on First Philosophy* (1641), and *Principles of Philosophy* (1645), Descartes set the agenda for modern philosophy. Alfred North Whitehead said, without too much exaggeration, that all philosophy is a footnote to Plato. It is not unreasonable to suggest that all modern philosophy is a footnote to Descartes. He set the stage on which the drama of modern philosophy has been played.

Descartes' methodology was one of systematic doubt. I can be mistaken about a host of things. I can think that the wall is red when in fact it is orange. I can mistakenly believe that the submerged stick is bent. I could even believe that I am in a crowded room filled with close friends when, in fact, I am dreaming. The point that Descartes noticed—and it is a commonplace one, one that most of us realize as logically possible—is that we can be deceived about virtually everything that we take to be true. What Descartes did was to take the commonplace fact and turn it into a methodology. Descartes said that if a thing *could* be doubted, if it was logically possible that what we took to be true *could* turn out to be false, then it *should* be doubted.[2]

The reason for that method of systematic doubt is as commonplace as the (logical) ability to doubt. Descartes wanted to arrive at a firm foundation, a foundation that was itself indubitable. Descartes, like the rest of us, did not want to build on a weak and shifting foundation. And the foundation he arrived at was the famous—"*Je pense, donc je suis*" or "I think, therefore I am." This proposition was thought to be indubitable because even the attempt to doubt was a form of thinking, hence, confirming the proposition itself.

Once one arrived at the firm foundation, then one could attempt to construct a system which was as indubitable as the foundation itself. One needed, thus, a methodology—and here, the development of a scientific method modeled on mathematics—that would be up to the task.

If one wanted a brief characterization of the Cartesian program, one might say that it involved an attempt to go from doubt to certainty. To us in the twentieth century, there is something eminently reasonable about the program. We accept as one of *our* commonplaces that theories need (firm) foundations. Indeed, that is one of the prime justifications for university offerings like Foundations of Education. A question might be asked, thus, regarding a claim that Descartes is one of the great revolutionaries in the history of philosophy.

When one looks at that history, a rationale for the claim becomes apparent. For medieval thinkers, and it really does not matter what tradition one looks at, the attempt had virtually nothing to do with striving to achieve certainty. Medieval thinkers—Jewish, Christian, Islamic—existed in a tradition which was assumed, which was given. Using the language we have adapted here, the rock-solid foundation was given in the Bible or the Koran. The task of the thinker was to build on that foundation, to construct theories that explained or justified it. St. Augustine, for example, claimed that the only way truth could be discovered was by means of the Inner Light—an understanding of things that was a function of the believer's relationship to Jesus.

Pushing back just a bit further, even thinkers like Socrates, Plato, and Aristotle would be somewhat dumbfounded by this attempt to reach certainty. For the Greeks, especially the Athenians, the polis (the city-state) was the world. Those who existed outside the walls of the city were considered barbarians, as somehow less than truly human. On the one hand, this gave the Greeks a rationale for thinking little of the rights of others and for enslaving them. On the other, it made them quite aware of how deeply their own humanity was tied to the polis. When, for example, Socrates was given the opportunity to leave the city, he chose death over exile. To leave the city would deprive him of the foundation which made the dialectic possible.

At this point, with Descartes as a background, we can start to make some explicit claims about modernism. We will assign letters to the claims and that, in turn, will give a ready way of getting at the competing claims of postmodernism.[3]

(A) *Thought can be divorced from its context.* Moderns believe that thought can and should be separated from the thinker, his or her background and intentions. It is possible to focus on the formal quality of thought, of propositions, of argument. Think of it this way: in order to know what a speech is about, in order to know whether the speaker is speaking truthfully or falsely, all that you need is a transcript of the speech. You do not have to focus on the speaker or the audience, or the interchange that has taken place. To reduce it further, it does not matter who is speaking or who is being addressed. The focus is on what is said: Are the arguments valid? Do they bear scrutiny? To reduce it even further, there is a difference between the thinker and the thought, the arguer and the argument. It is possible to focus on the thought, on the argument. Progress toward the discerning of truth or, at least, the avoidance of error, occurs when the focus is on such formal qualities.

(B) *Thought must be anchored in a firm foundation.* Cultures shift and people's belief systems evolve. Modernists believe that one needs some starting point, some foundation that does not shift, that does not evolve. Modernists look for a foundation of thought, a starting point that is not culturally determined, that is not a function of individual subjectivity or mere preferences. From such a foundation, one is able to evaluate critically cultures and belief systems. The attempt, metaphorically speaking, is to find a "point" outside of culture which is not itself culturally determined.

(C) *Certainty carries more weight than mere truth.* There are many things that are true and that I can know to be true without being certain of them. Indeed, Descartes pointed out a number of them. I *can* know that the stick is not bent without being certain of that. I can know that this is not a dream without being certain. Again, what Descartes was about was making much of the logical possibility of doubt. So, what moderns are after is certainty or, redundantly, absolute certainty. They are after a truth which is indubitable, which has been proven, and which is beyond suspicion. One then sees how important doubt is for modernism. The moderns will doubt and will be skeptical until they have been convinced by indubitable propositions or by means of deductive arguments based on those propositions. Moderns do not want to leap to conclusions. They want to go step-by-step, doubting whenever possible, until they arrive at absolute certainty. They would rather not know than know by means of a lucky guess. At heart, modernism is about avoiding mistakes. Doubt contributes to that avoidance. Guessing does not.

(D) *Science is the privileged method.* Once we arrive at that rock-solid foundation, once we arrive at certainty, one wants to build, and one wants to build with a method that is as certain as the foundation on which it rests. That method is called science and it is a privileged method, a method to which all other methods must pay heed. Poetry, religion, and art may be functions of one's own culture, but science is not, and if one wants to discover what is really true, one must go beyond the limitations of one's person and one's culture. Science is a ladder that reaches from an indubitable foundation to objective truth. All other methods can be reduced to culture and person. Science is privileged—the stars of the physicists are the real ones while Vincent van Gogh only sees and paints metaphorical ones.

(E) *Science points the way to objectivity.* Moderns maintain that there is something objectively "out there." The world has certain characteristics, certain features, whether it is being observed or not. If the proverbial tree falls in the forest, and there is no one to hear it, it does make a sound: modernism is the endeavor to hear that sound. Along with the belief in objectivity goes a claim that what one is trying to do is to build a set of theories that correspond with or reflect the way things are. We speak truthfully when our words and theories correspond with the way things are.

(F) *The ethical and the aesthetic worlds have contours of their own.* At the same time that one says the physical world has contours, moderns say that the ethical and the aesthetic worlds have contours of their own. The moderns' search is to find, to discover, and not invent, the best possible state, the best possible way for people to live together and to treat each other (Here one can see reasons for viewing Plato's *Republic* as a clear precursor of modernism). For the moderns, goodness and beauty are as real as solidarity and nature. Beauty does not exist in the eye of the beholder. Goodness is not a function of simple preference. Again, going back to Plato in *Euthyphro*, pious things are not pious because the gods prize them. Rather, the gods prize them because they are pious. Goodness, beauty and justice are not matters of opinion, but those of fact.

(G) *Science makes each person godlike.* Socrates distinguished between human wisdom and that of the gods. The former, as we saw, was worth little and involved the knowledge of our own limitations. The latter was the truly important. For moderns, if we do it right, if we start from a rock-solid foundation and if we use a reliable methodology (science) we can be sure of always speaking the truth. Given modernism, each person becomes his or her own pope, gifted with a sort of infallibility. The modern claim is that the way the gods know, say, the truth of mathematics is precisely the way mathematicians know the truth. Certainty is certainty.

Postmodernism, then, can be viewed as a reaction to (A) though (G). In regards to (A), postmoderns would say that thought is always tied to some extent, sometimes greater and sometimes less but always to a significant extent, to its context. To understand the thought is itself to understand the context from which it springs. Take, for example, a proposition as simple as "I love my country." On one level, it is merely a statement of relationship—the speaker has a certain affective tie with his or her country. But to really understand, to understand in a rich or pregnant sense, one has to know, among other things, who is speaking and when it is being said. There is a difference among, say, Benedict Arnold saying "I love my country" in his youth and in his ill-formed maturity, President Kennedy saying it during the Cuban missile crisis, and Timothy McVeigh saying it after the verdict for the Oklahoma City bombing had been rendered. To understand, the last thing you want to do is to depoliticize or to decontextualize thought.

In regards to (B), since thought is always tied to a context, it is not possible to get a foundation that is divorced from a context or from a culture or from a historical period. To look for some transcultural, ahistorical foundation on which cultures exist or from which they may be evaluated is to look for the conceptual equivalent of a unicorn. For the postmodern, there is no such thing.

In regards to (C), since postmoderns are, in a sense, locked into culture and context—although they can imaginatively leave their own context or literally travel away from it, they always wind up in *another* culture or context—they are much more wary of doubting things. View postmoderns as being on a great wooden ship at sea. Postmoderns will examine any of the "planks" of their beliefs. They will doubt, but if they do it in a systematic way, if they go in for the wholesale doubt of modernism, their ship will sink. As a matter of course moderns doubt, and believe only when they are forced to do so by their (scientific) method. As a matter of course, postmoderns believe, and only doubt when the context, somehow, presses doubt upon them, when something goes wrong.

In regards to (D-E-F), postmoderns, in the manner of Socrates, think certainty is the province of the gods. We are creatures of history and culture, and what we are after is justification or warrant. There is a court of informed opinion (opinion that we may share in common and that is called "public," or shared opinion within the discipline) in which certain things are said to be reasonable and others not so. In 1998, that court or arena, public or discipline-based, looks askance at astrology but with approval on astronomy. In effect, what we try to do is to give reasons that will satisfy reasonable people. There is, admittedly, a circularity here. Even, perhaps, more troubling than the circularity is the recognition that what is taken to be reasonable today may be viewed as unreasonable tomorrow. Both art history and child-rearing practices are littered with examples of such reversals.

Basically, what postmoderns are trying to do is to build coherent systems, systems that allow us, at this time, to predict, explain and control, systems that pass muster with specific groups at identifiable points in time. If a proposition fits in with our system, we call it true. If it conflicts, the system spits it out, and labels it false. Truth is not a function, for postmoderns, of a correspondence between our words and the way things really are, but is a function, instead, of relationships within a theory and/or relationships between theories and theory-holders. Indeed, questions about the way things really are, questions about the contours of the objective world are moot. The questions, in fact, are questions about the contours of theories.

In regards to (G), since truth is dependent on context, postmoderns hold whatever truths they maintain in a tentative fashion. Postmoderns do not claim papal authority; they are fallibilists, that is, they are aware that contexts are always changing and that even one's most cherished beliefs may eventually be discarded.

There is much more we could say about the dispute between modernism and postmodernism, but the preceding does give a way to look at Philosophy for Children practice. It would be nice to say, for purpose of clarity and symmetry, that there has been an evolution in Philosophy for Children from a straightforward modernist stance to a postmodern one. It would be nice, but, unfortunately it would not be completely accurate. The problem has something to do with the richness and complexity of the original Philosophy for Children novel, *Harry Stottlemeier's Discovery*, and the Socratic-Platonic and pragmatic traditions that feed it.

Lipman, as we mentioned previously, thought of Harry as being comprised of two parts—a formal reasoning part, based on Aristotelian logic, which was meant to directly improve the thinking abilities of children (those future students in university) and a philosophy part which was intended to attract students, to be used as an enticement or invitation to children. The latter was meant to be instrumental for the former, where children would learn rules of conversion, inference, and so on. To simplify, the intent was to write a purely pedagogical novel whose primary purpose was the direct tuition in logic. There were three things that got in the way of the achievement of the intent. The first had something to do with the use of the medium of a novel. The second was related to the model of community of inquiry presented in Harry. The third had something to do with Lipman's own relationship to formal logic. Those three things may have precluded the successful achievement of the intent, but in large part they are responsible for whatever richness and complexity Philosophy for Children offers.

Harry Stottlemeier's Discovery is not a perfect novel, but then again even the novel many people think of as the greatest American one, *Huckleberry Finn*, is seriously flawed. There are episodes in *Harry Stottlemeier's Discovery*, most notably a situation in which a boy is hit by a car and subsequently applies a rule of logic, which seem contrived purely for pedagogical reasoning. There are situations which seem to trade exclusively in stereotypes where characters are maddeningly one-dimensional—Lipman said that he would differentiate characters by means of their styles of thought, but sometimes the characters are only a single style of thought. And there are times, at least for this reader, when the novelist's art is reduced to pure didacticism.

Still, saying all of that, Lipman has written a novel and at times it is a very good one. Some of the characters, steadfastly, refuse to be one dimensional. Tony may be invariably analytical or mathematical, but Lisa is wonderfully complex. She is a good friend to Harry; she is crucial to the discovery of the initial logical rules; she is both analytic and intuitive; and she is the one who has the most significant doubts about the logical journey on which the children have embarked. Lisa, and other of the characters at different times, are full-bodied and complex. They refuse to fulfill simple didactic purposes. The situations, in turn, in which they find themselves reflect the complexity of the characters.

The gift-giving situation is particularly rich. Dale, a very minor character, has had a run-in with a school official, Mr. Partridge, over Dale's refusal to stand for the Pledge of Allegiance. Mr. Partridge attempted to "inquire" with Dale regarding the reason for his action, but, in fact, used a combination of mean-spirited rhetoric, tricks of logic bending, and outright intimidation to get Dale to stand for the Pledge, thereby violating Dale's beliefs or those of his parents (it is never clear whose beliefs are in question). When Dale refuses to comply, he is sent home to his parents, where the choice is made to transfer Dale to another school.[4]

On Dale's last day at school, his friends present him with some going-away presents. Since those friends feel some complicity in Dale's removal—Mr. Partridge used the method of inquiry that the community had been developing and he used it in a classroom setting while the children watched—the gifts that they give are particularly touching.[5]

The point, then, is that novels have their own dynamics. To the extent that they work—and the argument here is that *Harry Stottlemeier's Discovery* works as a novel—there is a complexity about them that resists reduction to a single purpose, didactic or otherwise. Novels involve the creation of alternate universes in which the players go about their business in ways similar to the ways in which we go about ours. And like us, those players are creatures of, at once, logic and psychology, reason and irrationality, hope and despair. The great debate about *Huckleberry Finn*, the reason that some school boards ban the work while others make it required reading, is whether the work is a satire on racial attitudes and epithets of the day or whether it is a reflection of those attitudes, and hence, racist. When one reads the work, and when one spends some time on the raft with Jim and Huck, it becomes clear that the sort of reductionism that school boards want to engage in, is somehow precluded by the complexity and vividness of the characters. When, for example, Huck considers turning Jim in to Jim's owner, reasoning first, that stolen property should be returned to its rightful owner, but then rejecting the argument, it is hard to claim that Clemens is engaging in simple satire or pure reflection of social attitude. It seems more accurate to say that he is doing both. Even if one assumes that Clemens' explicit purpose was satirical, it does not follow that Huck is in complete agreement. Creation of a fictional character is much like the creation of a child. Much as the parent might try, children tend to have minds and wills of their own. Their purposes are not necessarily those of their parents, and the purposes of fictional characters are not necessarily those of their author.

The second factor to be considered, the second reason why *Harry Stottlemeier's Discovery* cannot be reduced to a simple attempt at establishing a method of inquiry, is the mechanism that Lipman used to expose inquiry to his readers—the community of inquiry approach.

Lipman lifted the term "community of inquiry" from the writings of Charles Sanders Peirce. The American philosopher was a skilled logician, certainly the best logician among the triumvirate which included William James and John Dewey, and modeled the term on scientific practice of the late nineteenth century. When Peirce spoke of community of inquiry, he meant the agreed-upon practices and procedures that scientists used to inquire and to verify one another's work. Those procedures were, typically, modified and were explicitly maintained by all those who considered themselves scientists. In addition, membership in the community was not merely a function of agreement with established principle. It involved what we in the twentieth century would call "credentialing." One could not simply decide to join the community. One had to pass some sort of test that might involve the exhibition of special expertise, the possession of some degree, or some preexisting characteristic that would warrant membership in the guild.

Although Lipman may have had Peirce's community of scientific inquiry in mind, when he began to create it in the fictional setting, something interesting happened. The boys and girls had no special expertise. They were a very ordinary group of children with not much holding them together other than the mere fact that they were classmates. At the beginning they did not know what the methodology was about and they had no specific methodology with which to discover it. They were bound—very loosely bound—by a curiosity to discover something about the truth function of sentences. (Harry's Rule, discovered in the first chapter, is that a true all-sentence when reversed becomes false, while a true no-sentence when reversed retains its truth value. Throughout the course of the novel, the children never learn the exception to Harry's rule, that is, a true—all statement which is, at the same time, an identity statement).[6]

The children, then, were significantly different from a group of scientists. They were immature, they had no agreed-upon methodology or procedure, and credentialing was never an issue. If anything, one might say that they were in a sort of prescientific condition where the seeds of a methodology were present, but where the domain of study was wide open. Quite literally they could go anywhere with their search and, in fact, during the course of the novel they followed the inquiry into politics, religion, ethics, metaphysics, epistemology, and logic.

The community of inquiry that emerges in the novel is one that is, in a sense, characterized by self-doubt. Tony insinuates that doubt in the opening chapters by his "so-what" question. Tony wants to know what the extent *and* the importance of the discovery will be. We can turn this sentence around and that sentence around but how many sentences can we really do that to? And even if we can do certain things with sentences, what is the importance of the discovery? The community comes up with a defense which enables them to continue on with the process, but the "so-what" question hovers over the activity of the novel, a ghostly presence, until it reemerges in the final chapter when Lisa herself expresses severe problems with the endeavor.

This doubt plays a crucial role in the characterization of the community. There is a palpable reflectiveness to their actions. Because the children are plagued by doubts, they are constantly on guard. Kuhn's famous distinction between normal and revolutionary science[7] is especially applicable here. Normal science involves working within a paradigm and extending inquiry by means of the algorithmic rules implicit in the paradigm. Revolutionary science occurs when the old paradigm proves ineffective, unable to deal with anomaly, and scientists are forced to, in a sense, operate in the dark, proceeding by means of hunches and intuitions. During that revolutionary period, there really are two possibilities: the inquiry may prove to be the birth of a new science or the inquiry may prove to be without worth.

The sequence with Dale and Mr. Partridge is once again informative. By chapter nine, there is reason to believe that the community of inquiry may have arrived at a procedure that can help with the way classrooms are run and with the way people treat one another. It does seem, to the reader and to the community members, that educational and ethical progress is being made. Then, however, Mr. Partridge uses the methodology, or something that appears to be quite close to the methodology, to do something which is reprehensible: he uses the methods of inquiry to intimidate poor Dale. He uses the methodology as a form of indoctrination and he is successful enough to convince the children that what he is doing is a legitimate form of inquiry.[8]

Examples like that point to the tentativeness that characterizes the group. Like Socrates, they are willing to follow the inquiry wherever it leads. Like Socrates, they are aware of their own limitations and the limitations of their emerging method. Like Socrates, there is a sneaking suspicion that the method itself may be of limited utility (true wisdom belongs to the gods). There is a modesty to their behavior that is not characteristic of people who believe that the methodology they possess is, if not infallible, then completely reliable. There is a modesty to their behavior that may not be a characteristic of modernist science.

William James said that we are all thrust into a whirring, buzzing confusion. The task in front of us, the task in front of the young philosophers in the novel, is the Deweyan one of reconstruction of experience and of sense-making. As adults and as experts, we can bring the findings of disciplined inquiry to children—and, all too often, we only bring those findings to children—and tell them what has been discovered. The children in the novel—and Lipman explicitly means them to be models for his child readers—are on their own. What adults there are in *Harry Stottlemeier's Discovery* are largely unseen, functioning much like those disembodied adult voices in the Peanuts comic strips and cartoons. They offer little practical advice, and the children are left to their own devices. Again, this allows them to inquire into whatever catches their fancy, and engenders in them a sense of their own limitations.

The third factor which contributes to the initial complexity of Philosophy for Children is Lipman's attitude to formal logic as a method of inquiry. As mentioned earlier, Lipman spent decades, prior to the creation of the Philosophy for Children, teaching logic to university students. Even before that, during his own student career, he had doubts about the efficacy of logic as an instrument for developing what it proports to deliver—an enhancement in reasoning skills—and his teaching experience, in large part, confirmed those doubts. Perhaps that explains why every time an advance in logic is made by the community, some sort of cautioning advice, some statement of limitation comes with it, words to the effect—"Don't think that you know a lot, just because you know a few rules of logic."

There is a difference between the glibness of the smart graduate student or the crafty politician, and the deeper understanding of the person who has reflected much on her/his experience. The latter, like Socrates in the *Apology* is all too aware of her or his inarticulateness. What that person knows and understands, the relationship that she or he sees often precludes the ready answer and fluid speech of the graduate student or politician. To the extent that knowledge of logical rules encourages a sort of glibness on the part of the initiate, Lipman may be seen as telling his reader to be wary. He seems to be suggesting to his readers that they emulate the character of Socrates and not that of the Sophist.

Philosophy for Children is a product of many traditions. Especially as it leaves the United States and grows in Europe, Africa, South America, and Asia, it feeds on many diverse traditions. When one reads the literature in journals like *Thinking, Analytic Teaching*, and *Critical and Creative Thinking* one hears voices that are clearly Cartesian while others have a tone that is far more Rorty-like. One hears arguments about rigor and consistency, especially in the Australian journal *Critical and Creative Thinking*, that reach back to a British tradition that weaves its way through the positivist like writing of Wilson, Hirst, and Hare. The diversity of Philosophy for Children is, in effect, the diversity and pluralism of contemporary philosophy.

One is hesitant, then, to suggest that there is an overreaching principle, something that holds those traditions together, and that may, itself, have something to say about the modern-postmodern dispute. Still, it would be hard to consider X an example of Philosophy for Children practice if it did not, to a significant extent, make much of an understanding of community of inquiry.

We have suggested that although "community of inquiry" as a term originates with C.S. Peirce, the definition is very much an ongoing construction. At the very least, it assumes, as applied to children, that a group of children can sit down together and talk about matters of importance and of interest to themselves and that the talk itself can be part of an inquiry process that is significant both for themselves and for that into which they inquire. Stated another way, the assumption is that children can do philosophy in a community, and when they do so, philosophy can contribute to them—make them more thoughtful, more reflective, and possibly more humane—and they can contribute something to philosophy. From that assumption, one can begin to generate an incomplete—the definitional process is ongoing—list of the characteristics of community of inquiry. The list will include cognitive, affective, and socio-ethical features.

In *Democracy and Education*, John Dewey offers a two-fold definition of community.[9] He starts his discussion by means of a simple question: What is the difference between a community versus a mere aggregate? Stated another way, what distinguishes a family from a collection of people riding in an elevator? For Dewey, the distinction revolves around what he calls likemindedness and commerce. The former involves some shared beliefs, hopes, goals and so on, while the latter involves ways and means, protocols, for dealing with other communities and aggregates. When both are in place, a community exists. In the following, we will focus most of our attention on the first characteristic.

When one thinks of a community of inquiry, one thinks of a group of people who are bound together by a specific awareness—they are aware that there is something that they do not know. There is a kind of pebble in the collective shoe and that pebble engenders a burgeoning awareness. It spurs the community to some action. Previously, we were a collection of friends who got together to go to the movies.

Mary has a car and John has an uncle who can get us discount tickets, and things just go from there. But then, as we talk one night after a banal movie, we became aware of something problematic, something open-ended, something that sparks our curiosity. We become aware of our own ignorance and, through explicit or implicit agreement, we begin to work together to understand something, to discern some truth. We begin to evolve from a moviegoers club to a community which thinks and inquires about movies.

It is working together that defines us as a community. Not only do we share a curiosity, not only do we wonder at similar things, we recognize both a liberty and an obligation. The community frees me to contribute my own opinion and my own sense of things. I do not have to sit, an empty vessel waiting to be filled. I have the right to try on a position, to see how it fits, to test it. The community is a place in which I can formulate a position, thereby finding out what I believe.

Still, the community of inquiry is not merely what in previous decades was called a rap-session or what in educational circles is called brainstorming. Yes, I have the right to say what I think, but, at heart, the community of inquiry is a place where reasons are evaluated. I soon learn that I ought not say whatever comes into my head because I will be obligated to give reasons for what I say. When people are introduced to community of inquiry, they initially extol the comparative freedom of things, especially when they contrast it with a more traditional classroom setting. At last, they say, we have a right to talk and express our opinion. As they become aware of the nature of the endeavor, they understand that the right always came with a corresponding obligation. Say what you will, but always be prepared to justify what you claim.

It is not just that the other community members place demands on us for justification, it is not just that at some point in the inquiry process those demands become internalized, it is also that the very process of inquiry puts demands on us. In, for example, a community of ten, it might be said that there is always an eleventh member, and that is the inquiry itself. If we are to move closer to the truth or to deepen our understanding, there are certain things that we must do. The very process of inquiry demands it.

Those things include listening "hard" to each other. In his poem, "The Writer" Richard Wilbur relates the experience of a father who originally wishes his daughter well in the achievement of that which he takes to be childish endeavors. Then, when the course of events shows him the seriousness of those endeavors—"It is always a matter of life and death"—he wishes what he wished for her before, but now he wishes it harder.[10]

Ludwig Wittgenstein said that anything that could be said, could be said clearly and concisely and distinctly. That which could not be said (clearly and concisely and distinctly) must forever remain in silence.[11] What community of inquiry members realize, especially when dealing with relatively new language users (children) is that although Wittgenstein may be right, he is talking more of a regulative ideal than a description of actual practice. When we inquire, we are on new ground. We tend, linguistically, to stumble and fall. We tend to need all of the sympathetic hearing, all of the careful attention that our listeners can provide. We need the sort of hard listening of which Richard Wilbur speaks.

Another thing that must be done to create and maintain the community of inquiry might be called environmental. John Dewey said that education typically is indirect and not direct. Rather than teaching by telling, we are more effective as teachers when we create an environment that culls out intelligent response from students. Nowhere is Dewey's precept more applicable than within the community of inquiry.

That community must be characterized by a respect for persons that permeates the environment. If it is to be a community of inquiry, members must be willing to listen to one another, accept the other's perspective, and see it as valuable. Communities of inquiry develop what Thomas Hobbes would call rules of large and small morals, what we today would call ethical rules and those of manners. Not only do we have to respect each other as person and inquirer, that respect is exhibited in the following of rules and procedures relating to how we talk, how frequently we talk, and so on. Those rules will change from community to community; they will always be subject to review and revision, but a community of inquiry that had no rules of etiquette and manners would quickly degenerate into a less-than-pleasant and less-than-educational place.

Before moving back to our discussion of modernism and postmodernism, it will help to think a bit about what might be termed degenerate communities of inquiry. One is trying to create a community in which the problematic can emerge, in which one is constantly aware of the pebble in the shoe. Doing that is no easy task. Indeed, as Ann Sharp frequently points out, it is more of a goal than something that one achieves with much frequency. There is always the danger, especially in the classroom, that we fall into traps of pedagogy, therapy, or moral lesson-giving.

In terms of pedagogy, one should remember that the banking model of education is ubiquitous. The schools have curricula and agendas of their own. There are skills and bodies of information that licensing agencies and school boards have mandated. Teachers are under an enormous amount of pressure to ensure that the information gets across to children and that they get ample time to practice their skills. The pressure is always on to use community of inquiry to teach that which the curriculum mandates. One might argue, and in the United States many people have argued, that the community of inquiry develops reasoning skills and that the development of those skills will enable children to learn that which is mandated more efficiently. We will engage in community of inquiry and, as a consequence, scores on standardized tests will improve. Without teaching for the test we will do that which improves performance on the test.

Such an attitude is commendable, but what happens all too frequently is that the demands of the curriculum force teachers to use community of inquiry as an instrument for teaching the existing curricula. The temptation, always, is to use communities of inquiry as a mechanism for teaching that which the curriculum takes to be important. Rather than attending to the interests of the community members and following the inquiry where it leads, teachers wind up downplaying or ignoring those interests and following the curriculum where it leads. When this happens, the community of inquiry has degenerated.

In regards to therapy, the danger might be even greater. Think, for example, of the university lecture hall. Students sit in rows, with little chance for interaction with the lecturer or with themselves. By contrast, community of inquiry has a much more interactive focus. It depends, for its very existence, on the building of personal relationships. When people come together as a community, they do not just inquire together. At the same time that they are inquiring, they reveal a good deal about themselves. While revealing themselves, they frequently reveal what is troubling them.

The claim is frequently made that teachers are not counselors and they should eschew any sort of counseling role. It is a claim that sounds good in theory but once one enters a classroom, one sees the impracticality of that rule. In the course of not just a day, but of minutes, teachers, of necessity, play a host of roles including therapist, judge, and sometimes jury.

Therapy, of some sort, cannot be avoided, but the teacher in community of inquiry is wise to recall that the purpose of community of inquiry is not therapeutic. Community of inquiry might culminate in a series of therapeutic results (I became a better person because I became a better inquirer), but every time one engages in therapy, one does something which is outside the purpose of the endeavor and runs the risk of sabotaging the inquiry process itself. If the teacher is to engage in therapy, it might be done better outside the boundaries of the community.

Finally, teachers do have a long-standing and worthy tradition of direct and indirect moral tuition. In order to teach at all, they must create an environment in which children respect each other's rights, refrain from cheating and fighting, are punctual, and so on. In addition, although distinctions might be made between the simple teaching of the basics and creating a citizenry composed of decent and honorable individuals, there is ample reason to believe that schools would be held at fault if graduating students were merely literate. The teachable moment does not refer merely to mathematics and reading; it also has something to do with the use of drugs, with cigarette smoking, and with the dangers of promiscuity.

The community of inquiry provides many opportunities for the giving of moral lessons. Just as in any other classroom setting, community of inquiry depends on what we have called large and small morals. Teachers, legitimately, will want to underscore those rules as the community inquires, but it is always good to realize that the rules, themselves, can be questioned within community of inquiry. To the extent that the rules are accepted in an unthinking fashion, the purpose of the community of inquiry may be blurred. What the teacher wants to avoid, at all costs, is turning the community itself into a platform in which her or his beliefs, or the beliefs of the dominant culture, are forced on the child. Mr. Partridge used his power and his understanding of inquiry processes as a means of indoctrination and intimidation. Behavior like Mr. Partridge's should be avoided.

To return to the debate between modernism and postmodernism, what emerges is that Philosophy for Children has as much to say about it, as the debate has to say about Philosophy for Children practice. We listed seven characteristics of the debate. The first (A) suggests that thought can be divorced from its context. While it may be logically possible to do that, while this might be a goal of the inquiry process, the community of inquiry itself is a social construction that serves as context. Community members depend on one another to test ideas, to correct excesses, and so on. Every time the community is changed, by means of an addition or subtraction of a community member, the process of inquiry reflects the loss or gain in perspective and methodology that the individual represents. Even with something as straightforward, as transcontextual as Aristotelian logic, how the rules are interpreted, when they will be used, and with what degree of seriousness, are all functions of individual communities of inquiry, of individual context. This is not to say that transcontextual methodologies, privileged or not, cannot and will not be discovered. Rather, it is to suggest that if such methodologies are discovered they will be sensitive to the nuances of interpretation of individual communities.

The ongoing practice of community of inquiry, the fact that it is recursive rather than linear, constantly reflecting on its own practices, changing as new beliefs are added and old ones discarded, as members enter or leave the community, suggests that (B) and (C) are elusive. Foundations, rather than being starting points or endpoints of inquiry, might be viewed as convenient resting points. We "perch" on them for given periods of time, but at some point in the process of inquiry they may become themselves questionable. In a similar manner what is held steadfastly at one point later becomes problematic. The very notions of foundation and certainty may be quite useful in community of inquiry, but to do so they must be radically redefined: perhaps along the lines of a distinction between beliefs that are long-lived or central and those with a shorter life span or more peripheral scope. Indeed, this is precisely what has happened in the history of thought to Aristotelian logic. For a span of fifteen hundred years it was foundational until it was replaced by other, multivalued logics.

In regards to (D), (science is the privileged methodology), communities of inquiry as they have functioned in Philosophy for Children, both in the novels and in actual classrooms, may be said to be quite antagonistic to that claim. Lipman, by training and inclination, presented a model of community of inquiry which was as aesthetic as is was scientific, as intuitive as it was rule-based. His allusions in *Harry Stottlemeier's Discovery* to such an elusive but evocative concept as "grace" is illustrative. When Fran is bullied by two boys, perhaps because she is a girl, or perhaps because she is a girl and black, she pushes the boys and is chastised by her teacher. Fran protests by leaping gracefully from desk to desk around the classroom. Her protest has an aesthetic quality that turns the protest, like much of the protest during the Vietnam era, into an artistic experience. In Fran's case, it effectively silences her accuser.

Lipman, then, used and has always used the aesthetic as an effective means of inquiry. A quick look at the literature on Philosophy for Children in journals such as *Analytic Teaching* and *Thinking* will show practitioners around the world using theater, dance, painting, and history, among others, as ways of doing inquiry in communities. In some communities of inquiry, science is considered to be the best, the privileged one, but in other communities of inquiry, its findings take second place to inquiry within other disciplines. If scientism is defined as a naive belief in the ability of science to resolve all human problems, then community of inquiry is not guilty of scientism.

The issue regarding objectivity (E) and (F) (there is an objective reality out there, independent of our perspective, and it has certain contours, both natural and ethical and aesthetic) is a complex one for community of inquiry. Even if one rejects the claim that science is the privileged method of inquiry, the questions remains: Is there something to be discovered, is there something out there?

The early novels in the Philosophy for Children corpus did seem to hinge on a distinction between invention and discovery. There were some things, like light bulbs, that were made or invented, while there were other things, electricity, for example, that were natural forces and were waiting to be discovered. There was an explicit distinction between things that were dependent on human creation for their existence and those that existed independently of human intervention: those that existed objectively. The teachers manuals that accompanied those early novels gave students ample opportunity to distinguish between the two. More recent work, especially that of Martin Benjamin and Eugenio Echeverria, along with a good deal of feminist writing about Philosophy for Children in the late 1980s and early 1990s have cast doubt on the existence of an objective reality that is not a result of a process of human inquiry. At any rate, the early assumptions in Philosophy for Children about objectivity have been called into question.

Finally, in regards to (G), at a conference in Philosophy for Children held in New Jersey in the early 1990s, Lipman distinguished between two senses of "I can't believe I said that" in regards to participation in community of inquiry. The first sense related to the feeling one has, in rare moments, of saying something that bordered on the brilliant, something that surprises the speaker even as she or he speaks. The second case related to a more common feeling—a recognition that what one said was trivial or asinine or stupid.

At the extremes of community of inquiry one may feel touched by the gods or mired in one's own denseness. Still, the more typical feeling in community is one of questioning and redefining, moving ahead a bit, and then falling back. One works hard with a group of other people. The work is alternatively frustrating and wonderful (sometimes it is both at once) and the feeling that comes across is something about the nature of human inquiry. Moderns may have yearned to know things with a godlike certainty. Members in a community of inquiry may not achieve certainty, but when they are fortunate, they learn something of importance about their own humanity.

So what of the debate? Philosophy for Children, and its creation, community of inquiry, spring from two major sources, sources which themselves span the issues of modernism and postmodernism. Neither source is given to extremes. For Socrates, the emergence of a truth is a function of the process of a dialectic. A group of individuals, in the company of a skilled dialectician, works together to inquire into a specific issue. Each member has his or her own perspectives, his or her own view of the way things are. Each member, it may be presumed, has his or her own expectations of the dialogue and what may emerge, but each person must submit those beliefs and wants to the rigors of the dialogue. The question that hovers over the dialogue is this: will a specific belief pass muster within the dynamics of a specific group at a specific time? Socrates, alternately, presents himself as gadfly or midwife. As the former, he is constantly on the alert to spot sloppy reasoning and faulty assumptions. He is ever ready to sting the community, to force it to self-correct, to be as good at the inquiry process as it can be. And as midwife, he is there to attend, to help along the community as it gives birth to whatever it is capable of delivering. He amuses, he confounds, all in the service of those two tasks.

Socrates is the master of a method that he himself admits is awkward, and that generates a kind of inarticulateness in the teacher. Aware of his own limitations and the limitations of his own group, Socrates is on a journey of sorts, using the appropriate question to arrive at a destination not yet known. The method itself is highly sensitive to the subtleties of individual topics and individual groups.

When one first reads a dialogue, one is amazed at Socrates' dialectical skill. At times, he appears almost a magician pulling appropriate questions from some unseen hat. Upon rereading, however, the questions themselves seem to have the sort of inevitability that characterizes action and scenes in the best novels.

The method itself is both an art and a craft—which is simply another way of pointing to the complexity of the methodology. It involves rule-based behavior *and* intuitive leaps. When people are counseled to emulate the behavior of Socrates, the counsel entails careful and repetitive readings of the Platonic dialogues, along with discussion of the moves and counter-moves that Socrates performs in the dialogue. In the best Philosophy for Children training, it is exactly this sort of immersion in the character of Socrates which takes place. Given this immersion, the counsel to emulate Socrates begins to make sense. To summarize, there is a dialectical method; it is best exemplified in the character of Socrates; it is used best when the teacher imitates the behavior of Socrates, attending to the subtleties and nuances of individual situations.

For James and Dewey—remember that they were both, in effect, nineteeth century figures—there was an objective world out there, but, it was, in a significant way, unfinished. It presented itself initially as a whirring, buzzing confusion, but as one worked with it, as one tested and measured it, as one painted and told stories about it, as one prayed in it, it began to exhibit certain regularities, certain patterns, things that we have labeled contours. Still, in a significant sense the world was (is) unfinished. It waited on inquiry, and the inquiry itself would determine the nature of things. Paraphrasing William James, by our inquiry and activity, we can create a world that meets our deepest moral hopes, a world in which people can achieve their aspirations, or we can create a world inhospitable to morality and rationality. The indeterminism of William James—the iron hand of necessity covers most of the activity of the universe, but on occasion when options are living, and forced, and momentous, the universe waits for a choice that is free—suggests a world that is neither modern nor postmodern, but has elements of both.

John Dewey's notion of "reconstruction of experience" as definition of education is also one that spans the gap between modernism and postmodernism. As one reads Dewey in "My Pedagogic Creed," *Democracy and Education*, and *Experience and Education,* it becomes clear that when Dewey speaks of reconstruction of experience he means two things: discovering what is already there, finding preexisting contours, and making or inventing connections among things, putting schema on things that will enable us to predict and explain. To educate a person is, at once, to help her or him determine the contours of objectivity, and to mold the contours so that they are more in line with human aspirations and desires.

When Lipman takes over the notion of community of inquiry, when he adopts Peirce's term but redefines it for his own use, he too is spanning modernism and postmodernism. William James, especially in *The Varieties of Religious Experience,* took all perceptions with utter seriousness. Implicitly, he rejected a modern belief that views a scientific perspective as necessary condition for the determining of objective truth. Explicitly, he said that all perceptions could be viewed so that they would yield important information about the nature of the real. Although John Dewey cringed at James' embrace of the strange and the bizarre, there is a sense in which Lipman, to the extent that he understood the importance of perspective in community of inquiry, is more Jamesian than Deweyan.

The community of inquiry, in theory and practice, puts no significant bars on entrance into the individual community. There are no gatekeepers. If you are a classroom member you can be a member of the community. If you are an adult, and you can find enough people to work with you, you can form a community of inquiry. If you have internet access, you can join the Philosophy for Children list. The only thing that one must do is to observe the evolving rules of discourse (how we talk with one another, what is considered rude or a personal attack, and so on). No advanced degrees are required; no credentials showing competency are needed; no letter of reference from those competent in community of inquiry and supporting one's candidacy need be produced. You will be listened to and taken seriously, primarily because the assumption, the Jamesian assumption, is that all perceptions have something of worth to contribute to the inquiry process. A good part of that will involve the careful scrutiny of your statements and beliefs. Those beliefs may be rejected, they may be found wanting, but it will always be after examination.

We have looked at the intellectual context of Philosophy for Children specifically as it played out in the modernism-postmodernism debate. It is an article of faith within the critical thinking movement that sensitivity to context is essential to thinking well about things and to understanding them. Philosophy for Children came of age during the time of the debate between modernism and postmodernism, and the debate, in large part, was the context in which scholarship about Philosophy for Children proceeded. What the debate did and continues to do is to force us to reflect on the goals and the purposes of Philosophy for Children practice. That, we think, is a good thing.

When one tries to "resolve" the debate in terms of Philosophy for Children, when one asks if Philosophy for Children is a creature of modernism or a postmodernism, however, things get to be complex, so complex that the question admits no simple answer. It is not just because Philosophy for Children is not monolithic, and it is not just because there are Philosophy for Children practictioners who would consider themselves modern while there are others that are postmodern. It is because the significant springs of Philosophy for Children—Socrates, the Pragmatists, Matthew Lipman—say something which is, somehow, larger than the debate itself. Moderns are appalled at Richard Rorty's postmodern appropriation of John Dewey while Rorty, it may be assumed, takes the more traditional readings of Dewey to be wrongheaded. It may turn out to be the case that both have something important to say about Dewey—a postmodern reading of Dewey may reveal something about the American philosopher that a modern reading conceals, and vice versa. It may turn out that alternately viewing Socrates or the Pragmatists or Matthew Lipman from a modern, and a postmodern perspective may deepen and enhance our understanding of Philosophy for Children.

Before leaving this chapter, we might turn things around. We have looked at the relationship of the debate to the practice of Philosophy for Children. What of looking at it from another angle, what Philosophy for Children might have to say about the debate itself?

We mentioned earlier that the debate has been rancorous, acidic, filled with venom, and bordering on the violent. To say that protagonists in the debate have been disrespectful of their opponents is to make a huge understatement. Unfortunately that level of venom is not uncommon. When philosophers debate with one another, they understand the purpose of a debate is to win while leveling one's opponent.

Community of inquiry (Philosophy for Children) does not view the talk we have with one another as debate. I am not trying to score points against you, and you are not trying to demolish me. Rather, we are working together to discover some truth, make sense of something which was previously confused, find something to which we can give our assent. Stated another way, rather than trying to convince *you* of the truth of *my* position, I am trying to convince myself. I am trying to discover, through dialogue with you, whether my position is worthy of assent. We are not debating with one another; we are inquiring together.

To do that, we really cannot be bitter rivals. We have to be prepared to listen to the other person, to imaginatively assume his or her perspective, to suspend belief in our position while suspending disbelief in her or his, and so on. We must, to some extent, become friends with one another. The final chapter of this book will deal with the relationship of friendship to community of inquiry and moral education. Plato said that philosophy could only be done among friends. The history of philosophy, especially as it culminates in the modern-postmodern debate, may be viewed as a rebuke to Plato. Philosophy for Children, on the other hand, takes his remark seriously.

Notes

1. Jean-Francis Lyotard, *The Postmodern Condition: A Report On Knowledge.* (Minneapolis: University of Minnesota Press, 1984).

2. Much of the analysis of Descartes follows the argument sketched in Martin Benjamin and Eugene Echeverria, "Knowledge and The Classroom" in Ann M. Sharp and Ronald Reed (eds.), *Studies in Philosophy For Children.* (Philadelphia: Temple University Press, 1992), pp. 64–78.

3. Although the claims themselves are fairly standard in the debate, Lyotard (see endnote one) and Richard Rorty's *Objectivity, Relativism, and Truth* were essential in the compiling of the list of claims.

4. Matthew Lipman, *Harry Stottlemeier's Discovery.* (Montclair, New Jersey: First Mountain Foundation, 1985), pp. 43–47.

5. *Ibid.*, pp. 60–61.

6. *Ibid.*, pp. 1–4.

7. Thomas Kuhn, *The Structure of Scientific Revolutions.* (Chicago: University of Chicago Press, 1962.)

8. Ronald Reed, "Discussion and the Varieties of Authority" in Ann M. Sharp and Ronald F. Reed (eds.), *Studies in Philosophy for Children.* (Philadelphia: Temple University Press, 1992), pp. 32–41.

9. John Dewey, *Democracy and Education.* (New York: The Free Press, 1966), pp. 81–85.

10. Reprinted in Matthew Lipman and Ann M. Sharp, *Writing: How and Why.* (Montclair, New Jersey: First Mountain Foundation, 1980).

11. Ludwig Wittgenstein, *Tractatus Logico-Philosophicus.* (London: McGuiness, 1961).

Chapter 6

1988 to the Present

The past decade has been an interesting, turbulent, and often disturbing one—especially for Philosophy for Children practitioners in the United States. While Philosophy for Children has grown enormously around the globe, it seems to have stalled, if not diminished within the United States. In this chapter, we will give an overview of Philosophy for Children around the world, focus on two countries in which Philosophy for Children has made dramatic strides, look at one country in which Philosophy for Children has all but disappeared, and attempt to show how traditional Philosophy for Children has evolved in the United States.

In a 1996 report to the American Philosophical Association, Matthew Lipman and Ann Margaret Sharp "noted" the rapid spread of philosophy into the schools of other countries."[1] Of the fifty countries mentioned, some were in nascent stages. Armenia's Institute of Argumentation, for example, sent three of its faculty members to workshops sponsored by Montclair State University while the Scientific Educational Center in Tbilsi, Georgia sent two representatives for training. Others, however, were approaching maturity:

The size of the Philosophy for Children operation in Brazil can be seen from the fact that it now involves 100,000 children a year in studying philosophy, and has a center for Philosophy for Children in almost every state. It also has a Master's program at the University of Cuiaba and at Catholic University of Sao Paulo. Brazil has been active in offering philosophy lessons to street children"[2];

"Except for Brazil, Mexico has the most intensive set of Philosophy for Children operations in Latin America. Active centers are those in Mexico City, Puebla, Oaxoca, Monterrey, Tuxtla Gutierez, Cancun, Guadalajara, and San Cristobol de las Casas. A doctoral program in Philosophy for Children is now operating at Iberoamericana University in Mexico City"[3];

"Philosophy for Children exists in many states in Australia with a heavy concentration in Victoria and New South Wales. There is a Master's program

for Philosophy for Children at Deakin University and a certification program
at the University of New South Wales. A national organization, FAPCA, is
comprised of educational administrators, teachers, and professors of educational philosophy.[4]

From the beginning of its history, Philosophy for Children has always looked beyond its own (American) borders. In a most obvious
sense, any program that is philosophical must look to its own history,
and that glance is invariably intercontinental. In a less obvious way,
Philosophy for Children material and training has always had an international cast. The first secondary text source in Philosophy for Children, *Growing Up With Philosophy*, included articles by the English
philosophers John Wilson and Richard Hare, and by the Israeli educator Samuel Scolnikov. The next secondary text source, and in many
ways, still the principal Philosophy for Children text, *Philosophy In
The Classroom*, was perhaps the first of the critical thinking texts
that was clearly influenced by the writings of the Russian psychologist
Lev Vygotsky. And in regards to the biannual and triannual training
sessions sponsored by the Institute for the Advancement of Philosophy for Children, they have always had a significant number of participants from countries other than the United States. Simply, Philosophy for Children has never been parochial.

Still, one would have had to be awfully prescient to guess what
would happen to Philosophy for Children as it evolved in Brazil. That
country, which in many ways is a mirror image of the United States—
similar size and population, same number of political units or states,
and nearly identical difficulties in reconciling demands for unity with
those for diversity—has experienced an explosion in Philosophy for
Children.

Fifteen or so years ago, a pedagogical coordinator of a language
school in Sao Paulo read an article about Matthew Lipman and Philosophy for Children in a discarded American magazine.[5] The coordinator, Marion Burleigh, passed the article on to Catherine Young Silva,
who became fascinated with the idea of Philosophy for Children. With
a colleague, Sylvia Mandel, she travelled to Menham, New Jersey,
where she attended a workshop sponsored by Montclair State University. At that point, somewhere in 1983, Philosophy for Children was
little more than an idea in the minds of these women—an idea that
was spelled out in texts, in language, that was inaccessible to their
compatriots. The three Brazilian educators began the arduous task of
translating I.A.P.C. material, along with secondary sources, into Por-
tuguese while, at the same time successfully encouraging other col-

leagues to attend training at Montclair. In 1985, Silva and her colleagues founded the Brazilian Center of Philosophy for Children and also in that year invited Matthew Lipman and Ann Margaret Sharp to give lectures and workshops at universities in Sao Paulo, Porto Alegre, and San Luis de Marando. In Sao Paulo they prepared the first group of teacher educators in Philosophy for Children. That group would later begin giving workshops and courses to teachers all over the country.

Progress was slow but steady through the late 1980s, but in the early to mid 1990s, labor began to bear fruit. The number of teachers and students has increased over tenfold since 1992. A visit to the 1996 Brazilian Philosophy for Children conference in Petropolis gave reason to believe that the current trend will continue. In terms of numbers, the conference was one of the largest in the history of Philosophy for Children—over five hundred representatives from schools all over the country attended the three-day event. More impressive still was the knowledgeability and enthusiasm of the participants. Even the most novice of participants were familiar with the work of Lipman, Sharp, and Gareth Matthews. Virtually all of them would and did boast of successful implementation within their own classes. An American visitor was most struck by the optimism and joy of the educational enterprise as it unfolded during the conference, an optimism and joy not typical of most American educational conferences.

Melanie Young Wyfells, the daughter of the late Catherine Young Silva and current director of the Centre Brasileiro de Filosofia para Criancas, lists myriad reasons for both the growth and the quality of that growth. First and foremost,[6] she cites the importance of the work that Paulo Freire has performed in Brazil over the past twenty years. The late Brazilian philosopher and educator, who is best known in this country for his *Pedagogy of the Oppressed*, has created a climate in Brazilian educational circles where it is commonplace for teachers to have an almost visceral awareness of their political-educational responsibility to help create a generation of thinkers who can throw off the yoke of oppression that is endemic to what Friere calls a banking model of education (a model in which the teacher is expert and has the task of transmitting information to a relatively docile class of students), and who take responsibility for their own growth, for their own intellectual development. Freire's "plowing" of the educational field, according to Wyfells, has made possible the growth of Philosophy for Children.

Second, Wyfells points to the economic and educational poverty of Brazilian education, especially when viewed in contrast to the relative affluence of the United States. Brazilian teachers have not been bombarded, as their American counterparts have been, with hosts of slick, prepackaged educational programs. The cynicism with which attempts at educational reform are frequently greeted in the States has been noticeably absent in Brazil. In addition, the perception of draining poverty, hunger, and homelessness has encouraged a receptivity to educational reform that has been, all too often, absent in American discussions.

Third, there are the personalities involved. Catherine Young Silva was a warm, intelligent woman who took to Philosophy for Children with what her daughter calls a "missionary zeal."[7] Ms. Young Silva and a small band of co-workers viewed Philosophy for Children as a significant answer to Brazil's educational problems, and used their intelligence and their personal characteristics to spread what they took as "gospel." With the exception of Catherine Young Silva, that core group of ten to fifteen individuals is still largely intact and continues working as a cohesive unit.

Fourth, that missionary zeal became coupled, in the early 1990s, with the formation of a series of centers. The work of the centers, in large part, has been one of professionalizing and standardizing of procedures, that is, formulating minimum requirements regarding training in Philosophy for Children, scheduling training sessions, and organizing conferences. Ms. Wyfells claims that it is the professionalizing that is most responsible for the recent growth spurt in Brazil. "That is the reason we moved from 4000 children in 1992 to 150,000 in 1997."[8]

Finally, relating back to the missionary quality, Ms. Wyfells speaks of a "visionary obsession."[9] In Brazil, there is a vision of what a just society would be and there is agreement that Philosophy for Children is an essential element in building that society. The reform that Philosophy for Children practitioners in Brazil are most concerned with is, at heart, political. Philosophy for Children is seen as a pedagogy of liberation.

Philosophy for Children's history in Australia is analogous to that of Brazil. It began in the early to mid 1980s, championed by a single individual, and though the growth of Philosophy for Children has been less explosive than Brazil's, it may be steadier.

Since 1983, hundreds of schools have introduced Philosophy for Children into the curriculum, regional centers have been established, an organization, the Federation for Australian Philosophy for Children Associates came into being only to be replaced by the Federation of Australasian Philosophy for Children Association (F.A.P.C.A.) which includes New Zealand, and numerous universities now offer advanced degrees and certification in Philosophy for Children.

In addition to the similarities, however, there is an explicit dispute that has taken place in Australia, but has created little stir in Brazil, that says much about the tensions within Philosophy for Children. The dispute is about philosophy, and it is between, in large part, philosophers with a background in education and educators with a background in philosophy. Phrased as a question, the dispute asks "How much training in philosophy is necessary for doing philosophy with children?" We will return to that question after a brief history based on correspondence with Laurance Splitter, director of the Philosophy for Children Association housed in the Australian Center for Educational Research (A.C.E.R.) in Melbourne.[10]

Around August, 1982, Laurance Splitter had completed his dissertation on philosophy of biology and was awaiting the awarding of his doctorate from Oxford. While visiting New York, Splitter realized that his "true destiny lay somewhere in the intersection of philosophy and education. Not the philosophy of education, as traditionally construed, but something to do with bringing the discipline of philosophy into education."[11] Splitter heard of Lipman's work, travelled the thirty or so miles from midtown Manhattan to Lipman and Sharp's then trailer-enclave on the campus of Montclair State College, and talked with Lipman.

This was during the period of Lipman and Sharp's greatest productivity. (They would go on to produce five novels with accompanying teacher's manuals, thereby completing the K–12 curriculum by 1988). Splitter's discussion with Lipman convinced Splitter that Lipman's approach to bringing philosophy to education was exactly what was needed.

After receiving his doctorate in February, 1983, Splitter returned to Australia, intent on introducing Philosophy for Children to his compatriots. He quickly learned that a number of teachers already knew something about Philosophy for Children, and he set about establishing contact with them. In the meantime, he brought copies of *Harry Stottlemeier's Discovery* to "one of the state education department head offices sometime in 1983–4."[12] The department head was not interested because the material had too much of an American flavor and, to the extent that it would be comprehended, might be offensive to parents "of a more fundamentalist persuasion."[13]

Splitter reports that the attempt to work top-down was useful because it taught him something about the conservative nature of the educational establishment and because it pointed to the value of a more grassroots way of doing things. From that point on, while lecturing in philosophy at the University of Woolengang, which is located fifty miles from Sydney, he "set out on a fairly random trail of conferences, workshops, and awareness sessions."[14]

In January 1984, he attended a workshop organized by the Institute for the Advancement of Philosophy for Children in the Pocono Mountains of eastern Pennsylvania. There he met some of the people who would go on to be leading figures in the International Philosophy for Children community, including Catherine Young Silva of Brazil. He was also exposed to Lipman and Sharp's evolving notion of community of inquiry, which Splitter took to be an "answer to all the problems of education."[15]

Splitter returned to Sydney, convinced that if he was to champion Philosophy for Children in Australia, for reasons of his own inexperience in the primary classroom and for reasons of credibility, he would need to do a good deal of work with children. Like many people coming to Philosophy for Children from the discipline of philosophy, his experience with children, especially in a teaching situation, was limited.

He began in a primary school in Sydney, spending two terms with a grade five class, working from Lipman's *Harry Stottlemeier's Discovery*. On one level, he concluded that the experience was a failure: grade five, perhaps because of his own lack of expertise with the material and methodology, seemed to be too early for immersion in Harry. On another level, however, it was invaluable. "After ten years of seeing myself as a pretty smart university lecturer, it was a salutatory and humbling experience to sit down with a class of eight-year-olds and find that (1) they could do philosophy and (2) they wouldn't do it just because I wanted them to; they had to want to as well! These experiences confirmed my admiration for the teaching profession; could there possibly be a more important yet less celebrated profession?"[16]

In July 1985, the first residential training workshop was held at the University of Woolengong. Professor Splitter took on most of the administrative functions, but, for the most part, the workshop was conducted by Matthew Lipman and Ann Margaret Sharp.

Lipman's teaching and speaking style is low-key and academic. He has little of the charisma associated with many educational reformers of his stature. Couple that with Sharp's special expertise in philosophy and education, along with a infectious enthusiasm for community of inquiry, and one begins to see how and why Australian fears about American educational imperialism were allayed. At that first conference, many of the people who built Philosophy for Children in Australia over the next decade were present.

Immediately consequent to that conference, a handful of regional centers, or associations as they are called in Australia, were established. In addition, the conference spawned the Australian Institute for Philosophy for Children (A.I.P.C.) whose purposes included organization activities on a state and national basis and serving as a distribution center for curriculum materials, all of which were provided by the Institute for the Advancement of Philosophy for Children at Montclair.

By 1989, associations existed in Melbourne, Sydney, Adelaide, Canberra, Perth, Hobart, Launceston, Armidale, Brisbane, Warrnambool, and Darwin. Also, by 1989, AIPC had sailed into dangerous waters while Splitter himself was looking for deeper involvement in Philosophy for Children than his lectureship at the University of Woolengong afforded.

He resigned his tenured position at the university, dissolved the AIPC, of which he was director, and accepted a position as director of The Centre for Philosophy for Children under the auspices of the Australian Council of Educational Research. The support of ACER, under the leadership of Barry McGraw proved invaluable. ACER is a well-known publisher of educational materials, and a long established educational agency. Those qualities helped put the Centre on strong ground, and gave Philosophy for Children a security and stability it had not yet known in Australia.

In July of 1991, following the first National Philosophy for Children conference, The Federation of Australasian Philosophy for Children Associations (FAPCA) was formed. Its founding chairperson was Philip Cam, who would go on to edit a series of philosophical short stories for children. According to its constitution, FAPCA was to function as the coordinating body "for any and all Philosophy for Children associations—including the Centre at ACER—that did, or might, exist."[17] At present there are twelve members of the association, with only three or four of those actively functioning. "Given the size and demographics of Australia, it has proven very difficult for the FAPCA executive—hitherto shared between Melbourne and Sydney but, as of July 1997, to be located in Tasmania—to stimulate or assist the growth of local associations in other parts of the country."[18]

There are two issues that have proven, at once, to be most divisive and most fruitful during the formative years of Philosophy for Children in Australia: the problem of American packaged programs, and the dispute regarding the relationship of training in philosophy to teaching Philosophy for Children and creating Philosophy for Children materials. Splitter sees the two as closely connected:

> One of the issues that has proven most divisive in the formative years of Philosophy for Children in Australia is the relationship between the/an Australian curriculum, and that devised by the IAPC as exemplified in the programs that include *Elfie*, *Pixie*, etc. For a number of reasons, Australian educators do not readily accept 'packaged programs' which (as they might see it) are imposed on them. In the case of Philosophy for Children, it seemed to some that we were wanting to impose an American program that left virtually no scope for individual interpretation and adaptation. It is probably for this reason that Australia has seen the generation of several alternative or complementary (depending on one's point of view) programs, including *Thinking Stories* (edited by Philip Cam), *Books Into Ideas* (Tim Sprod) and the *Philosophy With Kids* series (De Haan et al). In my judgement, what is problematic here is not the development of such programs—indeed, they add to the richness and diversity of Philosophy for Children—but the development in the absence of any real sense of what a structured philosophy curriculum for Australian children might look like. (In this context, it must be remembered that there is virtually no tradition of philosophy as a school subject in Australian schools).[19]

We have tried to point out that even in the beginning, Philosophy for Children was never monolithic or, at least, not as monolithic as it may have appeared to its critics. Matthew Lipman, of course, was key, but Ann Margaret Sharp was a crucial driving force behind the idea, substance, practice and style of Philosophy for Children. So too, as we pointed out, were Fred Oscanyan and Gareth Matthews.

Still, all had remarkably similar educational and economic backgrounds. All were within twenty years of each other in age, all came from solid middle-class backgrounds, all attended prestigious American universities, and, of course, all were Americans. This Americanism comes out very clearly when one looks, once again, at that first novel—*Harry Stottlemeier's Discovery*.

When people from outside the United States want to criticize Philosophy for Children for its Americanism, for its focus on American topics and/or its implicit embracing of American values and themes, they point to the central dramatic scene of *Harry Stottlemeier's Discovery*—Dale's refusal to stand for the pledge of allegiance to the American flag. Yet there is so much more that can be considered American, so much more that makes up the very fabric of *Harry Stottlemeier's Discovery*.

There is a relationship between children and adults that is characteristically, though not exclusively American, and that resonates as American. As mentioned earlier, Lipman took the relationship of adult to child in large part from the way in which adult presences and voices figure in the Peanuts comic strips and cartoons. Those children live in their own world—the world of childhood—and there is a clear distinction between the child and the adult. The presence of the adult in the child world is distant, muted, almost but not quite audible, and non—threatening. There is somebody out there, some presence to depend upon and to whom one may be accountable, but in a real sense, in the confines of their own world, children are on their own: they have both right and obligation to think for themselves. At the same time, the efficacy of their thought and action is always in question, and is dependent on the approval of some adult. Tony in *Harry Stottlemeier's Discovery*, for example, comes up with a very good argument against his father's wish that Tony become an engineer, but Harry and Tony both have doubts that the argument will work in changing Mr. Melillo's mind. Dale systematically refutes Mr. Partridge—but, alas, to no avail. Even Harry, when he correctly applies his rules of logic to an adult situation, is gently but firmly rebuffed by his mother. Again, the experience of childhood in America is to be, at once, prized, encouraged, limited, and distinct. The continental cafe, the Irish pub, where children and adults mingle freely, and where the line between child and adult is blurred, is not the American experience, and Lipman's novel clearly reflects the American experience. Ken Kesey, the American novelist, pointing to the experience of his own childhood, thanked his mother for teaching him that there were no songs and then teaching him to sing. Lipman captures that characteristic tension in *Harry Stottlemeier's Discovery*.

There are two other factors that point to the American fabric in *Harry Stottlemeier's Discovery*—movies and baseball. We mentioned earlier that Lipman wanted to exemplify different types of thinking by means of his characters. One person would be analytic, another intuitive, another methodical, and so on. Lipman mentioned in workshops

in the early 1980s while he was creating the other, and different novels, of the corpus, that he was trying to do what Hollywood did in the
war movies of the 1940s—present representative characters. In that
fictional foxhole, there was an Irish boy and a Jewish one, an urban
tough kid and a hayseed, a pampered college boy and a wisecracking
kid from Brooklyn. Hollywood was attempting to present a mosaic of
sorts, and so too was Lipman.

Finally—and the list here is incomplete—there is the play on words
that is the title character's name in the original novel. Say it quickly,
and part of the name becomes "Aristotle." Lipman says that he hunted
around for a name, searching for something that would capture the
philosophical flavor of the novel, something that would anchor it in
perspective and method. He did, of course, come up with a very clever
way of doing that. Still, one should not forget other influences and
other intentions.

Lipman grew up in the New York City area during a time when
baseball was America's pastime and when the center of the baseball
universe was New York. There were three major league teams in the
city and it was not uncommon for young sports fans to be able to
rattle off the starting lineup, along with the pitching rotation of each
team. Indeed, since there were only sixteen teams then, a more avid
fan would be able to do the same for all major league teams. That may
explain why most of the male names, seem derived from major league
players of the 1930s, 1940s, and 1950s, and why, given some spell-
ing changes, Harry Stottlemeier shares his surname with former New
York Yankee pitcher, Mel Stottlemyre.

Lipman does what all good novelists do—he refines the story with
the things that are at hand, with the things that are part and parcel of
his own experience. When poets like Whitman and William Carlos
Williams counsel the writer to return to the things themselves, to ren-
der the concrete and the specific in the novel or poem, the counsel, in
effect, is to bring the situation in which the writer finds herself or
himself to the narrative. One brings this specific red wheelbarrow to
the poem, this graveyard angel to the story, that rainsoaked street
corner to the novel. And all of those exist in specific times and places.

The questions, then, since the narrative is so context-laden, are
can the story be translated into its contextual equivalents and, if so,
how? Is the translation, as it were, "light" so that references to American politicians are changed to references to Australian ones and references to baseball changed to cricket, or does that translation have to

be heavier and deeper so that the story springs from and represents something that is characteristically Australian.

Professor Splitter himself attempted the former. American references were changed to Australian ones. His translation of *Harry Stottlemeier's Discovery* retains both the style and structure of Lipman's version. Indeed, the episode with the flag and the interlude with Mr. Partridge remain virtually unchanged. For the most part, what Splitter changed were those references that would be most jarring to the ears of the Australian children.

The benefits of Splitter's endeavors are straightforward. Lipman has produced a clean, coherent introduction to philosophy and logic. The introduction is philosophically respectable and rich, in many ways covering the classroom topics of a university introductory philosophy course along with the first few weeks of an introductory logic class. At once, it is the pivotal novel in the Philosophy for Children curriculum, Lipman's best estimate on how creative and critical thinking might develop in children, and a middle term of sorts in the "argument" that is philosophy and logic. By a light translation of *Harry Stottlemeier's Discovery*, Splitter gives Australian teachers and children access to the traditional corpus of Philosophy for Children.

As Professor Splitter points out, the attempt at light translation was not considered sufficient. Both Australian educators and philosophers demanded material that was more deeply Australian. Thus began an endeavor on the part of those educators and philosophers to replicate Lipman's work. They discovered, in the process the very difficulty of the task—in a nutshell, creating a story that is philosophically respectable, of interest to children, and that will lead from and lead to other stories that are philosophically respectable and of interest to children is not an easy task.

So far, the Australians have been able to create works that are philosophically rich and do have appeal for Australian children, and it may be pointed out, to children in other countries. In particular, Philip Cam's collection of short stories, *Thinking Stories*, Volumes I, II, and III,[20] and San MacColl's and Chris de Haan's, *Kinderkit*, actually go beyond or extend Lipman's work.

The former, by means of the introduction of things more imaginative and whimsical, builds a connection to traditional children's literature which is absent from Lipman's more pedagogical novels. The latter, by means of more hands-on type activities for very young children, builds a similar connection to traditional classroom practice with kindergarten students. What they have not been able to do at this point is to create the sort of coherent curriculum that Lipman has produced—the K–12 curriculum in which books and teachers' manuals lead one from the other.

The problem of curriculum-building leads to, or is tied inextricably with that of teacher training. In the United States, there never has been any agreed-upon minimal training in philosophy and pedagogy. "Training" has ranged from one or two-day awareness sessions run by I.A.P.C. or I.A.P.C. representatives through the National Diffusion Network (a federally sponsored program in which programs designated as "exemplorary" were brought to local school districts and funded by federal grants) to the more elaborate models devised by I.A.P.C. and the Analytic Teaching Center of Texas Wesleyan University. The former typically involved a fourteen to twenty-one day residential training experience, usually held in a monastic retreat at Mendham, New Jersey, followed by practice teaching in the student's local or home district. That student teaching then was followed by another fourteen to twenty-one day residential training experience. In both residential training experiences, students were exposed to the I.A.P.C. curriculum materials and their attendant secondary sources (works like *Philosophy in the Classroom*, *Growing Up With Philosophy*, and later, *Thinking in Education*), as well as the sources and tradition from which Philosophy for Children sprang, including works by Dewey, Peirce, and Plato. Students were also given the opportunity to practice doing Philosophy for Children with the communities that were formed at the residential site. Those sessions were usually run by Matthew Lipman, Ann Margaret Sharp, Philip Guin, and other members of the international Philosophy for Children community, and involved ongoing criticism of students' participation as leaders and members of the community of inquiry. In addition, students with an aptitude and/or inclination could opt to pursue a master's degree in Philosophy for Children at Montclair State University.

The latter method, developed by Texas Wesleyan University in Fort Worth, involved student participation in a thirty-six credit graduate program culminating in a master's degree for practicing teachers in Philosophy for Children. Students enrolled in that program would take an initial intensive three-week summer course, worth six graduate credits. The course, which met from 8:00am to 5:00pm, Monday through Friday, would involve background in Philosophy for Children, immersion in the methodology through use of *Harry Stottlemeier's Discovery* in a community of inquiry setting, and then exposure to other primary material, depending on the make-up of the class. Thus, if the class was composed of early childhood educators, material used might include Ann Margaret Sharp's *Doll Hospital* or Matthew Lipman's *Elfie*. If, the composition of the class was mainly high-school or middle-school teachers, the materials would include Lipman's *Suki* or *Mark*. Students would read secondary material and would be given the opportunity to practice teaching while receiving advice about that teaching from their colleagues and from the staff at the Philosophy for Children teaching center at Texas Wesleyan. People from the Philosophy for Children community, in the United States and from around the world, helped teach the three-week summer course.

Students would then go on to take two blocks of courses simultaneously. The first block, called the concentration area, was devoted to courses in Philosophy for Children. Those courses included a seminar that related Philosophy for Children methods and materials to classic works in children's literature such as *Alice's Adventures*, *Through the Looking Glass*, *Stuart Little*, *Charlotte's Web*, and the *Phantom Tollbooth*. Other courses in the block looked at the relationship of Philosophy for Children to contemporary movements in feminism and critical thinking, along with more historical ones, including courses on the pragmatists, and Socrates, Plato, and Aristotle.

The second block, approximately one-half of the student's coursework, was comprised of traditional educational courses such as research methods, classroom management, and so on. Upon completion of both blocks, students performed a practicum in which they put into practice, in their own classrooms, things they had learned about community of inquiry, with an eye toward figuring out what might be problematic or what they might want to test. For example, the student might want to see if community of inquiry had an impact on students' reasoning skills. She or he would arrive at what was taken as a reliable measure, say the New Jersey Test of Basic Reasoning Skills, administer it as pretest to control and experimental groups, and then have community of inquiry with her or his students, typically two to three times a week for forty to fifty minute sessions. She or he would posttest, and then write a report which detailed her or his experiences in the classroom, along with the results of the testing. The report would be evaluated by three faculty members and, if found suitable, would be defended in a public forum.

As mentioned previously, there were other training experiences available in the United States (most notably at the University of Hawaii) but it is safe to say that during the period of 1974–1995, the

bulk of teachers trained in Philosophy for Children received that training from one of the two centers. During that period the Texas Wesleyan
Center graduated three hundred and five teachers with a concentration in Philosophy for Children, while over one thousand teachers
took part in the six-hour summer block.

The numbers for Montclair State University are harder to arrive at
since Montclair put a heavier emphasis, in their early days, on training
the educators of teachers, that is, Ph.D.s in philosophy or education,
and in later days, on the training of professors and teachers from
outside the United States. Also, during that period, Montclair did a
good deal of work with direct, onsite training of teachers in local (New
Jersey) public and parochial schools. Having said that, it is safe to say,
that Montclair State was the major producer of American teachers in
community of inquiry, with Texas Wesleyan a not-too-distant second.

There were differences in the programs, but the similarities were
striking, too. Just as the journals that each produced, *Analytic Teaching* for Texas Wesleyan, and *Thinking* for Montclair State, were meant
to have different emphases, with the former focusing on the practical
and the pedagogical while the latter dealt more with the theoretical
and the philosophical, the ongoing practice of each stressed the similarities. In particular, each had a nearly identical stance on the relationship of philosophy to community of inquiry. That stance was played
out in three conceptually distinct ways: the role of the teacher, the role
of the material, and the role of what might be called the ideal philosophical dialogue to the actual one in the classroom.

Just as John Dewey stated his creed early on in his career (and then
went on to justify it), there was an implicit creed that informed Philosophy for Children practice, as exemplified in the two United States
Centers. The first article stated that to do philosophy with children,
the teacher must have an extensive background in philosophy. Focusing on training of teachers, I.A.P.C. demanded a Ph.D. in philosophy
or a Ph.D. in education with an emphasis on philosophy. Foreign
nationals were expected to have at least an undergraduate degree in
philosophy and, it was hoped, that teachers in American schools would
have an extensive background in the discipline.

Working primarily with American teachers in the southwest, the
experience of the Philosophy for Children center at Texas Wesleyan
pointed to the fact that meeting that last requirement—teachers having an extensive background in philosophy—was virtually impossible
to assume. The Texas Wesleyan center, therefore, went about includ-

ing that training in philosophy within its master's program. The assumption behind the first belief was that to nurture a philosophical discussion among children one must be, oneself, philosophically astute.

At the same time, there was an agreement about the nature of the material. It was believed that the novel had to be philosophically rich and suggestive, that the novels had to be coherent in the sense that they led from one another, with skills and concepts building on one another, and that they would provide a model of the sort of inquiry which children in the classroom might emulate. At Montclair State University, the traditional corpus was seen as necessary and sufficient for achieving these purposes. Texas Wesleyan introduced a modification, stressing the importance of the traditional corpus, but extending the methodology to other Philosophy for Children material, that is, primary material written by people other than Matthew Lipman, and to major texts, such as *Alice's Adventures* and *Charlotte's Web*, within traditional children's literature. The belief at Texas Wesleyan during this period was that teachers could best come to understand and use the methodology through the use of I.A.P.C. novels and manuals, but that once the methodology was internalized, teachers would and should extend its use to other materials. The difference, then, between the two programs revolved around the status of I.A.P.C. material with, as mentioned previously, Montclair State University taking them as necessary and sufficient while Texas Wesleyan took them, simply, as necessary.

Finally, there was agreement about, borrowing from Jorgen Habermas but with a bit of transmutation, what might be called an ideal community of inquiry situation (I.C.I.S.). The philosopher spoke of an ideal speech situation in which that which was meant by the speaker was conveyed to the listener—in which I heard and understood what you said and what you meant to say.

In an analogous manner, one might say that the problematic in situations speaks to inquirers. When we are involved in a situation, when we are inquiring into a situation, when we as a community are on track, when we, like detectives on a trail follow the evidence where it leads, no matter how elliptical and abstruse the trail may seem, when we work together, taking account of each other's strengths and weaknesses to create meaning or discover truth, we are involved in what may be called an ideal community of inquiry situation. The model, in effect, is the history of philosophy viewed as, in Michael Oakeshott's telling image,[21] an ongoing conversation begun in the primeval ooze and continuing to the present day in which men and women try to determine what is good and true and beautiful. Socrates said something to which Plato responded, and Aristotle attempted a correction, then Augustine attempted to put that correction into a Christian context and on and on. The philosophical conversation, the history of philosophy then can be viewed as an ideal community of inquiry situation.

When the teacher does community of inquiry in his or her classroom, what she or he is trying to do is to emulate the I.C.I.S. The teacher must listen hard to the actual conversation and pay attention, of course, to what the real children in the classroom are saying. While listening to that conversation, however, the teacher must also be listening to the I.C.I.S. She or he must be able to hear the echoes of the voices of Plato and Socrates in what this student or that student says, and must let those echoes somehow reframe the actual conversation, and guide her or his own practice. Knowledge of the I.C.I.S. will help the teacher determine the type of question she or he will ask, will help her or him figure out how to guide the discussion. The teacher can only do this to the extent that she or he is knowledgeable about the history of philosophy. Training then, at Montclair State and Texas Wesleyan, revolved around this immersion in the history of philosophy.

To summarize, then, the implicit agreement was that teachers must be philosophically astute—they must be capable philosophers, the materials must be philosophically rich, and knowledge of the history of philosophy must inform the practice of teaching. These three received different emphases at different times during the lifespans of the two centers, but they were always present as articles of faith.

As Philosophy for Children moved to Australia, and as the "Australianization" of the curriculum took place, a series of related problems were brought up—those things that were more or less assumed in America were called into serious question within Australia. The dispute was not and is not as rancorous as that between moderns and postmoderns but, at the very least, it was and is quite lively and often heated.

Essentially, the dispute can be seen as one regarding decision-making. There was an original group of thinkers, most notably Laurance Splitter, who accepted almost *in toto*, the American belief that philosophy should drive decision-making about Philosophy for Children and that those most versed in the discipline should determine what the curriculum would be like.

Another group sprang up, populated more by practicing school teachers and school of education faculty members who, while well versed in philosophy themselves, thought that the practice of classroom teaching had an enormous amount to bring to Philosophy for Children, and that teachers, given their expertise in the classroom, should play a much greater role (far greater, say, than they ever had in the United States) in building the Philosophy for Children curriculum. The question then became: "How does one maintain the rigor and purity of the philosophy in Philosophy for Children while at the same time making use of the expertise of classroom teachers, who, themselves, may not be well versed in philosophy?" As Australian practice has shown over the past decade, while it is relatively easy to frame the question, the answer proves more elusive.

For the individuals involved in Philosophy for Children in Australia over the past decade, the dispute has been, frequently, fitful and painful. At times, to an outside observer, it has seemed that the scene was about to explode with Philosophy for Children being divided into two mutually exclusive camps. Fortunately, perhaps due to a combination of the works of FAPCA, coupled with the intelligence and good will of the parties involved, Philosophy for Children in Australia continues to thrive. We turn to Professor Splitter for a penultimate word on the state and future of Philosophy for Children in Australia:

> While recognizing the achievements of national and regional Philosophy for Children associations, including a rich program of workshops, conferences, demonstrative classes, teacher networks, research activities and tertiary level courses, it must also be acknowledged that there have been, and are, many problems including:
>
> (1) There is no unified curriculum structure which might address such question as "What does it mean to do philosophy in Australian schools of the 1990s?", "What learning outcomes can be expected?", and "What kinds of resource materials are most likely to achieve these outcomes?"
>
> (2) Records of teacher/student involvement, progress and achievement of declared aims and objectives have been, by and large, anecdotal.
>
> (3) There has been no agreed-upon minimum standard for the training of teachers or teacher educators in school-based philosophy. This has led, in turn to inadequate training of philosophy teachers, and inadequate support structures, particularly within individual schools and classrooms.
>
> (4) There is no systematic framework for assessment, evaluation and reporting in school-based philosophy.[22]

The Australian experience may prove invaluable for the worldwide Philosophy for Children community. It has exposed and made explicit a tension that has always hovered, a ghostly presence in Philosophy for Children, between the needs and goals of the philosophers and those of the educators. It has also given the practicing classroom teacher a voice in the ongoing Philosophy for Children conversation that she or he never had before and that voice has deepened and enriched the conversation itself.

There is a final point worth making about the Australian experience with Philosophy for Children in Australia. American pragmatism is part and parcel of Philosophy for Children in the United States. Most of the philosophers in this country live and breathe the pragmatism of John Dewey. Those professors in the United States who might be considered second-generation, that is, all of those with the exception of Lipman himself, Ann Sharp, Gareth Matthews, and the late Frederick Oscanyan, came into their maturity during a time when pragmatism, in large part due to the controversial work of Richard Rorty, was in its ascendancy. For them, rather than being remnants from some philosophical netherworld, Dewey and the other pragmatists were considered at once respectable and part of the mainstream. Lipman may have found Dewey on his own, but by the time that second generation came of age, Dewey, it seemed, was everywhere.

The Australian situation is and was different. When Dewey and the other pragmatists were introduced to Australian philosophers in the middle 1980s at Philosophy for Children workshops, the introduction was genuine. Of course they knew of Dewey, but few had read any of the primary Deweyan works. If they had, they were familiar with works such as *Logic: The Theory of Inquiry* and not with such obviously educational works as "My Pedagogic Creed," *Democracy and Education*, and *Experience and Education*. When they read those works they brought to them a fresh perspective which enlivened their own practice and contributed to an understanding of pragmatism. They provided, in effect, a new way of entering one of the major historical "streams" of Philosophy for Children.

That new perspective, itself, was a function of the steeping of the Australian tradition within a British one and/or a positivist one. Where American scholars learned philosophical vocabulary, manner and nuance from, in large part, the pragmatists, Australians received their education from Bertrand Russell, Rudolph Carnap, Ludwig Wittgenstein, John Wilson, *et al.* It is dangerous to label philosophical movements, but the Australians did seem to bring a clarity and precision to the conversation that was not always present prior to their arrival. Where, for example, American philosophers might key on explicating the notion of experience in Dewey's "reconstruction of experience," the Australians seemed more intent on getting the language right before passing on to what might be called extralinguistic matters.

The last case we will examine, before returning to the United States, is that of Germany. If the implementation of Philosophy for Children means either a light or heavy translation of I.A.P.C. material, then Philosophy for Children must be viewed as a failure in Germany. This is not to say that the Germans are not doing important and extremely interesting things involving philosophy with children. Rather, it is to say that those important and interesting things have come after, and possibly as a result of, a negative reaction to the I.A.P.C. way of doing philosophy with children.

At a conference in Australia in 1992, Professor Helmut Schreier gave one of the addresses at the F.A.P.C.A. International Meeting. In the course of the question-and-answer session following the presentation of his paper, he referred to the "preposition" in Philosophy for Children, and suggested that it might be one of the reasons for the lack of positive response in Germany to the I.A.P.C. programs.

According to Professor Schreier, although one may see Lipman as saying, in effect, that while philosophy, historically may be for the old and the white and the male, it is also for the young and the nonwhite and the female, that is, philosophy is for children, *too*, the implication that comes across, especially when reading the I.A.P.C. teacher's manual, is that philosophy must be changed, must be simplified, must, in effect, be trivialized if it is to be for children, if it is to be accessible to them.[23]

At that conference, a number of participants tried to point out the historical role of the preposition—that what Lipman can be viewed as saying is not that philosophy must be watered down in order to be accessible to children, but that in addition to being for adults, it is also for children. Lipman can be viewed as attempting to return to children (and to nonwhites and to women) their philosophical birthright.

Professor Schreier did not deal directly[24] with those responses at the F.A.P.C.A. conference, perhaps, because, in his opening remarks he had already done just that, but in recent correspondence he has amplified his concerns. While Professor Schreier is quick to point out that he is only speaking for himself, his concerns do seem to reflect the attitude of many German educators and philosophers. The concerns revolve around an understanding of the German classroom, most notably the role of the teacher in that classroom, and an understanding of the nature of philosophy itself.[25]

There is also criticism of the novels themselves. Most of the criticism revolves, not just around the American quality of the text, but also around the perceived woodenness of the plot. The texts, and interestingly, this is probably how Lipman sees them himself, are viewed less as novels than as teaching devices or occasion for instructions: A child is riding his bicycle, as a child does in *Harry Stottlemeier's Discovery*, down a busy city street. He sees an automobile approaching from an intersecting street, notices that a stop sign is posted facing the oncoming vehicle, and assumes that the car will stop. When it does not, the boy learns a lesson in the use and limitations of logic, and, perhaps, something about bicycle safety.

The German point,[26] about these and similar examples in the I.A.P.C. corpus, is that this is not just a misuse of the novel; it subverts the very use of the novel as teaching instrument. The novel has its own gestalt, its own dynamic. Lipman, so the German criticism goes, is right to think that the novel is a wonderful way to bring philosophy to children, a wonderful way to bring philosophy to life—Plato used stories, over and over again, to instantiate philosophical positions and Jean-Jacques Rousseau did it most explicitly in his philosophical novel, *Emile*—but by sprinkling artificial teaching situations throughout the novel, he is subverting his own very good idea. When Lipman crashes through what playwrights call the fourth wall—the wall that separates the writer from audience—he interrupts the gestalt of the novel, thereby impeding its very effectiveness as a teaching device. The intent to teach even a worthwhile lesson about formal logic mitigates against the novel's ability to instantiate, to teach, philosophy.

The perceived problem with the novels, however, only points to what many German philosophers and educators see as the fatal problem with I.A.P.C. materials and training in the use of those materials. When introduced to the huge teacher's manuals that accompany each novel, even when introduced in the course of one of the I.A.P.C. training programs mentioned previously, many Germans see the manuals as hopelessly rule-based and as simplistic.[27] Rather, so the criticism goes, than letting children talk and explore, rather than giving free vent to the child's imagination, rather than letting the child act as philosopher when the philosopher is doing philosophy, the manuals constantly intrude. The manuals are always there to instruct and to guide; the manuals are always there to teach lessons.

The Germans do not deny that the manuals are of use and they do not deny that the manuals teach valuable lessons. The claim, simply but dramatically, is that the manuals are not philosophical—they misrepresent philosophical activity, and when teachers, especially teachers with minimal training in philosophy, use the manuals effectively, they are giving a sort of anti-lesson in philosophy. Even worse, they may be creating a class of individuals similar to those Socrates labored so hard against: a class of people who mistakenly believe they know something (in this case, the nature of philosophy) when they really do not.[28]

The other significant claim is that while the I.A.P.C. program may work well in American schools, it is doomed to failure because the German system and, specifically, the role of the teacher are quite different.[29] Americans, so the argument goes, are quite used to viewing the teacher as a middle-manager of sorts. The teacher's function in the classroom is to act as mediator between the curriculum and the students. The curriculum is created independently of the teacher, usually by local or state boards in cooperation with large publishing houses.

In Texas for example, a state board, consisting of educators, parents, and political appointees determines a set of what are called "essential elements." These elements specify what children are to learn and when they are to learn it. Indeed, the hope, when a state commission led by perennial Presidential hopeful Ross Perot specified the original essential elements, was that students in, say, the fourth grade in the Rio Grande Valley, would be receiving the same type of instruction about the same material at the same time of day as students in the suburbs of Dallas.

The system in Texas—and Texas is only an extreme example of what has been occurring in the United States, at least since the landmark Holmes report—has been set up as a delivery system, almost as a caricature of what Paulo Friere called the "banking model" of education, where experts "deposit" knowledge in the previously untutored. The textbooks and other curricular materials are meant to deliver that important information. The tests, standardized or otherwise, are there to assess the efficacy of the delivery system, with school systems that fall below state averages in danger of reprisals from school boards, parents, and the press. Those reprisals include publication of school-by-school test scores, transfers of principals and teachers, and closing of low-scoring schools. Simply, the pressure on teachers to deliver a prepackaged program is enormous.

Lipman's program was and is meant to counter this banking view of education. It says to the teacher that education is not the sort of thing that can be delivered; that if, using Dewey's phrase, you are attempting to help the child reconstruct her or his experience, you must sit down with the child and as much as you talk with him or her, you must listen. The child is not viewed as an empty vessel waiting to be filled, but as an active inquirer who comes to the community with a set of goals and interests specific to him or her. These goals and interests begin the dialogical process—the teacher says to the class "what did you find problematic or questionable or worth talking about in that which we have just read?"—and in the course of the conversation, those goals and interests must be constantly monitored by the teacher.

It should be remembered that there is a basic assumption behind Lipman's work. The assumption is that children are "typically" or "naturally" philosophical, that children tend to ask the same types of questions that philosophers ask—what makes me me, where do things come from and where do they go, and so on—and that schools should be places where those typical or natural inclinations are nurtured. Lipman was not attempting to impose a set of curricular material on children, but was trying to create a context in which children could do, well and systematically, that which they were inclined to do. The novels, the manuals, and I.A.P.C. training are all geared to achieve that goal.

Still, and here we return to the German criticism, it should be remembered that Lipman was attempting to create that context within the larger one of American schooling. If the program was to be successful, it could not be viewed as being radically different from the banking models of the schools. If teachers and school boards are to accept an I.A.P.C. approach and I.A.P.C. material they will have to view them as significantly like that which they were doing already.

Thus, at least in part, the teacher's manuals represent an attempt to give American teachers and school boards that with which they are familiar. Although not meant as keys to the text or an instrument for the delivery of a pre-existing curriculum, they can be seen as reinforcing a system that looks for such keys and instruments. Lipman was aware of this problem during the time leading to the construction of the original teacher's manual, but thought they (he and Ann Sharp and Frederick Oscanyan) could counteract this problem by means of a manual which was significantly different from other teacher's manuals—*Philosophical Inquiry* would be heavy on questions and light on answers—and by means of embedding the use of the manual, whenever possible within extensive training by the I.A.P.C.

For the Germans, however, this attempt is a failed one.[30] They ask a startingly simple question in regard to both the intent and the use of the original manual: "Would Philosophy for Children be considered to be a success if upon reading *Harry Stottlemeier's Discovery* and setting up an agenda based on the children's interests, no questions about the formal logic arose?" If we assume that such a situation is possible, then if Lipman answers "yes," he is saying that formal logic is not essential to *Harry Stottlemeier's Discovery*. But if he does say "yes," then he seems to be contradicting earlier statements where he spoke of the logic as being the "spine" of *Harry Stottlemeier's Discovery* and, hence, presumably essential.

If he answers "no" to the question, if he says that *Harry Stottlemeier's Discovery* would not be considered a success without the introduction of formal logic, then he would seem to be counseling the teachers, in this hypothetical situation, to ignore the children's interest, and to use the manual to teach direct lessons—to use the manuals in ways that manuals are traditionally not used by teachers in the United States. That, in turn, would make the teacher mediate between curriculum and student and that, if used in Germany, would turn German teachers into American ones.

The German teacher has a degree of autonomy in the classroom that is unheard of and, perhaps, undreamed of in American schools. The teacher is responsible for educating the child where education is viewed as being highly complex, deeply situated and, at heart, personal. The teacher is the person within the situation, and the teacher, given her or his knowledge of the situation, is the one who has the best chance of determining what is appropriate for that situation. This is not to say that the teacher is infallible or will always make the appropriate decision, and this is not to say that teachers cannot and should not be influenced by outside forces such as school-advising panels, parents, and teachers. Rather, it is to say that anything that goes beyond recommedation, anything that attempts to determine the teacher's behavior, is and should be viewed as a threat to the autonomy of the teacher. Again, I.A.P.C. materials have been viewed as a threat to that autonomy, have been viewed as an attack on what is considered good teaching in Germany, and, as a consequence, have been rejected by German philosophers and educators.

There is another sense, however, in which the I.A.P.C. program has been quite successful in Germany. While it is true that Germany is conspicuous by its absence from the list of official Philosophy for Children centers published by the I.A.P.C., the debate about the I.A.P.C. material has had an invigorating effect on the practice of doing philosophy with children in that country. Once one determines, rightly or wrongly, that I.A.P.C. material is not appropriate for a German context, one has to say, assuming that there is some sense in which it would be reasonable to do philosophy with children, what that would be. Moreover, with the reunification of Germany, consequent to the fall of the Berlin Wall, and with the attempt to weld together a capitalistic system with a (formerly) communistic one, there is heightened discussion about the role of education in the new country. The ground is a fertile one for the discussion of the nature of philosophy with children.

The ground has given rise to a series of articles in some of Germany's leading journals, the publication of perhaps the most systematic description of Philosophy for Children around the world,[31] the formation of two national groups devoted to philosophy with children, and the first worldwide conference on philosophy, children, and nature. Training in philosophy with children is part of the ongoing curriculum at the University of Hamburg, and Professor Schreier, in addition, to the vast amount of work he has produced in Germany, has contributed stories to the Australian *Thinking Stories* volumes.

What, finally, is the state of Philosophy for Children in the period 1988–present within the United States? The answer is mixed, in part due to the fact that almost any comparison with the explosive growth of Philosophy for Children during the period 1974–1987 would pale, but also because there is reason to believe that although that growth has not stalled, it has slowed considerably.

Matthew Lipman's productivity certainly has not diminished. While his appearances at international conferences have been curtailed, his published works represent a significant advancement and extension of that which came before. His *Thinking in Education* (1993) has replaced his own *Philosophy in the Classroom* as the definitive work on philosophy for children, as the single work that all Philosophy for Children practitioners must read. *Natasha: Vygotskian Dialogue* was praised by Jonas Soltis as being one of the clearest and most accessible renderings of the Russian psychologist. His collection of articles on Philosophy for Children, *Thinking, Children, and Education*, republished from the pages of *Thinking*, is a valuable addition to the field of secondary sources on Philosophy for Children.

Lipman has continued to expand the corpus of K–12 material with the publication of two novels, *Nous* and *Kio and Joao*, and perhaps more significantly, with the inclusion of two of his stories in the Australian *Thinking Stories*. Readers who complain of the pedantry and predictability of his writing are likely to be surprised at the whimsy and fairy tale quality of his "Anybody's, Nobody's and Lady Sadie." Freed from the demands of curriculum building, the Lipman one encounters in those stories is quite different from the more familiar author.

Ann Sharp's stature has grown during this period. In the early days of Philosophy for Children, she was most concerned with the development of the teacher's manuals and with finding ways to connect philosophy with education. In the period 1988–present, she has written a score of articles on Philosophy for Children. Her interests have ranged from metaphysical questions through political to, most recently, religious ones. She has co-edited two works providing scholarly expositions to two of Lipman's novels entitled *Studies in Philosophy for Children: Harry Stottlemeier's Discovery* and *Studies in Philosophy for Children: Pixie*, and with Laurence Splitter has written *Teaching for Better Thinking*. Her novel, *Doll Hospital*, has been published and is used in many Latin American and Asian countries, and she has contributed work to *Thinking Stories*.

Her most notable achievement, however, during this period may be the way that she has spearheaded the growth of Philosophy for Children outside the United States. She has been a dogged traveller and determined advocate for Philosophy for Children over the past sixteen years, creating enthusiasm for and interest in Philosophy for Children almost everywhere she goes. Professor Sharp is the single person most responsible for the worldwide web of Philosophy for Children centers (see appendix).

She was also instrumental in setting up the first Ph.D. program in Philosophy for Children. With Professor Tere de la Garza, she helped define the curriculum, and recruit professors and students for the program at Iberoamericana University in Mexico City. Finally, her work with Matthew Lipman has led to the formation of a doctoral program at Montclair State University which has a concentration in Philosophy for Children.

Gareth Matthews continues to explore the philosophical imagination of young children. To his groundbreaking *Philosophy and the Young Child* and *Dialogues with Children*, published in the 1980s, he added *Philosophy of Childhood*, which was the first Philosophy for Children book to be reviewed in the influential *New York Times* Sunday book section. He continues to do regular reviews of children's literature for *Thinking*, and is a sought-after speaker at conferences, especially European ones, on philosophy and children. Given his fluency in German and his familiarity with German culture, he is probably the most important American influence on the debate going on in Germany regarding philosophy with children.

Both Lipman's *Thinking* and *Analytic Teaching*, formerly published by Texas Wesleyan, but now edited by Richard "Mort" Morehouse of Viterbo College in Wisconsin, are approaching their third decade of publication. Both have become international journals with recent issues devoting more space to Philosophy for Children around the world—most notably, articles from Australian, Brazilian, and African educators and philosophers.

What may be called the second generation of American Philosophy for Children practitioners—those trained in Philosophy for Children 1974–1987—continues to be quite active. Scholars such as Mark Weinstein and David Kennedy of Montclair State University, Michael Pritchard of Western Michigan University, Tom Jackson of the University of Hawaii, John Thomas of Pacific Lutheran University, Tony Johnson of West Chester University (Pennsylvania) and Ronald Reed of Texas Wesleyan University have produced twelve books and scores of articles on Philosophy for Children during the period 1988–present.

Finally, in 1990, the British Broadcasting Corporation took note of Lipman's works and did a three-part documentary examining Philosophy for Children along with Russian and Israeli experiments in education. The documentary won awards in England, and has been shown there frequently. Videotapes of that documentary have been made and are now a staple of Philosophy for Children training workshops.

Still, with all that has been happening in Philosophy for Children in the United States 1988–present, and while being aware of the fact that comparison with the boom of years of 1974–1987 may be invidious, there are reasons to believe that if Philosophy for Children in the United States is in its adolescence, that period is somewhat tortured. The reasons for that state may include the following:

(1) Philosophy for Children, in contradiction to much of what has gone on in Germany, Australia, and Brazil, has never advocated a turnkey approach to teacher training. Where as in other parts of the world, teacher-trainers with a sufficient background in philosophy, say with a Ph.D. in philosophy, have trained teachers in Philosophy for Children methodology with the expectation that those teachers would return to their districts and would train teachers in the methodology who, in turn, would return to their individual campuses doing the same, this was never the expectation in the United States. The fear, expressed over and over again, in I.A.P.C. workshops, was that a turnkey approach to teacher education would quickly lead to a watering down of philosophy and Philosophy for Children. The I.A.P.C. has steadfastly maintained that teacher educators have a sufficient background in philosophy. While the nature of that sufficiency has evolved over the past decade—there has been a recognition that one could have expertise based, say, on classroom practice which would be the equivalent of an advanced degree—there has never been dispute about the sufficiency condition itself.

Once the turnkey approach is rejected, if teacher education is to grow and prosper, it is necessary that more and more people who meet the sufficiency requirement be recruited as teacher-educators. During the period 1974–1987, as mentioned previously, a second generation of Philosophy for Children practitioners and teacher-educators was formed. Unfortunately, for Philosophy for Children in the United States, there has not been the formation of a third generation of academics interested in Philosophy for Children.

Something curious happened at the Second Decade conference held on the campus of Texas Wesleyan in 1987. At that time, scholars from around the United States met to present papers, exchange ideas, and consider the future of Philosophy for Children. One scholar had the temerity to ask Lipman what would happen to Philosophy for Children after Lipman's retirement. That reply has faded from memory, but the facts are that Lipman is still around, and many of the second generation scholars are now considering their own retirement. Without the replacement of that second generation with a third, Philosophy for Children in the United States will either move to a turnkey approach or it will cease existing.

(2) Philosophy for Children's connection with the culture of the public school has been circumscribed over the past decade. I.A.P.C. has shifted its focus to Philosophy for Children worldwide. Major initiatives have taken place in Australia, Spain, and Brazil, and new cen-

ters are appearing in Russia, and throughout Africa. In order to sustain those initiatives, most of the energy of the I.A.P.C. members, of necessity, has been there.

The cost has been to the health of Philosophy for Children within the United States. There has been no single organization to act as advocate for Philosophy for Children within the United States in the way that I.A.P.C. did it 1974–1987. There has been no single organization to make its presence known at state and national educational conferences. There has been no single organization in the United States to function the way that F.A.P.C.A. does in Australia.

Also, the suspension of the National Diffusion Network in 1994 dealt a serious blow to the connection of Philosophy for Children to the culture of the public schools. NDN designated certain educational progress as meritorious, and then provided funding so that school districts could have their teachers and administration trained in those programs. NDN allowed Philosophy for Children an almost daily presence in schools around the United States. With the elimination of NDN, so too the elimination of that daily presence.

(3) Philosophy for Children's exposure in both the American media and the American scholarly press during the period 1988–present has been minimal. There has been nothing in the United States media to match or even approach the attention given to Philosophy for Children by the BBC special. While there have been numerous television and radio programs throughout Europe, Australia, and Brazil about Philosophy for Children during the period, the American media has been, for the most part, silent about Philosophy for Children. Certainly, there has been nothing approaching the coverage afforded to Philosophy for Children during the period 1974–1987, when Lipman appeared on national television, and Philosophy for Children was featured in *Time* magazine and the *New York Times*.

That silence has been matched by scholarly journals. While *Analytic Teaching* and *Thinking* continue to publish works by Lipman, Sharp, Matthews and second generation Philosophy for Children practitioners, virtually none of their work appears in mainstream journals such as *Phi Delta Kappan, Harvard Educational Review, Educational Theory,* or *Educational Leadership.* If there are references to Philosophy for Children in these and similar journals, they have escaped notice.

(4) Philosophy for Children's relationship to the current climate in the public schools is, at best, tenuous. The last twenty years have

witnessed an explosion in educational programs and innovations. The American teacher, unlike his or her counterpart in third world countries, is likely to be exposed to dozens of books, current materials, and programs in the course of a semester, each one promising to solve all the ills of education. It is understandable that a certain jaded quality attaches itself to the teacher's experience of the American educational scene. That jaded quality can only be exacerbated by the demands of accountability and the constant stress of the standardized test. There is a bottom-line mentality that has invaded the public schools and, for programs to be embraced, they must show some connection to a rise in scores on standardized tests.

In the early days of Philosophy for Children, theclaim was typically made that one could do philosophy with children in the classroom, one could engage children in dialogue about the good, the true, and the beautiful, and that, as a fortunate byproduct, their scores on standardized tests would go up. From 1974 up to the middle 1980s at least thirty experiments were performed in the United States and around the world. Those experiments suggested, in effect, that one could have one's cake and eat it, too—that community of inquiry generated improvement of scores on standardized tests.

Since the late 1980s, there has been very little discussion of such bottom-line issues, and hardly any major statistical studies on Philosophy for Children performed within the United States. There may be many good reasons for this. Indeed, in the final chapter, we will argue that there are. At this point, however, it is sufficient to suggest that Philosophy for Children's apparent disregard for bottom-line issues puts it at odds with the climate of the American public schools.

(5) Philosophy for Children is a victim of the success of the movement it helped create. As one of the oldest and most established programs of the Critical Thinking Movement, Philosophy for Children encouraged many educators to regard the teaching of thinking as the primary task of the school. Philosophy for Children provided a systematic, coherent way of dealing with the development of thinking in the classroom, where, previously, thinking was dealt with by means of the occasional worksheet or brain teaser.

Because of its understanding of the amorphous quality of thinking—thinking is critical and creative and caring, thinking involves both skill and intuition, thinking is both an art and a craft—Philosophy for Children has had to stress the importance of long and intense training. Of all the critical thinking programs existing in the United States, it may be the hardest to adequately describe and the one with the most arduous apprenticeship. School districts looking for quick and efficient cures are more apt to avoid Philosophy for Children and involve themselves in programs that present thinking as a series of discrete and connected skills that can be mastered by a series of identifiable exercises—exercises which themselves demand little formal training on the part of the teacher.

(6) Philosophy for Children has not expanded much beyond the themes and methods of the original corpus. In *Harry Stottlemeier's Discovery*, Lipman, as mentioned previously, certainly opened the door to an extension of Philosophy for Children into aesthetics, art history, and art criticism. For a period in the late 1980s and early 1990s there was talk of the creation of a series of novels that would be a philosophic exploration of art and aesthetic experience. Unfortunately, that exploration has never taken place.

In a similar fashion, there was considerable talk about extending Philosophy for Children methodology to music, dance, drama, and natural science. The last mentioned was to be the elusive *Tony* of the traditional corpus. Supposedly, Lipman, Fred Oscanyan and others have tried to do a novel about natural science (to be called *Tony*), but none has ever been published. The benefits would not merely have involved an extension of the curriculum, but would have brought newer, more concrete, less verbal methodologies to Philosophy for Children, which, at times, suffers from abstractness and wordiness. At any rate, the hopes for expansion of theme and methodologies that were present since the formation of the traditional corpus have not been met.

After looking at the educational context of Philosophy for Children, we will attempt to give a brief, impressionistic feel of what community of inquiry is like. That chapter will reflect Ronald Reed's experiences with Philosophy for Children, and will be used as a springboard to exploring what, at once, may be the most distinctive characteristic of Philosophy for Children while receiving the least attention—the relationship of intellectual and moral friendship to the development of character. It will be the thesis of the final chapter of this book that one of the effects, though not necessarily the goal of community of inquiry, is the development of friendship and that this friendship may provide the key to solving many of the problems that beset Philosophy for Children in the United States during this period. In turn, it may provide a suggestion for general educational reform in this country and, perhaps, others.

Notes

1. Matthew Lipman and Ann Margaret Sharp, "International Developments in Philosophy for Children," unpublished manuscript, p. 1. (The manuscript will be published in Proceedings of the American Philosophical Association in 1997).

2. *Ibid.*, p. 2.

3. *Ibid.*, p. 5.

4. *Ibid.*, p. 2.

5. Information about the Brazilian experience is taken from personal correspondence between Melanie Wyfells and Ronald Reed, April–May 1997.

6. Personal Correspondence—Wyfells/Reed.

7. Personal Correspondence—Wyfells/Reed.

8. Personal Correspondence—Wyfells/Reed.

9. Personal Correspondence—Wyfells/Reed.

10. Personal Correspondence between Laurance Splitter and Ronald Reed, May 1997.

11. Personal Correspondence—Splitter/Reed.

12. Personal Correspondence—Splitter/Reed.

13. Personal Correspondence—Splitter/Reed.

14. Personal Correspondence—Splitter/Reed.

15. Personal Correspondence—Splitter/Reed.

16. Personal Correspondence—Splitter/Reed.

17. Personal Correspondence—Splitter/Reed.

18. Personal Correspondence—Splitter/Reed.

19. Personal Correspondence—Splitter/Reed.

20. All are published by Hale and Iremonger, Sydney, Australia.

21. Michael Oakeshott quoted in Ann Margaret Sharp, "Women, Children and Philosophy," Ann Margaret Sharp and Ronald F. Reed (eds.) *Studies in Philosophy for Children* (Philadelphia: Temple University Press, 1992) p. 47.

22. Personal Correspondence—Splitter/Reed.

23. Taken from notes made by Ronald Reed at that conference.

24. The irony of the response to Professor Schreier's original remarks did not go unnoticed.

25. Personal Correspondence—Schreier/Reed, June 1997.

26. Personal Correspondence—Schreier/Reed.

27. Personal Correspondence—Schreier/Reed.

28. Personal Correspondence—Schreier/Reed.

29. Personal Correspondence—Schreier/Reed.

30. Personal Correspondence—Schreier/Reed.

31. Barbara Bruning, Philosophieren mit Kindern. (Hamburg: Verlag fur Kinder und Eltern, 1996).

Chapter 7

The Educational Context
of Philosophy for Children

Philosophy for Children's emergence as an internationally acclaimed educational program is a recent phenomenon. Indeed, it exploded on the educational scene in the late 1960s and early 70s. As discussed in other chapters, Philosophy for Children is significantly the brain child of Matthew Lipman and his associates. Lipman was born in 1923 and during his 70 plus years has been both a keen observer of and a participant in many of the twentieth century's most significant social and educational events. With this in mind, this chapter focuses on the connections between the educational trends during the second half of the twentieth century and the emergence of the movement known as Philosophy for Children.

At roughly the same time that Lipman completed his doctoral studies at Columbia and began his career in academe,[1] academics like Arthur Bestor, a history professor from the University of Illinois, gained notoriety for his denunciation of public education in America. Titling his critique "*Educational Wastelands*," Bestor attacks progressive education in general and "life adjustment" curricula in particular. Bestor's views are reminiscent of the perspective articulated in the 1930s by a group of conservative educational philosophers known as essentialists. Essentialism—as these educational ideas and beliefs came to be known—favored a traditional or back to basics approach to the education of our children and youth. Specifically, the basic tenets of essentialism are as follows:

1. the purpose of education is intellectual discipline and moral discipline and these two are intimately related;

2. the curriculum of the school is an ordered series of subject matters, intellectual skills, and essential values that are to be transmitted to all who come to school;
3. teaching is essentially transmitting; and
4. the role of the school in society is preserving and transmitting the essential core of culture.[2]

These conservative tenets have dominated American education from the mid-nineteenth century to the present. Whether the critic is Arthur Bestor, Richard Mitchell or, more recently, William Bennett and E. D. Hirsch, Jr., conservatism has been the dominant ideology in our public schools.

To the extent that Lipman had thought about the education of children and youth during the early days of his career, he probably shared the bias of many Arts and Science professors toward the watered down curriculum and the lack of intellectual rigor that apparently characterized America's public school and the education of the teachers who worked there. Undoubtedly, Lipman agreed with Bestor and other critics that public education needed reforming, but it should be noted that Lipman's eventual contributions to the reform of education had more in common with Dewey's version of progressivism than with the essentialist ideas identified above. Still there is a connection between Lipman's ideas and the focus on excellence often associated with criticisms leveled by Bestor and others.

The connection becomes apparent in the late 1960s and 70s as Lipman devoted the last third of his life to turning philosophy inside out. Though Lipman began his career teaching philosophy to graduate and undergraduate students, he gradually rejected the all too common belief that philosophy should be the capstone or culminating discipline in the educational hierarchy. Lipman suggests that philosophy is best suited to serve as an introductory discipline, for it prepares students to think in the other disciplines. From Lipman's perspective, philosophy is not the monarch of the disciplines, but it should be recognized for its ability to cultivate higher order, complex thinking in every discipline.

Lipman argues that while each discipline may have its own distinct culture and content, their methodologies are more alike than different. Lipman contends that, "to a considerable extent, logic and scientific method are generic . . ."[3] From this perspective it follows that courses in generic methodology are needed for all students, and the earlier the better. To make the connection more explicit, curriculum reformers of the 1950s sought to develop curricula and text materials that challenged students to think as a scientist, mathematician, historian, or social scientist. This drive toward excellence—especially in the areas of science and math—received an added boost with the Soviet's successful launch of Sputnik. Alarmed by Russia's superiority in space exploration, efforts toward developing secondary curricula aimed at enabling our best and brightest to pursue careers in science and math became a high priority. Often with the support of the National Science Foundation, university and college professors focused on developing math and science curricula that sought to prepare gifted students to think mathematically or scientifically. In short, these curriculum efforts sought to recruit and initiate promising children and youth into the scientific and mathematical professions.

In seeking to replace the all too common "banking" methods of education—where the teacher talks and the student listens and absorbs—with curriculum material that emphasized "discovery, inquiry, and inductive reasoning as the methods of learning,"[4] these reformers anticipated Lipman's contributions of the late 1960s and 1970s. Using language very familiar to those of us involved in Philosophy for Children, these earlier reformers believed that challenging the more gifted students to figure out solutions to problems basic to the discipline would ensure that such students would understand and come to appreciate the key principles of the disciplines being studied. Rather than attempting to "cover" the field, new curriculum packages focused on a few key concepts and sought to help students understand how a scientist, a mathematician, or a historian might think. Rather than filling their heads with a sanitized version of what had become established fact within the field or discipline, this new curricula sought to teach the structure of the academic discipline.

These curriculum efforts of the late 1950s and early 1960s were significantly elitist in that most of the reformers were concerned largely with those promising children and adolescents committed to and capable of pursuing a college education. Their curriculum efforts focused on a rather small group of students. To the degree that these reformers devoted their time and energies to the education of the masses, they attempted to develop text material in the disciplines that were invulnerable to teachers' ignorance or incompetence. The unwillingness to involve teachers and teacher trainers in these efforts exemplifies the bias that these Arts and Science oriented reformers had for teachers and teacher trainers. Though Lipman's more recent efforts to turn philosophy inside out are compatible with these earlier efforts to help students to understand and to think in the disciplines, his approach is different in that it seeks to make philosophy accessible to *all* children. Still, Lipman's belief that the nature of the text material is more important than the teacher in converting classrooms into communities of inquiry suggests that he has not fully transcended the bias that Arts and Science professors have of teachers and those who train them.

While this drive for educational excellence during the mid to late 1950s produced some interesting and creative curriculum materials, it had little real impact on schooling as a whole. As already noted, this lack of impact is due in part to the elitism exhibited by most of the reformers. Jerome Bruner and his MACOS curriculum is a notable exception to this trend. As Bruner's efforts suggest, embracing excellence as a worthy educational goal is not limited just to the conservative reformers. To achieve excellence for all students requires more of a transformation of our educational system than just developing a special curriculum for the talented or privileged few. In a sense, Lipman's efforts almost two decades later sought to build upon and extend this drive for excellence. Advocating the construction of a rational curriculum, Lipman suggests that "each particular subject area should be more than just a heap of information to be doled out scoop by scoop, day after day. Each subject should unfold, build on itself, question itself, illuminate from within."[5] For this to occur two preconditions are required. First, the curriculum must be offered in narrative rather than in expository form; and second, philosophy must assume its natural educational role as the foundational discipline for children and youth.

Obviously, Lipman was not ready in the 1950s to make turning philosophy inside out his life's work, but one wonders why the educational excellence movement faded so quickly during the late 1950s and early 1960s. In response, we note that just as the emphasis on developing our children and youth's understanding of math and science gained significance as the Cold War heated up in the 1950s, the educational emphasis and the national mood shifted toward a more compelling, albeit domestic problem. As the nation began to seriously address issues of civil rights during the late 1950s and 1960s, the educational efforts aimed at correcting the problems of racism and discrimination soon overwhelmed the excellence reforms of the 1950s.

As David K. Cohen explains, "the fifties movement for excellence thus had been replaced at the top of the national educational agenda

. . . by an even more intense movement for equality."[6] This drive for equality would eventually become part of Lyndon Johnson's Great Society and War on Poverty agenda, but, from the beginning, the civil rights movement was significantly an education movement. Tracing its roots back to the efforts of the NAACP to ensure that those responsible for public education in the South took the equal half of Plessy's "separate but equal" doctrine seriously, the movement gained momentum in 1954 when the Supreme Court ruled that "separate but equal" has no place in public education.

For many blacks, school desegregation was the long awaited panacea. The integrated society would soon be a reality and equality of opportunity would be theirs. If the blacks were euphoric, many southerners were outraged. But as schools opened year after year with little or no change, neither the jubilation expressed by the blacks nor the anger with which whites reacted was justified.

Apparently "with all deliberate speed" meant different things to different people. Integration might be proceeding deliberately but it was not proceeding very quickly. Those who had been so wildly enthusiastic about the prospects of an integrated society after Brown had to wait fourteen years before the courts began to actually enforce the principles established in the Brown decision. It was not until the Green (*Green v. County School Board of New Kent, Virginia*) case that the Supreme Court charged local authorities "with the affirmative duty to take whatever steps might be necessary to *convert* to a unitary system in which racial discrimination would be eliminated root and branch." A few years later in the Swann case (Charlotte-Mecklenburg), the Supreme Court mandated busing for the purpose of achieving a racially integrated school system.

While technically not an educational reform movement, the focus on equity would dominate American education throughout much of the 1960s and 1970s. The activist role performed by our federal judiciary—including the Supreme Court—on questions of social equity in our schools contributed to their being viewed as the nation's school board. The impact that the federal judiciary played in shaping school policy during the late 1960s and 1970s, which in turn dramatically impacted the lives of real people, is captured eloquently in J. Anthony Lukas' magnificent work, *Common Ground: A Turbulent Decade in the Lives of Three American Families*. The consequences of judicial rulings on the nature of schooling in America was profound, but there were other equally important educational efforts aimed at correcting historical injustices. For example, compensatory educational programs were designed to provide access to equal educational opportunities for those previously denied. With President Johnson's administration declaring war on poverty, substantial federal dollars were earmarked for educational programs designed to ensure that heretofore excluded groups had access to equal educational opportunities. The Elementary and Secondary Education Act of 1965 is illustrative of how the federal government sought to address the problem of equity in our society. This act made substantial federal funds available, along with mandates designed to eliminate discrimination in our public schools, to local school districts willing to document compliance. This combined carrot and stick approach influenced many school districts across the country to desegregate and to abolish at least the most obvious forms of discrimination.

In short, both legislative and judicial social policy became educational tools used to destroy school desegregation and to condemn racial, ethnic, and gender discrimination. Though not immediately impacted by such educational efforts, Lipman was undoubtedly aware and generally supportive of them. By today's standards, Lipman's earlier efforts to dramatize philosophy—most notably *Harry Stottlemeier's Discovery*—were not sensitive enough to issues of gender and class, but Lipman did make a concerted effort to include among the children comprising Harry's friends and classmates representatives from different racial and ethnic groups. Employing what was often referred to at the time (late 1960s) as fox-hole journalism, Lipman made sure that the community of inquiry modeled by Harry and his friends had representation from various racial, ethnic, class, and gender groups. Though his critics suggest he did not go far enough in this area, Lipman clearly understood and appreciated the need for confronting the problems of equity in our society and schools.

As a major weapon in the heralded "war on poverty," the many remedial and compensatory programs concerned with righting old wrongs raised—but often did not meet—expectations. Though not a total failure, the belief that centuries of racism could be eliminated through school reform proved to be unrealistic. As society became increasingly disillusioned with our failure to solve our most significant social problems, we as a nation began to question one of our most cherished myths; that through education everyone could rise. As it became painfully apparent that our schools could not eradicate poverty or racism, a kind of cynicism about education began to permeate society, eventually invading the educational establishment itself.

Reeling as we were in the late 1960s and 1970s from one social crisis after another, it seemed almost useless to have either excellence or equity as our national educational goal. If—as some social scientists claimed—education makes no difference, then why, some began to ask, should schooling be such an all-consuming and sometimes oppressive part of childhood. Among those raising such questions were a group of critics who wondered whether the purpose of schooling should be either excellence or equity. To many of these romantic critics schools were not instruments for reforming and improving our society, but institutions intent on maintaining the inequities of the status quo. This critique reached its zenith in 1970 with the appearance of Ivan Illich's masterful *Deschooling Society*. Distinguishing between education and schooling, Illich suggests that as schools become more bureaucratic and as their credentialing function expands, there is a corresponding decrease in the educational level of society. Believing that the modern school had become a dehumanizing institution that was beyond reform, Illich carries the romantic critique to its apocalyptic terminus by calling for the end of the modern institution of schooling.

Though Lipman shared many of the biases of these critics concerning the drudgery and incivility that characterized much schooling in the modern world, he retained the essentially liberal position that a properly constructed rational school experience is a necessity for any society aspiring toward democracy. Lipman wrote *Harry Stottlemeier's Discovery* as these romantic critics were at the height of their popularity. Motivated in part by his belief that both his college students and their professors had been mis-educated, Lipman differed from these critics of schooling in the western world in that he believed that by using a curriculum grounded in the skills and traditions associated with philosophy to transform the school classroom into community of inquiry, the young could be spared the mis-education of older generations.

Lipman's belief that college students and adults have been mis-educated is reminiscent of Paul Goodman's earlier work *Compulsory Mis-Education* (1964). Characterizing schools as concentration camps, students as prisoners, and teachers as babysitters or guards, Goodman concludes that schools are inefficient and "do positive damage to the young."[7] Mirroring the society of which they are a part, schools are not true communities. Instead, they have become bureaucratic institutions that thwart human growth. Since there is neither a true community in school or society, children and youth are not allowed or enabled to grow up, to mature, to develop their unique skill and capacities.

Proclaiming himself to be an Aristotelian, Goodman explains that "without a polis or true community to help them grow up, the young become either resigned or cynical."[8] Critical of the belief that schooling is the only path to success, Goodman favors using the city or polis itself as the primary educative enterprise. But if there is no polis—no true community—then the city is likely to be as mis-educative as the schools.

We can imagine Lipman appreciating Goodman's Aristotelian sensibilities, but we can also imagine Lipman being appalled at the naiveté of Goodman and other romantic critics for suggesting that educative experiences occur naturally when such artificial barriers as schooling are removed.

While he shared Goodman's commitment to community and the romantic critics' belief that education should be interesting and meaningful, Lipman believed that these goals could best be achieved by transforming classrooms and schools into communities of inquiry where children and adults seriously examined philosophical ideas of importance to them.

Though their solutions are problematic, Goodman and other romantic critics articulated an ethos of despair and cynicism that characterized many school in the late 1960s and early 1970s. Reflecting a society frustrated with an unpopular war, alarmed by the social unrest at home, and questioning whether anything made a difference any more, many schools lost their sense of purpose or vision. Gerald Grant captures this ethos of hopelessness in his outstanding work, *The World We Created at Hamilton High*. In selecting Hamilton High (the school is real though the name is fictitious) as the subject for an illustrative institutional biography of a contemporary schooling, Grant chose well, for Hamilton High "is America in microcosm. Hamilton High experienced all the overlapping social revolutions that fell, in a particularly powerful way, on schools in this society in the last thirty years."[9] Though Grant accurately portrays the intellectual chaos and moral relativism that characterized Hamilton during these turbulent decades (1950s through 1980s), he also chronicles how the school faculty and administration collectively transformed the school in the 1980s, creating a more positive ethos. Out of the original deconstruction of the original white, suburban, upper-middle class ethos came the opportunity to create a new positive ethos that more appropriately reflects the polity of the contemporary Hamilton High. In describing Hamilton High of the 1970s and 1980s as bowing down to the twin deities of bureaucratic legalism and therapeutic contractualism, Grant suggests that too many schools operated without a vision of what they could or should be. According to Grant, "bureaucratic legalism was the primary expression of the moral order of the school...if something was not legally forbidden it was usually assumed to be tolerated, or at least it was possible to make a stiff argument that it was."[10] The student handbook, rather than explaining to students Hamilton High's intellectual and moral mission, announced to students in legalistic terms the criminal behavior that was not allowed. As Hamilton High and other schools turned to bureaucratic legalism both to fill the vacuum created by the deconstruction of the old order and solve the intellectual, moral, and sometimes physical chaos produced by the social and demographic upheavals of the time, visions of what education could and should be were the major causalities.

Accompanying this overreliance on bureaucratic legalism was the tendency to embrace an extreme relativism or "anything goes" attitude. At Hamilton High and other schools this manifested itself in numerous ways. For example, the roles between teacher and therapist became blurred. Teachers, except on occasions where unequivocal legalistic mandates had been broached, often behaved—sometimes out of fear—like therapists. Rather than challenge a student caught cheating on moral grounds, teachers often looked the other way or referred the student to a counselor to find out why they chose to cheat. Having no moral or educational vision to guide them, both teachers and students often rebelled against *ought* and *should* "as an intrusion of external and coercive authoritarianism."[11]

Grant found this reliance on bureaucratic legalism and contractualism as manifestations of a corrosive individualism that—beginning in the late 1960s—dominated our schools well into the late 1970s and 1980s. Much like Grant, Lipman refused either to be paralyzed by cynicism or to accept the "brittle moral formulas favored by fundamentalists." There is no evidence that Grant knew of Lipman's work, but, in facilitating Hamilton High's reconstructing itself into a community based on a strong positive ethos, Grant operationalized the goals of the Philosophy for Children program.

While Lipman and Grant were fashioning a sophisticated response to the cynicism and moral relativism permeating many of our schools, others sought a more simplistic, if not very effective, solution to this problem. To many Americans, our schools were reneging on their promise to teach the basics to every child. The widespread belief that—due to experimentation and innovation—our schools had abandoned teaching the "3Rs" created a perceived crisis in our educational system (Berliner and Biddle suggest that this crisis is manufactured).[12] This crisis mentality fueled a "back to basics" movement that empathized traditional approaches to the teaching of reading, writing, and arithmetic, advocated old fashioned discipline (including corporeal punishment), and fostered respect for the flag, motherhood, and apple pie.

This "back to basics" movement manifested itself in many ways, but no one captured its tone better than Gene Lyons' article, which first appeared in the September, 1979 issue of *The Texas Monthly*. In his article titled, "Why Teachers Can't Teach," Lyons declares that, "the business of teacher education in Texas—as everywhere else in America—is a sham, a mammoth and very expensive swindle of the public interest, a hoax, and an intellectual disgrace."[13] Lyons' scathing and sometimes irresponsible condemnation of American education offered little that was new, but proved to be prophetic, especially in Texas. Strangely reminiscent of Arthur Bestor's critique of schooling in America discussed earlier in this chapter, Lyons article received the Magazine Publishers Association prestigious National Magazine Award and portions of the article appeared in *Phi Delta Kappan*'s special Reform in Teacher Education issue of October, 1980.

Lyons' article captured, if not created, the public mood toward public education in Texas and the nation. His assertion that teachers can't teach because they do not know anything to teach fueled the flames of educational reform that swept over Texas and the nation during the 1980s. Noting that teachers' performance on standardized tests are often worse than the scores of public and private high school students, Lyons concludes that "teacher education is a massive fraud." The products of teacher education programs are now teaching from Amarillo to Brownsville, from Orange to El Paso. Many such teachers, Lyons contended, "cannot read as well as the average 16 year old, write notes free of barbarisms to parents, or handle arithmetic well enough to keep track of the field trip money."[14] He blamed not the enlisted personnel, i.e. the teachers but the officers—deans, professors of education, school administrators, and state and federal bureaucrats. Critical of schools or colleges of education for "coddling ignorance" and for turning "out hordes of certified ignoramuses, he chastises the National Educational Association for supporting what he calls no fault education. Lyons suggested that NEA's opposition to competency testing for both teachers and students was self-serving.

Visiting Southwest Texas State University, the largest producer of teachers in the state, Lyons commented upon the anti-intellectualism that permeates the campus. Sitting in on several education courses, Lyons characterized them as farcical. His venture through the "wonderland of teacher education" compelled him to conclude that the monopoly controlling teacher education must be broken. The interlocking directorate—that overly friendly relationship among colleges or schools of education, school superintendents, and the Texas Education Agency—must be dismantled. According to Lyons, alternative routes to certification were needed to make it possible for non education majors, knowledgeable in their fields, to enter the teaching profession.

Though condemned by educationists, Lyons' article struck a chord with politicians and the public. It is more than coincidental that shortly after the appearance of this article, the Texas State Legislature passed a comprehensive reform bill mandating many of Lyons' proposals. This new legislation successfully emasculated the Texas Education Agency and effectively destroyed the interlocking directorate alluded to above. Alternative routes to teacher certification were authorized and teacher salaries were raised to attract and retain qualified people into the ranks. A four-step career ladder for teachers was approved and attempts were made to equalize funding for students across the state. With increased funding came more regulations and accountability, including competency tests for both students and teachers. Though Texans like to think of themselves as independent and autonomous, similar kinds of legislative actions mandating educational reform took place in virtually every state in the union.

Lyons' salvo captures the frustration felt by conservative businessmen, concerned parents, and social and political leaders alarmed over the apparent decline in our children and youth's performance on numerous national standardized tests. While Lyons, politicians, and other concerned citizens clamored for a return to an authoritarian system where the basics dominate the curriculum as the "quick fix" to this very real problem, others—most notably Christopher Jencks—suggested that the solution lay in a return to complexity rather than the basics. According to Jencks, the problem lies not in the teaching of basic skills, but in our schools' inability or unwillingness to teach complex reasoning skills.

Whether the basics—reading, writing, and arithmetic—or the more complex fourth "R"—reasoning, declining literacy became an accepted fact of life in America of the late 1970s and 1980s. To many back-to-basics advocates, literacy meant mastery of some predetermined competencies or essentials. To others like Maxine Greene, literacy was "an opening, a becoming, never a fixed end."[15] Greene agreed that students should be well grounded in the three Rs, but truly literate persons go "beyond what they are taught and begin teaching themselves." Paraphrasing Gilbert Ryle, Greene explains that literacy ought "to open gates, not close them."[16] Literacy, so defined, aims at freedom, i.e., the ability to see things, not just as they are but as they should or could be; the ability to conceptually structure and restructure the world.

Many, if not most, of our high school graduates are not literate in the way Greene uses the term. Examples of this kind of illiteracy abound, but few can compare with the graphic illustrations Richard Mitchell offers in his scathing and sometimes irresponsible condemnation of American education. Mitchell, in *The Graves of Academe*, comments on the responses of students who attended a rock concert in Cincinnati where eleven people were trampled to death. Angry at a columnist of the Chicago *Sun Times* for suggesting that "those who would climb over broken bodies to reach a seat in the auditorium could be called 'the new barbarians,'" one young concert goer rationalized the tragedy by writing that: "People die *every three second* [sic]. What would you do if you paid $15 for a ticket?"[17] Such cavalier disregard for human life is shocking and, if representative, lends credence to Mitchell's assertions that today's youth are neither literate nor free.

While numerous grammatical and stylistic errors are apparent in these students' written responses, they are not deficient in basic skills. They understand, for example, the value of a ticket as well as the tenuous nature of human existence, and they are obviously capable of expressing themselves adequately in print. Still, Mitchell's conclusion that they are neither literate nor free is hard to refute. They are illiterate because they have no values of their own, and they are not free because they have uncritically accepted the beliefs of others. Defining literacy as "a way of the mind, the habit of thinking . . ." and not just a collection of skills, Mitchell concludes that in a democracy, "basic minimum competency won't do."[18] If ours is to be a viable democracy, we need a literate citizenry, individuals who do more than idolize media personalities; individuals capable of and engaged in critically examining themselves and their world.

While Greene and Mitchell agreed that our schools fail to produce enough such citizens, neither resorted to a back-to-basics approach. Both recognized that the declining test scores, though symptomatic, were not the problem. While test scores did decline in the 1960s and 70s, it does not logically follow that our schools were failing to teach the basics. A careful examination of the evidence suggests that the youth of the mid 1970s performed far better on basic skills than their counterparts did a few years back. The problem lies not in the teaching of basic skills, but in teaching complex skills, lending credence to Jencks' suggestion that "if schools need to do anything today—and it is doubtful that schools alone can solve the problem—it is to get back to complexity, not to basics."[19]

To support his conclusion, Jencks noted that nine-year-olds examined in 1974 by the National Assessment of Educational Progress performed better on reading and writing skills than a similar group tested in 1970. Similar results were registered using McGraw-Hill's Comprehensive Test of Basic Skills and Iowa's comprehensive statewide testing program. As Jencks noted, though there are students who need help in mastering basics, "there are proportionately fewer of them in today's primary schools than any other time in the past."[20]

If our elementary schools are teaching the basics as well as, if not better than, before, the assertion that our high schools are graduating large numbers of students who cannot read and write becomes suspect. Jencks argues that today's high school students know as many words as did their predecessors of a few years back, but they have trouble drawing correct inferences from what they read. They understand what a paragraph says, but experience difficulty deriving meaning from the passage. When writing, they make no more grammatical errors, but their thoughts are not as coherently expressed as those of their counterparts of a decade ago. Today's students possess less information and cannot reason as well as did their predecessors, due not to a deficiency in basic skills, but resulting from students' unwillingness and inability to deal with complexity. It is with the teaching of such complex skills that our schools should be concerned if "literacy," as defined by Greene and Mitchell, is to be our goal.

While the merits of literacy seem obvious, many of today's youth are oblivious to its value. Though the exact cause or causes for their attitude cannot be pinpointed, the impact of the media, particularly television, is generally believed to be significant. Since most television programming is aimed at a mental age of twelve, it is likely to expand the horizon of younger children while simultaneously stunting or impeding the intellectual growth of students in their teens. Jencks points out that the data, which show a rise in test scores among elementary school students and a decline among secondary school students, supports this interpretation.

While today's television offers the viewer an expanded world view, it does little to assist our children in coping with this complex world. If the influence of television is as pervasive as it seems, then it is no longer surprising that students have little patience with activities requiring sustained complex thought or that they fail to exercise thoughtful judgment when balancing immediate reward against possible consequences. Nurtured on such a diet of inane programming, students rarely demonstrate restraint, and all too often reject anything, including school activities, that is not immediately entertaining.

Perhaps our schools' failure to provide meaningful experiences for the young contributes to the media's impact. Though much of today's popular entertainment is clearly superficial, each half hour or sixty minute television show is presented as a dramatic whole. In contrast, much of the information provided in school is transmitted piecemeal with little or no concern given to assisting students in making sense out of what is, to many, a fragmented puzzle. Students, like everyone else, discover meaning as they come to understand how the part relates to the whole. Television programming, however inane, is meaningful, because shows are almost always presented as integrated wholes. Ironically, a return to the teaching of basic skills in isolation reinforces the negative impact that the media has upon today's youth. When school experiences are not related to other aspects of students' lives, these experiences are meaningless and have no lasting value. As a consequence, students, unable to make sense out of such empty educational experiences, look elsewhere for meaning in their lives.

If education is to regain some of the ground it seems to have lost in recent years, ways must be found of making education meaningful. As adults, we easily understand the connection that mastery of certain skills has to future success, but we must not assume that children readily understand this relationship. Children need to understand how things relate to the present, and they are poorly served by well-meaning adults who refuse, laugh at, or avoid treating children's questions seriously. All too often, information packaged in the form of a didactic textbook functions in this manner. Students, through no fault of their own, fail to understand how they are to be enlightened by such information. To them it has no context, which in turn makes it meaningless.

Matthew Lipman argues that it need not be this way. He believes that a textbook can be meaningful even to children. A textbook should "be an adventure filled with discoveries, indeed it should be a paradigm of discovery."[21] In developing philosophical novels for children, Lipman succeeded in creating text material that children find enjoyable and, when used by a skilled teacher, enables students to relate their school experiences to other aspects of life. Though Jencks', Greene's, and Lipman's arguments are compelling to us, they did not win the "literacy" wars of the 1970s and 1980s. Collectively, they provided a counterweight or buffer to some of the more extreme "back to basics" solutions, but during the mid to late 1980s, their vision of literacy encountered a new, more sophisticated, albeit misguided attempt to recapture what never was and what should never be.

In 1987, E. D. Hirsh's *Cultural Literacy, What Every American Needs to Know,* appeared on the American scene. In asserting that there is an index, a provisional list of the terms and phrases "actually possessed by literate Americans" and by developing a cultural literacy dictionary and text material targeted toward specific grade levels, e.g., "What Every Sixth Grader Needs to Know," Hirsch sought to make this information known by literate Americans the possession of all Americans. Hirsch agreed that every American needed to know such information, because it is "only by piling up specialized communally shared information "that one can prosper, succeed and participate in the larger social order." Since today's youth, argues Hirsch, have not stored as much of this common background information as their predecessors, they are less able to read at an adequate level, to grasp the implications of the written word, to relate it "to the unstated context which alone gives meaning to what they read."[22] Such shared or common knowledge must be known by reader and author alike if they are to communicate at all. Even journalists write for a common reader, assuming at least in vague terms what the reader already knows and does not know. "Without appropriately shared background knowledge, people cannot understand newspapers" and without the ability to understand a free press, democracy is doomed. Hence, Hirsch concludes, a certain amount "of shared canonical knowledge is inherently necessary to a literate democracy."[23]

Such canonical knowledge is more than just the knowledge necessary to function in a local setting or community but less than the knowledge of a specialist. It is the knowledge that should be taught to all Americans. Such knowledge is admittedly superficial, yet essential for sustaining our cultural heritage and national unity. This extensive curriculum "is simply a minimal description of elements that should be included in every child's schooling."[24] Equally essential, suggests Hirsch, is the intensive curriculum, i.e., in depth study of selected topics and subjects. As long as it builds upon the foundation laid by the extensive curriculum, the intensive curriculum need not be the same for all. It can and should respond to local concerns and individual interest. Though Hirsch recognizes the importance of the intensive curriculum, the crucial issue for him is the extensive curriculum. For this reason Hirsch and his colleagues have compiled a list of 5,000 items to serve as the initial step toward developing a national consensus on what it is that every American needs to know. Also available from Hirsch is a dictionary providing associations that every literate American supposedly makes to each of the items on the list. In developing this list and dictionary, Hirsch and his associates are heirs to Noah Webster, William Holmes McGuffey, and other men of conservative persuasion who succeeded, through their readers and other texts, in transmitting their essentially religious and authoritarian version of our cultural heritage to generation after generation of school children during the nineteenth century.

For much of the twentieth century, we have abandoned such an approach with, suggests Hirsch, disastrous consequences. The time has come, Hirsch argues, to revive this approach, taking from it what is essential for cultural continuity and laying aside that which is no longer viable. Whereas Webster grounded his curriculum prescriptions on his Christian faith, Hirsch uses anthropological arguments to buttress his call for cultural literacy. Hirsch admits that what constitutes cultural literacy for society differs to some extent from what it was twenty-five years ago or what it will be twenty-five years from now, but he adds that stability, not change, is the chief characteristic of cultural literacy. Hirsch argues that the 5,000 items that comprise his list and dictionary are descriptive in that they represent the information that literate Americans know today. It is prescriptive only in the sense that it can serve as a guide for developing curricula materials so as to insure Americans access to this body of knowledge.

Despite Hirsch's disclaimers, his is a prescriptive list. While he suggests that the items are provisional, open to challenge and change, he suggests that the knowledge represented by the list consists of the unifying facts and values of our intellectual heritage. As Henry Giroux notes, "culture" for Hirsch, "is seen as the totality of the language practices of a given nation and merely 'presents' itself for all to participate." Such a view "expresses a single, durable history and vision . . ."[25] Like Webster and McGuffey before him, Hirsch offers us his version of what one needs to know. Admittedly his version offers more flexibility than that of Webster, but it still represents the perspective of the privileged and the powerful.

To illustrate that his is the perspective of the privileged one need only to use Hirsch's example of how his father wrote business letters that alluded to Shakespeare. These allusions were effective for conveying complex messages to his associates, because, suggests Hirsch, "in his [father's] day, business people could make allusions with every expectation of being understood." Perhaps as Wayne C. Booth suggests, the upper crust of New England or the aristocratic South in the recent past might have understood Hirsch's father when he wrote to an associate, "'here is a tide'" but the average citizen, then or now, would not recognize the phrase as an abbreviated version of "buy . . . now and you'll cover expenses for the whole year, but if you fail to act right away, you may regret it for the rest of your life."[26] Booth notes that his illiterate grandmother would not have understood Hirsch's father, but "would have correctly recognized his as a privileged product of a higher education that she neither understood or consciously desired."[27]

Hirsch's example suffers from another problem. Using such references appropriately and understanding their use requires more than just passing or superficial knowledge of them. Knowing that "there is a tide" is a Shakespearean phrase is qualitatively different from knowing the meaning of the phrase in the context of the play and thus being able to use it to convey meaning in a different context. Clearly Hirsch's father and his associates had more than just a cursory knowledge of "there is a tide" for them to use it as he suggests they did.

Hirsch's arrogance blinds him to these problems. Once again individuals, like Booth's grandmother, are on trial here. It is up to the individual, albeit one exposed to Hirsch's extensive curriculum, to become culturally literate by appropriating this prescribed body of knowledge. Such individuals, Hirsch proclaims, "need traditional information at a very early age,"[28] even if it means learning it by rote. In the nineteenth century school "rote recitation was the commonest form of 'teaching'."[29] Once again, Hirsch follows suit, suggesting that "our current distaste for memorization is more pious than realistic. . . . Observe for example how children memorize the rather complex materials of football, baseball, and basketball even without benefit of formal avenues by which that information is inculcated." According to Hirsch "at an early age when their memories are most retentive, children have an almost instinctive urge to learn specific tribal information."[30]

Why then are so many of today's youth, as well as most other Americans, ignorant of the basic facts of our culture? Hirsch suggests that today's adolescents are ignorant of the dates of World War II, for example, because they have never been taught such information. More likely they encountered it somewhere in their schooling but failed to store it, because it had no meaning for them. Hirsch is right. Children have an amazing capacity to memorize things, but they are not likely to retain that which has been committed to memory unless it has meaning for them.

It may be possible to use Hirsch's list to develop a curriculum that speaks to today's students, but Hirsch's view of history suggest that his list will be used differently. As already noted, Hirsch advocates the revival of the nineteenth century approach to education. If Hirsch has his way the text material based on his or some other list will mimic the nineteenth century texts of Webster, McGuffey, and other men of the conservative persuasion. Such textbooks "selected their themes as to disguise the real world, not to reveal it; to repress anxieties, not to confront them; to foster complacency among the established groups rather than to include the dispossessed."[31]

There is a danger of history repeating itself. As already suggested, Hirsch's view of history runs counter to our nation's commitment to pluralism. His proposed reform is grounded in a mainstream version of history and culture, a version that has often denied or ignored the contributions and experiences of women and minorities. Just as Webster and other textbook authors of the previous century avoided controversy at all costs, Hirsch's proposal deftly sidesteps "the disquieting problems of sexism, racism, class exploitation, and other social issues that bear down so heavily on the present."[32] Hirsch might respond that one must be taught the basic facts of our cultural heritage before one can critically assess their value. Such an argument reveals not only the inherent arrogance of Hirsch's position, but also his rather pessimistic view of human nature and his suspicion of democracy.

Hirsch denies that his proposal is in any way elitist. Going further, Hirsch argues, much like Mortimer Adler in *The Paideia Proposal*, that genuine democracy can only be achieved if everyone has the same quality, as well as quantity of education. Still, as Booth points out, Hirsch's proposal sounds less like the education of free men and women, than the training of functionaries. As already noted, Hirsch considers our common cultural heritage, the body of knowledge that every American needs to know, to be relatively stable. From this perspective it logically follows that students are to absorb, more or less uncritically, this body of relatively stable knowledge. Or as Hirsch puts it, "only by piling up specific, communally shared information" can children become culturally literate. In turn, from such a perspective, the teacher becomes a transmitter, or to use Hirsch's verbs, *giving, conveying, covering,* or *offering* the information that each child must receive. The teacher is crucial for, according to Hirsch, "our children can learn this information only by being taught it."[33]

Clearly this is not an education conducive to democratic values. It is, to borrow Freire's term, banking education; an education better suited for maintaining a hierarchical, authoritarian society than for fostering genuine democracy. Implicit in Hirsch's "democratic" view is that those who possess the relatively stable body of knowledge should offer it to all. If some choose not to or are unable to partake of it, then they must suffer the consequences. Such a perspective presupposes the existence of one correct view of our common heritage. Teaching and learning is merely giving and receiving "a preconstituted body of knowledge."[34] Such an educational system is more likely to produce the modern day equivalent of Webster's "quiet Christian" than a reflective critical thinker our modern democracy needs.

Clearly Hirsh's view of democracy is antithetical to that of John Dewey and Matthew Lipman. It is no coincidence that his ideas fits conveniently with the thrust of the educational reform proposed by William Bennet, Chester Finn, and others of the Reagan administration. From this perspective, due to the successes of progressive educators like Dewey and Lipman, the revered traditions that constitute our cultural heritage have been all but lost during the last twenty years. Hirsch embraced this conservative educational perspective and blamed Dewey and his disciples for the cultural relativism that permeates the modern world. Since there are no common, much less absolute standards by which ideas and actions can be measured, the contributions of the western intellectual tradition cannot be held superior to others. In the late 1980s Hirsch emerged as the eloquent spokesperson for the perspective that not only is our nation at risk but so is the civilization upon which it is based.

At roughly the same time that Hirsh exploded on the scene as the latest champion of a "back to basics" approach to education, the critical thinking skills movement had become a hot item in education circles. Even some conservatives embraced a sanitized version of critical thinking recognizing that our "high tech" world demands mastery of the higher order thinking skills. Others argued that a critical thinking citizenry is a prerequisite for any viable democracy. Still others claimed that the teaching of critical thinking helped contemporary students avoid the pitfalls of prejudice, ignorance, bigotry, and intolerance. As John McPeck explained, "being in favor of critical thinking in our schools is . . . a bit like favoring freedom, justice, or a clean environment, it meets with general approval from the outset.[35]

Not everyone agreed that critical thinking could or should be taught. Even John McPeck argues, in his monograph *Critical Thinking and Education,* that critical thinking cannot and should not be taught as a separate course or subject. He contends that all thinking, "including critical thinking" is thinking about something and cannot be developed in isolation, independent of particular fields of study. McPeck argues that each field of knowledge is so distinct that the critical thinking skills germane to one field are not transferable to others.

McPeck's monograph, published in 1981, is a scholarly work which raises important questions about the recent push to teach critical thinking in our schools whenever possible. McPeck agrees that to think critically is a desirable human trait but argues that "the statement 'I teach critical thinking' *simpliciter . . .* is vacuous because there is no generalized skill called critical thinking." McPeck defines critical thinking as "the appropriate use of reflective skepticism within the problem area under consideration." In short, critical thinking is the judicious use of skepticism, but the criteria for such use "are supplied by the norms and standards of the field under consideration."[36] McPeck is in favor of critical thinking as an educational goal, but argues that it can best be taught or fostered through epistemologically oriented curricula purposefully designed to teach the structure of the disciplines.

The Philosophy for Children approach to critical thinking shares many of McPeck's concerns about teaching critical thinking. According to Lipman, "Often what is called 'critical thinking' is quasi-philosophical" in that many approaches to the teaching of critical thinking emphasize the skills in isolation from any narrative context. In so doing, Lipman explains, "Such courses generally fail to provide an initial philosophical experience . . . upon which a reflective discussion can be focused."[37] All too often such an emphasis on the acquisition of thinking skills results in the exercises and drills being thought of as worthwhile in themselves. In such an approach, little or no emphasis is given to Socratic inquiry.

Lipman offers instead a humanities discipline that serves to introduce to children ideas drawn from the philosophical tradition. While this tradition is difficult and complex, children can encounter in it issues that touch them as deeply as they touch adults, "questions about the nature of truth, of friendship, of fairness, and of rightness." According to Lipman, thinking skills "should be taught in the context of a humanistic discipline" that is "committed to the furtherance of humanistic inquiry into significant but problematic concepts."[38]

Lipman's approach raises additional questions such as, can children do philosophy and is the Philosophy for Children program genuine philosophy? Obviously, in taking seriously Bruner's assertion that "any subject can be taught to anybody at any age in some form that is honest,"[39] Lipman answers both questions in the affirmative. While not everyone agrees with Lipman on this point, the successful implementation of the Philosophy for Children program in elementary and middle schools throughout the world has effectively silenced many of his critics. Even McPeck recognizes that children have the capacity to do philosophy. As Paul Wagner suggests, the verdict on whether philosophy can or should be taught in elementary and middle schools rests on the success or failure of Lipman and Gareth Matthews as pioneers in this venture.[40] To the extent that Lipman's program honestly engages children in the philosophical enterprise, the Philosophy for Children approach to critical thinking meets McPeck's admonition that critical thinking be taught in the context of a discipline.

Another mistake often made by those who advocate the teaching of critical thinking is what McPeck calls the philosopher's fallacy. Many educators assume that by teaching students the rules of formal logic and how to identify numerous informal fallacies, they are developing critical thinkers. Such a position, McPeck contends, "merely assumes that there is (or will be) a persuasive transfer of training across disciplinary boundaries." McPeck reminds us that "this assumption has never been substantiated."[41] McPeck suggests that while logic may be necessary for critical thinking, it is not sufficient for it. His contention that "logic can help to eliminate hypotheses, conjectures, and plausible solutions, [but] it cannot provide them"[42] is correct, but goes too far in minimizing the role that logic plays in critical thinking. Granted, logic's contribution to critical thinking may be largely negative, but the ability to recognize faulty reasoning is an essential critical thinking skill.

While Philosophy for Children materials introduce fifth and sixth graders to formal logic and to numerous informal fallacies, the program avoids the philosopher's fallacy. Characters in the novel *Harry Stottlemeier's Discovery* discover the rules of reason and attempt to apply them to occurrences in their everyday lives. Equally important, children in the novel discover that logic is not enough. Harry, the novel's main character, becomes particularly upset when one of his classmates transfers to another school due to a conflict between his family's religious beliefs and school policies. Frustrated over the inability of members of the class to help "Dale," Harry admits that he, too, feels ashamed, adding, "But it wasn't just a little problem which someone can't solve because he's stated it wrong." His newly discovered logical rules concerning the effect of reversing "all" or "no" sentences are of little use here, and he knows it. The children in the novels repeatedly discover that formal logic and the rules of reason are just tools to assist in distinguishing good thinking from bad. Collectively these kids learn that such tools offer no guarantees that complex problems can be solved by simply applying the rules.

Still, logic has its uses. In a later chapter Jane Starr accuses Sandy Mendoza of stealing her briefcase. Harry, using his newly acquired knowledge of hypothetical syllogisms, demonstrated that Sandy could not have taken Jane's briefcase. At this point Lisa volunteers that she thinks Mickey stole the briefcase. Perhaps based on her intuitive understanding of Mickey's personality, she reasons that taking the briefcase and hiding it behind the water fountain is just the kind of thing Mickey would do. Using logic, the best Harry could do was to prove Sandy's innocence, while Lisa's shrewd guess was confirmed by Mickey's subsequent confession. While acknowledging Lisa's guess, Mr. Spence, the teacher, concludes the episode, asserting that "guessing isn't a substitute for careful investigation."[43]

Characters in the Philosophy for Children novels model different styles of thinking in their collective struggle to figure things out. Students in the classroom quickly note that certain characters are risk-takers, while others are more cautious; some are analytical, while others are experimental; and still others are speculative. The Philosophy for Children program assumes that logic and other styles of thinking go hand in hand. By modeling the interplay of logic and other modes of thinking in situations common to most, if not all, children, the Philosophy for Children program helps them to understand how and to what extent logic impacts upon their lives. In this way the Philosophy for Children approach to critical thinking avoids McPeck's objection to treating the teaching of logic and the teaching of critical thinking as synonymous.

In a chapter entitled "Reading, Testing and Critical Thinking," McPeck asserts that researchers in critical thinking "have adopted a basic skills approach to critical thinking in the same way as their counterparts in reading research."[44] McPeck counters that critical thinking, like reading, cannot be reduced to a few mechanical decoding skills. Whether or not others interested in the teaching of critical thinking are, as McPeck suggests, guilty of reducing a comprehensive, complex process to a few decoding skills, the Philosophy for Children approach to critical thinking does no such thing. While the mental acts introduced in the novels can be identified as specific reasoning skills, i.e., deduction, categorization, constructing analogies, definition, generalization, and instantiation, alone they do not constitute critical thinking. Only as they are used in the service of reflective inquiry on problems of significance to the individual do they evolve into critical thinking. In a sense such application cannot be taught at any level. The best that can be done is to create an environment that exposes students to the critical use of such tools and stimulates them to emulate the critical thinking they observe in others. The Philosophy for Children approach to critical thinking aims at creating such an environment by converting classrooms into communities of inquiry. In this way, Philosophy for Children is more than a basic skills approach to critical thinking.

In the last chapter of his monograph, McPeck suggests that we move "forward to basics." This means teaching a subject so that its epistemology is a fundamental component. More important than learning the facts of a given field of study is an awareness of why certain information is regarded as factual. McPeck explains that such an approach aims at replacing "the dominance of facts and skills by an understanding of their justification."[45] McPeck suggests that if we are serious in our desire to teach critical thinking in our schools, we should begin by having curriculum specialists from subject areas work with epistemologists to develop epistemologically oriented curricula in the different fields of study. McPeck notes that appropriate training for teachers would also be needed to ensure that this new approach is accurately implemented. By developing curricula and teaching it to students in this epistemologically oriented manner, students could be taught to think critically as they study the broad and general fields of knowledge. For the humanities, the Philosophy for Children approach puts into practice the kind of epistemologically oriented approach McPeck advocates. By developing curricula that span the elementary, middle school, and high school years, Lipman has, to a considerable degree, made the structure of philosophical inquiry available to and relevant for children and youth. In this way, Lipman has continued and expanded the quest for excellence begun by the curriculum reformers of the 1950s.

Though aware of the difficulties inherent in teaching critical thinking, both McPeck and Lipman embrace it as a worthy educational goal. Not everyone agrees. For example, Mel and Norman Gabler of Longview, Texas opposed the use of text materials that encouraged students to think for themselves. The Gablers and other members of the New Right considered the critical thinking skills movement as a renewed offensive in what Tim LeHaye identifies as "the battle for the mind."

In a sense LeHaye is correct. There is a "battle for the mind" between those who wish to indoctrinate humankind to a particular point of view and those seeking to educate human beings to think for themselves. In this battle, the New Right and advocates of critical thinking are natural enemies.

By its very nature, critical thinking requires questioning of conventional attitudes and keeping an open mind. But it is this championing of a healthy skepticism, of open mindedness, that makes this movement the natural enemy of the New Right. To the New Right, "open mindedness is not some inviolate concept that every educator has the duty or even the right to encourage."[46] Christian fundamentalists like the Gablers and Alice Moore of the Kanawa County (West Virginia) textbook controversy believe that anything which encourages questioning of institutional values has no place in the classroom. Articulating a position representative of the New Right, Moore proclaims her belief "in indoctrinating my children" beginning with the "assumption that God exists." She explains that "concerning my children's rearing, I am doctrinally dogmatic, and dictatorical."[47]

Such indoctrinating may have an unintended effect. By refusing to deal openly and honestly with controversial issues, parents and schools run the risk of creating an enticing aura of mystery around some forbidden fruit. Consider a different approach. Even when we believe that traditional values are the best, we must allow them to be accepted or rejected by each new generation. Let the arguments for the old values be given their fullest expression by one capable of presenting the best possible case for them. In turn, allow a fair and strong case for all alternative points of view to be presented. If the traditional values are better and students are accustomed to evaluating positions on the basis of evidence, we have nothing to fear.

Such an educational scheme is based upon humility, a humility grounded in the recognition that while progress toward knowing the truth is possible, absolute certainty is not. Those adhering to this point of view are open to opinions different from their own. By considering other points of views, they may encounter additional evidence that refutes part or all of their original stance. They may learn, after carefully examining the additional evidence, that it is incorrect or irrelevant, thus enhancing their original position.

The New Right suffers from no such humility. Since they know the truth with absolute certainty, they believe it unnecessary to consider other points of view. Their dogma contributes to their ignorance since, as John Stuart Mill pointed out more than a century ago, those who refuse to consider other points of view do not truly understand their own. Without understanding and then rejecting other points of view, they have no grounds for preferring their own opinion or point of view.

Though LeHaye coined the phrase "the battle for the mind," the conflict is not new. It originated at least 2,400 years ago when the Athenians killed Socrates for "corrupting the youth by his teaching." In his own defense, Socrates tried to explain to the Athenians that "he was a teacher unlike any they had ever known."[48] Many Athenians recognized Socrates as a wise man, though he denied it, professing to have "no wisdom, small or great." After years of questioning politicians, poets, artisans, and others who claimed to be wise, and discovering that they were not, Socrates recanted. Perhaps he was wiser than others, he reasoned, since at least he knew that he knew nothing. Socrates' awareness of his own ignorance made him wiser than other fallible human beings who claimed to be wise. He dedicated his life to questioning these individuals and revealing to them their ignorance.

While his method was less than diplomatic, Socrates believed it contributed to the "improvement of the soul." By helping others to see their own mistakes and errors, Socrates provided these fallible human beings with the necessary first step toward improving themselves. As a teacher, Socrates did not tell his students what to think. Instead he criticized their thinking, thus enabling them to improve their thinking skills and increase their knowledge.

Socrates was right. The Athenians had never known a teacher like him, i.e., a teacher who never told his students what was right, good, or true, but only what was bad, evil, or wrong. They did not understand or agree that his negative approach is the only way fallible human beings have for "improving their souls."[49] Socrates is still right. As fallible beings, we can never know what is absolutely right, good, or true. Our only hope for progress is to discover the errors and weaknesses of our established norms and truths and use these discoveries to improve ourselves and our world. Socrates exemplified critical thinking at its best. Just as his claim to wisdom was a negative one, the uses of critical thinking are largely negative. It cannot lead us to the absolute right, good, or truth, but, by helping us to recognize faulty reasoning, it can help us to avoid going wrong. Only by following Socrates' lead can we improve our souls.

The Athenians turned a deaf ear to Socrates' apology, perhaps because of the catastrophes that had racked their society in recent years. The Spartans had defeated them in the Peloponnesian War, destroying the walls of the city and establishing a puppet government there in 401 B.C. When democracy was restored three years later, many Athenians longed for a return to normalcy. Socrates and the critical inquiry he embodied became a casualty of this desire for peace and stability.

If the New Right has its way, a similar tragedy could occur in our society. Just as Athenians desired peace and stability after years of turmoil, many Americans "are troubled, frightened, and mad as hell over what they have seen happening to their country in recent decades."[50] Some genuinely fear that our society is disintegrating. While not everyone is for prayer and Bible readings in the school, many are willing to try it in the hope that it will produce peace and stability again. Perceiving today's children and youth to be callous and insensitive to the rights and needs of others, many Americans mistakenly seek to "return to a golden age that never was" by putting "McGuffey Readers back on the shelves."[51] The problems are real and complex, but embracing the New Right agenda is not the answer. Just as the Athenians feared Socrates, the New Right fears the commitment to criticism an open society requires. If, like the Athenians, we falter and allow the New Right to silence our commitment to critical inquiry, then we place our way of life in jeopardy.

Now, more than ever, our society needs quality critical thinking skills programs to improve our souls. While advocates of critical thinking generally embrace this Socratic ideal, not all so-called thinking skills programs achieve this goal. Some programs, in the name of citizenship education, seek to impose a prior perspective on the impressionable minds of our young. Others, including various values clarification techniques, foster the "everything is relative" attitude so fashionable today. While the former is indoctrination, the latter produces intellectual and moral chaos. Neither is critical thinking.

If critical thinking in the Socratic sense is a worthy educational ideal, then Lipman's Philosophy for Children approach is a move in the right direction. More importantly if the critical thinking skills movement is to be victorious in this modern day "battle for the mind," we must not forget that "the unexamined life is not worth living" or that the unexamined life is incompatible with a free and open society.

In describing the connections between Matthew Lipman's academic career and the trends and issues impacting educational practice in the second half of the twentieth century, we have focused on the tension between excellence and equity as worthy educational goals. We hope that we have made it clear that while the desire for excellence is often associated with the conservative persuasion—including those clamoring for a return to the basics—there are similarities between the philosophy of Philosophy for Children and the 1950s and 60s emphasis on academic excellence.

In a similar fashion, Lipman's attempt to operationalize Dewey's call for schools to become embryonic democracies fits with the more liberal emphasis of the 1960s and 1970s on equality of educational opportunity. We have tried to show that in the 1980s the question became "What did we learn from the educational critiques of the previous decades?" and "how can we overcome the ethos of despair that these critics identified?" Is it possible to find or create common or middle ground between the equally worthy educational goals of excellence and equity? As we have discussed, Philosophy for Children and other genuine critical thinking skills programs evolved as significant and sometimes desirable alternatives to those seeking to turn back the clock in an attempt to recapture a golden age that never was. In short, "literacy"—what it is and how to achieve it—became the dominant educational theme of the 1980s. Depending upon your definition,

Philosophy for Children is either an exemplary means of achieving literacy or anathema to it.

As discussed above, Philosophy for Children is a phenomenon of the late twentieth century that both reflects the educational context that spawned it and seeks to refashion that very context to make education more meaningful for today's children and tomorrow's citizens. Though significantly the brain-child of a single individual, Philosophy for Children is a growing, vibrant entity. As it evolves and matures, Philosophy for Children's potential for influencing the educational context of the next century will increase. Evidence of that expanding presence is already visible as Philosophy for Children at Montclair State University has joined forces with a major initiative aimed at renewing both our schools and teachers who work in them. This evolving relationship between Philosophy for Children and Goodlad's network for education renewal is the focus of the following and final section of this chapter.

If "critical thinking" and "literacy" were the educational buzzwords of the 1980s, the simultaneous renewal of schools and the education of educators is *the* educational phrase of the 1990s. In his 1990 seminal work, *Teachers For Our Nation's Schools,* John I. Goodlad explains that the fate of our schools and the education of our teachers are inextricably connected. Goodlad argues that dramatic and comprehensive reform is required for our teachers to achieve their potential and become genuine stewards of our democratic heritage.

Presenting nineteen postulates as the necessary prerequisites for his blueprint for the renewal of both schools and their teachers, Goodlad challenges schools/colleges of education and the universities of which they are a part to join forces with their counterparts in K–12 schools to ensure a more democratic future for our children and youth.

Montclair State University in New Jersey is one of a select few institutions of higher education meeting this challenge and accepting Goodlad's invitation to participate in the National Network for Educational Renewal. The invitation to join Goodlad's network resulted, in part, from Montclair State University School of Education's long standing commitment to critical thinking as a worthy educational goal and especially to its connection with Philosophy for Children. The Institute for the Advancement of Philosophy for Children is located at Montclair State University, and the associate director, Ann Margaret Sharp, is a faculty member in the School of Education and Professional Studies.

Key to Goodlad's blueprint is the creation of a new structure to facilitate this simultaneous renewal. Called a "Center of Pedagogy," it is both a concept and setting. Transcending traditional borders, this new structure unites university faculty responsible for the education of educators (including faculty from the Arts and Sciences as well as from the professional schools) with their counterparts in our nation's schools. These three groups (Arts and Sciences faculty, professional education faculty, and teachers) come together to renew the quality of both the education of educators and the places where they work. Conceptually, a "center of pedagogy" is "where the art and science of teaching are brought to bear on the education of educators and where the *whole* is the subject of continuous inquiry."[52] Since a "center of pedagogy" is much like a community of inquiry writ large, it is not surprising that Goodlad's network and Philosophy for Children have become collaborators in developing better teachers for better schools.

Notes

1. Ronald F. Reed and Ann F. Wichter, "Matthew Lipman: Restoring the Con-
    nection Between Education and Philosophy," in James Van Patten, ed., *Aca-
    demic Profiles in Higher Education* (New York: Edwin Mellen Press, 1992),
    210. For more biographical information about Lipman and why Philosophy
    for Children became his mission in life, see Tony W. Johnson, *Discipleship
    or Pilgrimage? The Educator's Quest for Philosophy* (Albany, N.Y.: State
    University of New York Press, 1995), pp. 115–118, 122–131.

2. G. Max Wingo, *Philosophies of Education: An Introduction* (Lexington, MA:
    D.C Heath, 1974) pp. 62–63.

3. Matthew Lipman, *Thinking in Education* (Cambridge, UK: Cambridge Uni-
    versity Press, 1991), p. 263.

4. Diane Ravitch, *The Troubled Crusade: American Education, 1945–1980*
    (New York: Basic Books, 1983), p. 232.

5. Matthew Lipman, "Dramatizing Philosophy," unpublished manuscript, 1993,
    p. 211.

6. Arthur G. Powell, Eleanor Farrar, and David K. Cohen, *The Shopping Mall
    High School: Winners and Losers in the Marketplace* (Boston: Houghton
    Mifflin, 1985), p. 292.

7. Quoted in Henry J. Perkinson, *Two Hundred Years of American Educa-
    tional Thought,* (New York: David McKay, 1976), p. 286.

8. Ibid., p. 285.

9. Gerald Grant, *The World We Created at Hamilton High* (Cambridge, MA:
    Harvard University Press, 1988), pp. 5–6.

10. Ibid., p. 183.

11. Ibid., p. 184.

12. David C. Berliner and Bruce J. Biddle, *The Manufactured Crisis: Myths,
    Fraud, and the Attack on America's Public Schools* (Reading, MA: Addison-
    Wesley , 1995)

13. Gene Lyons, "Why Teachers Can't Teach," *Texas Monthly* (September, 1979),
    p. 128.

14. Ibid., p. 123.

15. Maxine Greene, "Literacy for What,?" *Phi Delta Kappan* 63 (January 1982),
    p. 326.

16. Ibid., p. 327.

17. Richard Mitchell, *The Graves of Academe* (Boston: Little, Brown, and Company, 1981), pp. 190–191.

18. Ibid., p. 202.

19. Christopher Jencks, "The Wrong Answer for Schools Is: Back to Basics," *The Washington Post*, February 19, 1973, p. C1.

20. Ibid.

21. Matthew Lipman, Ann Margaret Sharp, and Frederick S. Oscanyan, *Philosophy in the Classroom* (Philadelphia: Temple University Press, 1980), pp 8–9.

22. E. D. Hirsch, Jr., *Cultural Literacy: What Every American Needs to Know* (Boston: Houghton Mifflin, 1987), p. 2.

23. E. D. Hirsch, Jr., "Cultural Literacy," *The American Scholar* 52:2 (Spring 1983), p. 165.

24. Hirsch, *Cultural Literacy*, p. 127.

25. Stanley Aronowitz and Henry A. Giroux, "Schooling, Culture, and Literacy in the Age of Broken Dreams," *Harvard Educational Review* 58:2 (May 1988), 191.

26. Hirsch, *Cultural Literacy*, p. 9.

27. Wayne C. Booth, "Cultural Literacy and Liberal Learning: An Open Letter to E. D. Hirsch, Jr,." *Change* 20:4 (July–August,1988); 13.

28. Hirsch, *Cultural Literacy*, p. 31.

29. David Tyack, *Turning Points in American Eucational History* (New York: John Wiley, 1967), p. 178.

30. Hirsch, *Cultural Literacy*, p. 30.

31. Tyack, *Turning Points*, p. 184.

32. Aronowitz and Giroux, "Schooling Culture, and Literacy " p. 194.

33. Hirsch, *Cultural Literacy*, p. 14.

34. Aronowitz and Giroux, p. 194.

35. John E. McPeck, *Critical Thinking and Education* (New York: St. Martin's, 1981), p. 1.

36. Ibid., pp.5, 7, and 8.

37. Matthew Lipman, "On Children's Philosophical Style," *Metaphilosophy* 3 and 4 (July/October 1984): 323.

38. Matthew Lipman, "Philosophy for Children and Critical Thinking," *The National Forum* 6. no. 5 (Winter 1985): 20.

39. Jerome Bruner, *In Search of Mind: Essays in Autobiography* (New York: Harper & Row, 1983), 180.

40. Paul Wagner, "The Universe, Philosophy, and the Public School," *Journal of Thought* 20, no.2 (Summer 1985): 13.

41. McPeck, *Critical Thinking and Education*, 14.

42. Ibid., p. 16.

43. Matthew Lipman, *Harry Stottlemeier's Discovery* (Montclair, N.J.: First Mountain Foundation, 1982) pp: 57, 90.

44. McPeck, *Critical Thinking*, 131.

45. Ibid., 148.

46. Joe L. Kincheloe, *Understanding the New Right and Its Impact on Education* (Bloomington, IN: Phi Delta Kappa Educational Foundation, 1983), p. 17.

47. Ibid.

48. Henry J. Perkinson, *Since Socrates: Studies in the History of Western Educational Thought* (New York: Longman, Inc., 1980), p. 2

49. Ibid., p.11.

50. William Martin, "Two Cheers for the Moral Majority," *The Texas Humanist* 7:4 (March–April, 1985): 12.

51. Gerald Grant, "The Character of Education and the Education of Character," *Daedalus* 110 (Summer 1981): 147.

52. John I. Goodlad , *Educational Renewal: Better Teachers, Better Schools* (San Francisco: Josey-Bass, 1994), p. 11.

Chapter 8

Phenomenology: A Personal Statement

Ronald F. Reed

What is the experience of Philosophy for Children, of community of inquiry like? What does it feel like from the inside? How does it feel to the newly initiated, how does it feel to those with a long history? How does it feel to teacher and how does it feel to student? In this chapter, we will attempt to provide some partial answers to those questions based on our experience with Philosophy for Children. The assumption behind this chapter is that experience may be held to yield some truth, facilitate some understanding, that escapes theory. As usual, we are taking William James seriously.

I arrived in Berea, Kentucky, a day and a half after my departure from Rochester, New York. There were a series of delays caused by technical difficulties and the threat of snow and ice along the east coast. When the plane finally skidded to a stop in Lexington Airport, the weather forecast said that a layer of ice was expected to cover the city by nightfall. The student who met me told me that it would be impossible to drive the seventy miles to Berea that night. We would have to stay in her mother's home overnight, and when the weather cleared, make the drive. I remember trying to sleep on a too-small couch; I remember the sound of a mantel clock ticking throughout the night, sounding the hour and the half-hour; I remember wondering why I was there and what good would come out of this fiasco.

We made it to Berea by late afternoon, in not the best of spirits. The drive was grueling and treacherous, the student seemed unfamiliar with the road—the same gas station appeared and reappeared—and my luggage was still travelling somewhere in the Midwest: it would arrive six days later.

I checked into a motel, went to leave my things in my room, but then realized that I did not have any things with me, so I reluctantly got into the car and the student drove me to a classroom on the Berea College campus. The first sessions had already begun and I was late.

A tall, balding man was sitting at the end of a long rectangular table, talking. Matthew Lipman was speaking about the nature of Philosophy for Children, and where the idea came from, and what it was meant to do, and how Philosophy for Children was different from other programs. At his side was a younger woman, who seemed impatient with the procedure. At one point, she turned to him and said, "Mat, you are acting just like a college professor; you are lecturing." I don't remember what Lipman replied, but he did continue on, while the woman, Ann Sharp, rolled her eyes.

It was hard to figure out what was going on. I had read an article about Philosophy for Children by Fred Oscanyan in the journal *Teaching Philosophy*, and had seen a notice about a training session to be held in January 1979, conducted by Oscanyan, Matthew Lipman, and Ann Sharp. Oscanyan had focused on the formal logic in *Harry Stottlemeier's Discovery* and presented community of inquiry as a new, dialogical way of teaching logic. As a recent doctoral student at a very traditional university, one with a heavy concentration in philosophy of science and logic, I was intrigued by any program that even attempted to humanize the teaching of that often forbidding discipline. But here was this man, who looked like and sounded just like my former professors talking about the "spine" of Philosophy for Children, the logic, and in turn, giving a credible university like lecture on the subject. There was something strange about that. I'm not sure if all the fifteen or so academics seated around the table felt that strangeness, but I was pretty sure that most of them did.

But then Lipman said that he was talking too much, and he suggested that we read from a new novel he had written called *Harry Stottlemeier's Discovery*. Lipman and his associates had been testing the novel in schools in New Jersey and New York, and by this time, Lipman had also gone on to create a sizeable portion of the traditional corpus, with *Lisa, Suki, Mark,* and their respective manuals completed or just about to be completed. Still, there was an experimental quality to the way Lipman handled the instructions and began the reading. It was clear that he was still ready to be surprised, both by the novel itself, and the reactions of the participants to the novel. The facade of the expert, the veneer of the all-knowing university professor wore off as soon as Lipman became involved with *Harry Stottlemeier's Discovery*.

It was late afternoon. I was especially tired and cranky, and looking around the group, it felt like my feelings were not minority ones. Most of the people in the room were recent Ph.D.s in philosophy, most were people who had worked very hard to overcome the many obstacles that are placed in the path of doctoral candidates, and, as a consequence, had, perhaps, an inflated sense of their own worth. Now Lipman was telling them, telling us, that we would each read, aloud, a few paragraphs of *Harry Stottlemeier's Discovery*, and that we would continue until we finished a chapter.

The reading was eventful. It disclosed something about the nature of reading itself. By the time one has been in school for twenty-five years, as most of us in the room had been, reading is largely taken for granted—it is assumed that the individual reader can sit down with a text and extract whatever meaning the text contains, especially if the text is written for eleven-year-olds and the readers are Ph.D.s in philosophy. What became apparent as the reading went public was that as Socrates might say, when people with great reputations are put to the test, sometimes those reputations are not completely deserved.

When we read, we did stumble over words, miss words altogether, sometimes changing a negative to positive thereby changing the meaning of a sentence, or read so quickly (or slowly) that meaning was obliterated. What became apparent to me at that initial reading was that we were all capable of making very basic mechanical errors and, presumably, when that happened in private (silent) reading, the errors were likely to go unchecked.

The reading also disclosed something about the importance of voice, and by extension, the importance of perspective. I had read *Harry Stottlemeier's Discovery* before coming to Berea, liked the novel very much, and was struck by how much the narrator of *Harry Stottlemeier's Discovery* sounded like Chaim Potok of *The Chosen*, *Davita's Harp*, and *The Promise*. There was something about an urban, New York-like accent, both cultured and street-sophisticated that Lipman and Potok shared, something about the cadences of their sentences, that I was familiar with, that I grew up hearing. I found Lipman (and Potok) easy to read and appealing precisely because I heard their voices almost every day of my life, in the neighborhoods in which I grew up. If asked, prior to the public reading, given my familiarity with the voice, and given my familiarity with the philosophy and logic of the text, I would have said that I had a clear idea of what Lipman meant.

When I heard the text read with different voices, with a female voice, with a southern accent, with an Asian one, the text itself, became, alive in ways in which previously it had not. The changes in inflection enabled me to hear things that were previously obscured by my own assumption of familiarity with the text based on familiarity with voice.

Looking back, twenty years later, I would say that initial reading taught me something invaluable about community of inquiry: how the public nature of inquiry contributes to self-correction, and how perspective is crucial to meaning making and meaning discovery. At the time, however, I was just aware that something very interesting was taking place.

Lipman and Sharp then functioned as a team, asking the group to think about what they had read and then formulate questions about what the group took to be problematic or questionable or interesting or philosophic. In theory, the request seemed straightforward, but the practice of our group showed the limitations of that theory. I would not want to say that we were prone to pontificate, but I only refrain from saying that because I was part of the group, and I prefer to refrain from being hard with myself. There was a good deal of theory building, and there was a good deal of endeavoring to get to the underlying structure, but we did find it difficult to get to the problematic. In effect, we fledgling experts were more concerned with dispelling the problematic than with, simply, exposing it.

After a time, Lipman and Sharp did get us to pose a few questions: future experience with other groups would show the paucity of those questions, but, at least, we had accomplished the task. Then, Lipman told us that we had set up an agenda, and that for the next few hours, possibly the next few days, we would try to answer the questions that we had raised.

I remember looking at a large clock that hung on the front wall of the classroom. The discussion did not go well. Indeed, I thought it was dreadful. It replicated every bad experience I had in classrooms, and I felt like the same fourth-grader who had sat in a classroom on Lincoln Road and Nostrand Avenue, watching the hands of the clock making excruciatingly slow progress around a circle, while I only yearned for freedom. But, now there was no bewitching hour, because it looked as if Lipman and Sharp would go on forever. When it appeared, finally, as if they were wearing down, when it looked as if they were willing to give up on this noble, but apparently futile attempt at community building, when it seemed as if we would never stop posturing, Fred

Oscanyan came into the room, was introduced, and Lipman and Sharp, their energy mysteriously restored, renewed their endeavors. The session ended after eleven o'clock. I drove back to the hotel, with three other participants, and we were all eagerly plotting ways to make our escape from this unbearable situation.

The following day started poorly. Another sheet of ice covered the street, auto traffic was impossible, so the word came down that the session would be delayed an hour. That would give us the opportunity to walk the two miles or so to the Berea campus. I had time to buy a toothbrush and toothpaste, and to make the first of a series of futile phone calls, trying to recover my wandering luggage.

The first session was inauspicious. Lipman, ignoring our agenda, carried on a conversation begun with one of the participants over a point regarding sentence conversion. That went on for almost half an hour, but then we returned to the agenda. For the rest of the morning, we replicated the misery of the previous evening.

Something happened, I still do not know what it was, or why it occurred, or even when it began, but sometime—let's say it was the middle of the third day—something very strange occurred. We, perhaps because we were becoming bored with our behavior, stopped acting as Ph.D.s and started to function the way I thought, but had never really envisioned, philosophers would act when they were doing philosophy. People were focused on a single topic, they were listening to each other, testing each other but also helping one another, building on one another's ideas, doggedly trying to figure whether Harry Stottlemeier has discovered a rule of logic, invented it, or possibly done something else.

What originally drew me to philosophy were the early Socratic dialogues. Without making too much of psychoanalytic explanation, there was something about the communal experience of doing philosophy, as Plato revealed it in the dialogues, that was attractive to a lonely, only child. When I pursued academic philosophy, I found that attraction irrelevant. Philosophy was private, was individual, and on those occasions when groups were involved, the interaction invariably was competitive. One did not work with the other; one tried to win an argument. The ideal of a group of friends or near friends, sitting down, trying to discover some truth or uncover some meaning was, in the context of academic philosophy, a naive, and romantic delusion.

I suppose, in retrospect, I could offer a number of good reasons explaining why I think Philosophy for Children is important. In fact, this book, in large part, is an attempt to do that. Still, what drew me to Philosophy for Children was not its educational benefits, was not its potential for instigating social and political reform, was not even its ability to contribute to what Dewey might call the ideal of democracy. The thing that attracted me on the third day of sessions at Berea was something more basic, more experiential. Here was a place—a geographical place, a physical one, but also an intellectual and spiritual one—in which we could have the experience of doing philosophy. Marrianne Moore had praised poetry, although she disliked it, because it provided a place for the genuine. I felt a similar way about philosophy and now I had found that place. It was, quite simply, a wonderful feeling.

Of course, it did not last. Egos emerged, and with them, inevitable pettiness. There was gamesmanship, and bickering, along with the press to get things done, to expose people to as much of the curriculum as possible. In addition, Lipman, Sharp, and Oscanyan had to figure whom they wanted to encourage to continue with the program, and whom they wanted to encourage in other pursuits. There was, in effect, business to do, but still there were times, all too brief to be sure, tantalizingly so, when we were getting it right, when we were doing philosophy.

Ten days and the session was over. The weather had cleared, a mid-January thaw, and people exchanged phone numbers and addresses, as we waited for the Berea bus that would take us to the airport, and then on to our destinations. By the time I got on the plane, the whole experience seemed so ephemeral as to qualify as a dream.

As part of our experience with the program, we were to do Philosophy for Children with children in our home city. A local university set me up with a group of eleventh-graders at a public high school, and then, through a series of clerical mix-ups, with a group of fourth-graders in a small, experimental school in one of the suburbs of Rochester.

As (bad) luck would have it, I started with the high school students. They had no desire to be in the program, indeed knew nothing about it, and when I tried to explain what we would do—read a story and then talk about it—their lack of interest, their outright hostility, was visceral. We finished the first session by getting through a reading of a page and a half of *Harry Stottlemeier's Discovery*, and asking a few basic questions about the text. We had an agenda, but not much else.

I met with the class every day, forty-five minutes a class. The classroom teacher was in the class with me at all times, and although she was not familiar with Philosophy for Children, she was in favor of any program that would give children the opportunity to think and would provide a way in which their ability to reason and to solve problems could be improved. The class members were all bright, intelligent students who were in the equivalent of an honors class in world literature. And I was enthusiastic about the subject, had some knowledge about philosophy and logic, was trained in I.A.P.C., methodologies, and was recommended by Lipman, Sharp, and Oscanyan. Finally, I was not all that different from the teenagers in the class. I was not *that* much older than them, had had similar educational experiences to them, and knew—or at least thought I knew—what they liked and what they found interesting. It seemed crystal clear to me that once they realized that they were being given the opportunity, *in the classroom*, to talk about things that interested them, they would value the program as much as I did.

The trick was to create an environment in which they could see what was crystal clear to me, in which they could have that wonderful experience of doing philosophy. I tried as hard as I could that week, but the mechanics of the trick eluded me. By Friday, I was ready to write the Berea experience off as wonderful and inspiring, but, also, as unique, as nonreplicable.

The following week was spring break, so there were no sessions with the high school students. I went to the private, experimental school with little expectation that things would be better than they were with the high-school students. I was depressed by the earlier experience and was not comfortable with the fact that I would be using a novel, *Harry Stottlemeier's Discovery*, that was intended for older students.

It is hard to describe the initial experience with that group of twelve ten-year-olds without lapsing into too many superlatives. I explained what we would do, and the children not only understood what I was talking about, they seemed to find it eminently reasonable.

We read aloud the first chapter of *Harry Stottlemeier's Discovery*, taking turns, handing a single copy from hand to hand. The reading was warm, expressive, and when the students stumbled on words, they were helped, gently, by the others. Notably, the classroom teacher refrained from any sort of intervention during the reading.

When I asked what they found most interesting or most problematic, one student said that she found Harry the most interesting, and another student said that he did, too, while a third student questioned why. Before I could do anything, before I could remind the children that we were trying to set up an agenda, the class was off on a discussion that burrowed through the character of Harry until it arrived at precisely the question that had motivated my group at Berea—was Harry a discoverer or an inventor or something else? I did manage to insert a few of the exercises from the teacher's manual on the distinctions between discovery and invention, but, for the most part, my presence was of little significance. I felt like an umpire at a well-played game—my task was more to admire than to enforce.

Not every class went like that. There were days when the children seemed cranky, or out-of-sorts, or just plain dull. There were days when the press of school business interrupted us, when plans for an assembly or fund-raiser took precedence over Philosophy for Children, but there continued to be days when the discussion was rich and fruitful, when it felt like we were actually doing philosophy. On a few of those days, too, I thought that I was becoming more of a member of the community, that I was helping in the doing of the philosophy.

I returned to the high-school group with renewed enthusiasm. While we never reached the artlike quality of the private school dialogues, while we never achieved the apparent "natural" qualities of the private school group, we did seem to make progress. Although we never went much beyond the mechanical, we did begin to develop rules of etiquette and ethics that helped us to listen to one another and to explore one another's ideas. It was as if the high school experience presented a very distant, black-and-white, abstract view of community of inquiry, whereas the private school experience brought it (community of inquiry) closer, presented it in technicolor, and made it concrete.

Life goes on. I became involved with scores of communities of inquiry, as teacher and participant. Sometimes I was the novice, but other times I was viewed as the expert. I worked at Montclair and in training sessions in Pennsylvania and New Jersey, dozen of times. I attended Philosophy for Children training sessions around the world, some lasting as long as an academic year, others covering barely a day. After a while those initial groups came, for me, to represent the twin poles of Philosophy for Children training—the group that had neither an idea nor feel for community of inquiry versus the group that understood community of inquiry deeply and organically. The task of the trainer, always, was to know which sort of group she/he was dealing with, and then find some way to help the group to make some progress—to help one group discover the craft or mechanics of dialogue while helping other groups become more artistic in their practice of the form.

That was a good lesson for me to learn, this notion of progress being tied to the type of group with which one is working. I think it helped me to become a better teacher, but the longer I was involved with Philosophy for Children, the more I trained and educated groups, the more I helped create and nurture communities of inquiry—here for three weeks, there for a semester—the more I became troubled by the transitory, the ephemeral nature of community of inquiry.

We had this ideal of a group of intelligent, well-intentioned people getting together to talk about matters of significance, of interest. As we approached the ideal in practice, as we approached the ideal of community of inquiry, we discovered over and over again that we cared, deeply, about the topics; that we cared, deeply, about the procedures we adopted from inquiry into those topics; and that we cared, deeply, about our co-inquirers, about our friends in the process of inquiry.

And then, of course, the inevitable happened. The class would be over, the training session would end, this one would hop into a car and head back to Wisconsin, that one would leave in a taxi that would find its way to an airport, another would be last seen walking down a gravel walk in some suburban forest. How to say this, but the experience of community of inquiry always brought with it a sense of inauthenticity: we claimed to be doing important works, it felt, while we were doing it, like important work, but then a metaphorical bell tolled, and people just got up and left. It was as if community of inquiry was like a vacation, a respite that we treated ourselves with, *indulged* ourselves in, but when the real world beckoned, we packed our bags and were gone.

It seemed to me that we were always beginning things, and that even if those of us involved with Philosophy for Children did effect a significant change in public education, we would still be missing out on the really transforming possibilities of Philosophy for Children— the way that Philosophy for Children could change us, by providing a new way in which we could do philosophy. It was as if we were given the opportunity to choose between, literally, having a dialogue with Socrates and having a Socratic-like dialogue, and had chosen the latter. Nothing wrong with the choice we had made. Indeed, the choice likely would have all sorts of benefits. Still, the feeling persisted that if we would take this notion of community more seriously, if we did ignore metaphorical bells, if we kept the community going when training was over, we might, in effect get Socrates to speak.

It is interesting to look at old photographs of Philosophy for Children workshops from the 1970s and early 1980s. In this one Lipman and Sharp stand together squinting into an autumn sun. Fifteen people with whom I have shared an intimate and grueling three weeks. Sessions begin at 8:00am and continue on to 10:00 or 11:00pm, seven days a week. Now, sitting in this chair, this office, eighteen years later, I can only remember three or four names.

In another photograph, Lipman stands at one end of a long line, but Sharp is nowhere to be found. The group is larger, and judging from the clothing, it is a very cold winter day. The photograph is taken in 1989 because at the far end of Lipman's view is the BBC producer who filmed the documentary that year. I remember her face, but not her name. If pushed, I could identify six of the thirty or so people appearing in the photograph. And yet, for a brief period of time we knew each other very well, cared about each other, depended on each other and considered ourselves a community of inquiry. In a certain sense, one feels like betrayer and person betrayed. "I thought we had established a certain bond. I thought that for more than three weeks I would continue to react to you and you to me. I thought that we had become friends in inquiry, but now I cannot even remember your name."

But then one realizes that while there are people who do not stand out, there are also people who somehow persist beyond the end of the specific community, who consistently force themselves on consciousness. There are relationships that are formed within the community of inquiry that do not reflect the ethereal nature of the individual community of inquiry. We have become co-inquirers with the other, and the inquiry persists even when its specific community disbands.

Sometimes that happens quite literally. You go back to your home in Ohio and I to mine in Texas, but we correspond with one another, now a letter, now the telephone, now e-mail. We explore one of the interests we shared at that training session in Montclair, New Jersey. We meet at another training session, and expand our interest, and then we work on a paper together, do a presentation. The community of inquiry at Montclair was our starting point but when it ended, we became members of a smaller but more enduring community of inquiry, a community of, if you will, intellectual friends. We continue to talk with each other, and, agree, explicitly to do our inquiry together and in light of each other—I present my findings for your consideration and you do the same for me.

More frequently, however, things are far more nebulous than that. Our correspondence post-inquiry, might be sparse and infrequent. We lose each other in the press of our own lives, but every once in a while you reappear, force yourself into my conciousness. I hear you, my intellectual friend, begin to speak as I perform my own deliberation. "What should I believe? What is worthy of my belief? How should I act? How should I treat this person?" I hear your voice, recall snippets of argument patterns, remember how you would react in this situation, and you have become part of my deliberation. I am reacting to you as certainly as I did that cold winter morning in 1982.

I did not become involved in Philosophy for Children because I wanted to make friends, intellectual or otherwise, with people. That was not my goal and, I would argue, that should not be the goal of community of inquiry. The goal should have something to do with the uncovering of meaning and the discerning of truth. The effect, however, might be quite different.

Speaking simply from my own experience, those communities of inquiry that I have experienced in Germany, Australia, Brazil, Mexico, and the United States have become places where I have met people who have become for me what Edmund Wilson was for Scott Fitzgerald—an intellectual conscience. Consciously and sometimes not so consciously, I relate my behavior to them. Whether they know it or not, they have contributed to and continue to contribute to my intellectual and ethical development.

In the final chapter of this work, we will examine the relationship of friendship to community of inquiry, and try to move beyond the anecdotal to suggest that any program that did not have this as an outcome would be ignoble and unworthy of our attention. On the other hand, a system which typically generated such outcomes would have much to recommend it.

Chapter 9

Friendship and Moral Education

Outside of talk shows, the topic of friendship, until this decade, has attracted little scholarly attention. While it was a significant topic for ancient and medieval thinkers, it makes little dent in modern philosophical thought. Elliot Deutsch attempts to explain this near-absence:

> Friendship is among the most cherished of human goods. Yet how neglected a topic it is in philosophy. It does not even appear as an entry in the eight-volume *Encyclopedia of Philosophy* or in any of the standard dictionaries of philosophy. The reason for this paucity of philosophical analysis is not entirely clear, but it seems to rest on a certain aversion in modern ethical theory to deal with particular relationships, and especially those that appear to have partiality built into them. Lawrence Blum noted that 'friendship is a largely unfamiliar territory for modern moral philosophy, dominated as it has been by Kantian concerns or with utilitarianism, neither of which is hospitable to particular relationships which are both personally and morally significant.'[1]

In educational circles, especially in contemporary ones, the talk decidedly is not about friendship, intellectual or otherwise. If friendship involves a sort of rough equality, then everything in the banking model mitigates against the development of friendship between students and teachers. In effect, the relationship between teacher and student is analogous to a cross-species one in which the reciprocity that historically is attached to friendship seems lacking. The talk in contemporary American educational circles is about things thought to be more basic and more direct—how the teacher can transmit, most efficiently, that which the student needs to know.

When friendship does make its way into contemporary educational discussions, it is typically within teachers' lounges, and not in scholarly journals, and focuses on the negative aspects of friendship. What does the teacher do when select groups of students engage in the exclusionary behavior that is typically connected with the friendship relationship? John and Philip have become best friends and when they sit near each other in sixth-grade mathematics they talk constantly, disrupting class. How does the teacher deal with this relationship so that she/he minimizes disturbance of classroom teaching? Mary, Joyce, and Alice have formed a clique of seventh-grade taste. They monitor the behavior and dress of their classmates, determining who is in and who is not. Their judgements on fashion and style have come to terrorize those perceived as inferior. What is the teacher to do?

Such is the contemporary educational and philosophical terrain, a geography inhospitable to discussions of friendship, one unconcerned with them because they are thought trivial or disruptive. Yet not all modern or contemporary philosophers take things to the extreme of, say, Jean-Jacques Rousseau, who recommended removing the child from the corrupting influence of society and educating children on an individual basis (one tutor, one child), or the contemporary home school movement, which again sees society as a corrupting influence and recommends that children be educated by their parents. C.S. Lewis, in this century, devotes a significant amount of his attention to what, in a backhand slap at the collectivism to which he was opposed, he called the "least necessary love." For Lewis, friendship was always a function of some activity, was always related to an affective relationship to that which was perceived as "truth," and could never be nurtured directly:

> In our own time Friendship arises in the same way. For us of course the shared activity and therefore the companionship in which Friendship supervenes will not often be a bodily one like hunting or fighting. It may be a common religion, common studies, a common profession, even a common recreation. All who share it will be our companions; but one or two or three who share something more will become Friends. In this *kind* of love, as Emerson said, 'Do you love me?' means 'Do you share the same truth?'—Or at least, 'Do you care about the same truth?' The man that agrees with us on that same question, little regarded by others, is of great importance and can be our friend. He need not agree with us about the answer. . . . That is why those pathetic people who simply 'want friends' can never make any. The very condition of having Friends is that we should want something else besides Friends. Where the truthful answer to the question 'Do you see the same truth?' would be 'I see nothing and I don't care about the truth; I only want a Friend,' no friendship can arise—though affection of course may. There would be nothing for the Friendship to be *about*; and Friendship must be about something, even if it were only a enthusiasm for dominoes or white mice. Those who have nothing can share nothing; those who are going nowhere can have no fellow travellers.[2]

Lewis goes on to distinguish friendship from companionship and love.[3] The former involves a simple taking part in an activity. We are companions in this hunt, in that workshop activity, in this neighborhood project. We are something more than mere members of an audience. We are aware of each other as companions, and we suit our actions and reactions so that they are congruent with the actions of others. In the repair of this inner-city house, for example, we are assigned specific tasks, the tasks themselves have a sort of logical order—sanding precedes painting—and to do our tasks well, we must have an understanding of that logic, a respect for the process. Still, as Lewis points out, that feel for the other which characterizes the friendship relationship, need not be and, typically is not, present. In effect, the companionship relationship is only about the task, while the friendship relationship, though always about the task, involves something more.

The relationship we call erotic love, according to Lewis, although it does share many characteristics with the friendship relationship is different from it in two significant ways. First, while both take individuals away from the group, encouraging a sort of privacy, the goal of erotic love *is* that privacy, whereas friends, somehow, look to increase the pattern of relationships. "Lovers seek for privacy. Friends find this solitude about them, this barrier between them and the herd, whether they want it or not. They would be glad to reduce it. The first two would be glad to find a third."[4]

In terms of activity, though lovers do many things together, their love is not mediated by activity in the way that friendship is. The lover simply delights in the other, while the friend it may be said, delights in the delight the other takes in the shared activity, delights in the way the other "cares for the same truth." In Lewis's telling image,—"we picture lovers face to face but friends side by side; their eyes look ahead."[5]

Finally, for Lewis, there is an irresponsibility and lack of necessity about friendship that make it similar to philosophy, art, and the universe itself:

> Hence (if you will not misunderstand me) the exquisite arbitrariness and irresponsibility of this love. I have no duty to be anyone's Friend and no one in the world has a duty to be mine. No claims, no shadow of necessity. Friendship is unnecessary, like philosophy, like art, like the universe itself (for God did not need to create). It has no survival value; rather it is one of those things which gives value to survival.[6]

Of course, once I do enter into the friendship relationship, all sort of other duties, along with a new set of desires are created, for example, the desire to enter into activity with the friend, and given the nature of time and space, the inability of people to do all things at once, the corresponding desire to refrain from activity with those who are not our friends. Simply, given the opportunity of going to the movies with my friend and a mere companion, everything else being equal, I choose the friend. The friendship relationship, then, involves the "particularity" that Kantian adherents frown upon. It involves choosing the friend over others, and it does involve a secession of sorts from the group. Lewis sees this as the reason that authority frowns on friendship—we might view it as a reason why the schools have difficulty with the topic:

> It is therefore easy to see why authority frowns on friendship. Every real friendship is a sort of secession, even a rebellion. It can be a rebellion of serious thinkers against accepted clap-trap or a faddists against accepted good sense; of real artists against popular ugliness or of charlatans against civilized taste; of good men against the badness of society or of bad men against its goodness. Whichever it is, it will be unwelcome to Top People. In each knot of friends there is a sectional 'public opinion' which fortifies its members against the public opinion of the community in general. Each therefore is a pocket of potential resistance. Men who have real Friends are less easy to manage or 'get at'; harder for good authorities to correct or bad authorities to corrupt. Hence if our masters, by force or by propaganda about 'Together- ness' or by unobtrusively making privacy and unplanned leisure impossible, ever succeed in producing a world where all are Companions and none are Friends, they will have removed certain dangers, and will also have taken from us what is almost our strongest safeguard against complete servitude.[7]

As an aside, it is interesting to connect some of the above claims to what we have said about relating the community of inquiry model to the banking model of education. The latter, intent on passing infor- mation from expert to novice, abhors anything that threatens the ef- fective and efficient transmission of that information. If Lewis is right that friendship relationships are pockets of resistance to the estab- lished norms and mores, if friendship relationships are, at heart, anti- authoritarian (and note that authority, as Lewis points out, can be good and well-intentioned or evil and ill-intentioned), then it is easy to see why school authorities, within a banking model, could abhor stu- dent friendship. Friends are much harder to manage. In a banking model, this means that they are much harder to teach.

The friendship relationship within community of inquiry takes a somewhat different turn. Earlier, we spoke of the feeling of freedom that accompanies intitial experience within community of inquiry, that feeling that here I am allowed to think and to talk. The feeling that many people report is one of "having the teacher leave the room" and being in a place where there is no external authority. We also mentioned, however, that the feeling is transitory. At some point a deeper understanding of community of inquiry emerges and one realizes that with freedom comes a series of obligations, and with the overthrow of one authority, the formation of another. (The authority of truth, of rules of inquiry, and so on). When thinking about the friendship relationship in community of inquiry, especially as contrasted with the banking model, one may be prone to assume, mistakenly, that since there is no authority structure, the very question of "pockets of resistance" (to authority structures) will never arise. As we shall see, it does.

Keep in mind the rebellion that is friendship—"of real artists against popular ugliness or of charlatans against civilized taste; of good men against the badness of society or of bad men against the goodness." For movements that exist within the progressive tradition of American education, and to the extent that John Dewey is one of the prime influences, Philosophy for Children exists within that tradition, it is tempting to have a very romantic view of the child. Aware of the dangers and rigidity of the banking model, one is tempted to swing to the other extreme, but just as Dewey invariably argued against the extreme of either-or thinking, we are better served by taking a more moderate stance.

Children are capable of great kindness and intelligence. They can be like the wonderful children in that private school, those fourth-graders who were so generous with their talents, coming to the aid of a fledgling community of inquiry teacher. But they are capable of being mean-spirited and coarse. They are capable, if we take community of inquiry to be a good thing, of acting as "—bad men against the goodness." Almost any teacher with significant experience in community of inquiry can report times when things were going very well, when the children were inquiring into a situation of interest and importance to them, when they were seized by the problematic nature of a situation, but then the enterprise was derailed by a few children who, for whatever reasons, no longer wanted to play.

That experience of sabotage is incredibly frustrating for the teacher. Building a community of inquiry and getting it to function is extremely hard work. Seeing that hard work destroyed because of the whim of a few individuals who may just be having a bad day is, at best, distressing. Communities of inquiry can be destroyed by outside forces—the press of the curriculum, the existence of Mr. Partridge-like principals, the demands of standardized testing—but they can also be destroyed from within. They can be destroyed by cliques of friends who "turn against" the enterprise, and attempt to destroy it for the sheer perverse joy of being able to do so.

Simply, friends can be enemies to the community of inquiry in very much the way that they are enemies to the banking model. But there are other ways in which friends, even if they are pockets of resistance, *especially* if they are pockets of resistance, can be essential to the health of a community of inquiry.

When we work together for an extended period of time, we are apt to take things for granted. One of those things, as Lipman pointed out when relating his experience of teaching logic, is about the importance or worth of what we are doing. A complacency sets in, and with it a sort of intellectual flabbiness. What the pocket of resistance can do is work as a Socratic gadfly, to sting the community awake, and by questioning the very process of inquiry, by refusing to play the game, may make the game of inquiry itself more productive. Those reluctant friends may serve the same purpose that Lisa plays in *Harry Stottlemeier's Discovery*. By questioning the importance of what the children are doing, she helps them to do that which they are doing (inquiring), better. If community of inquiry is about self-correction and self-reflection, then the teacher must value the occasion of resistance—the pockets of resistance that emerge from the friendship relationship—no matter how distressing they are.

It would be a mistake, however, to focus solely on the abrasive quality of friendship in community of inquiry. There is another way that friendship functions in a community of inquiry that, teachers report, is quite beautiful. The community disbands for the day and then two friends continue the inquiry. As they walk home, they expand the discussion that was begun in the Philosophy for Children class. The expansion is productive. They make progress and they experience the joy of discovery. The next day they bring that discovery to class, and that discovery refines the deliberation of the community. Because two friends have left the community and gone off on a search of their own, the community receives immeasurable benefits. As Lewis might point out, friendship somehow deepens and refines the activity of inquiry which defines this community, and when brought back to the community deepens and reinforces it.

So far, we have talked about the benefits and harms of friendship to different models of education and to authority in general. We have assumed a general understanding of friendship on the part of the readers, and have used that understanding as we distinguished the love that is friendship from erotic love and from simple companionship. At this point, it is appropriate to go into a more detailed analysis. To do that, we will follow the analysis presented by the philosopher Bhikhu Parekh in "An Indian View of Friendship." Note, Professor Parekh's title is most informative. Rather than presenting an analysis of friendship as it functions in an Indian context, he uses his Indian context to shed light on a concept that is important for all cultures. After benefiting from that illumination, we will go to that source to which all analyses of friendship must go—Aristotle.

Parekh identifies seven characteristics of the friendship relationship. "First, it is non-biological in the sense that unlike parents and children, it is not based on the ties of blood or heredity."[8] Mothers and daughters, fathers and sons, cousins, can become friends, but, as Parekh suggests, the friendship relationship is not based on biological considerations. It, the biological relationship, is neither necessary nor sufficient for the formation of the friendship relationship and may, in fact, set limits on it. As close as I am with my father, I may never experience the same quality of intimacy I share with my best friend because of the competing demands of the biological and the social, and the way biological relationships tend to generate cultural expectations. Of course, as both my father and I age, as his authority over me lessens, and my autonomy grows, it may become possible for the biological relationship to exist as faint echo, and for the social relationship of friend-to-friend to achieve primacy.

"Second, friendship is a voluntary relationship."[9] You and I can be forced to be companions. It can be mandated that we march in lockstep through this activity and that. What cannot be mandated is that we become friends. We have to choose that on a day-to-day basis. We have to affirm on a daily basis, have to nurture it through all sorts of reciprocal actions. Moreover, either one of us can choose to walk away from the relationship. "Since it is entirely voluntary and neither embedded in a network of other relations nor reinforced by social sanctions, friendship is one of the most mortal of all human relationships."[10]

"Third, friendship is a relationship between two individuals."[11] Corporations cannot be friends with one another. You may love your country, but you cannot be friends with it, and while you and I may have our own circle of friends, each relationship is dyadic—I am friends with Mary in a way different from the way in which I am friends with John, and if John and Mary are friends with each other, their relationship is different from mine with Mary or with John.

"Fourth, since friendship has no basis outside of itself and is a free creation of two individuals, it is entirely dependent on what they care to make of it. It takes whatever form they choose to give it, has such content and depth as they succeed in putting into it, is a unique expression of the kinds of person they are, and reveals their individuality to a much greater degree than most other human relationships."[12]

The friendship relationship is analogous to the craft/art matrix we found in the discussion of the dialogue. One can learn rules and mechanisms for nurturing the dialogue. One can practice them over and over again and, in the course of that, become more Socratic. One can look at other people running dialogues and see obvious mistakes—here you did not listen to what was said, here you listened but discounted too quickly, there you tried to insert your own agenda—but even after doing all of that, there is something impregnable that remains, and somehow that seems most important. One can mimic things that Socrates does but one cannot mimic all that he does, precisely because what Socrates is doing is artful. He goes beyond the rules of the craft to make certain moves that seem as unpredictable as they are inevitable. He brings something to the discipline, something that we call his art, that is based on who he is, and his specific relationship to the dialogue. To emulate Socrates, completely, one would have to be Socrates.

In a similar manner, when you and I became friends, there are certain conditions that must be met—reciprocity, mutual attraction, and so on—but how those conditions are played out, what they mean in terms of our specific relationship, is a function of the individuals that we are. Friendship is a creative act, and as in any creative act, craft and art apply as we determine what our friendship will be.

"Fifth, friendship is open-ended and admits of degrees. One person is 'just' a friend; another is a 'good' friend; yet another is a 'close' or an 'intimate' friend—a 'fast' friend, as Indians call it. Friendship covers a large spectrum ranging from a perceptible degree of warmth to a near total merging of two selves, and after occupies a place somewhere between the two extremes. There are levels or types of friendship and by our actions, by our tacit and explicit agreements, we define what sort of friends we will be, how deep our relationship will be."[13]

"Sixth, friendship is reciprocal and involves mutual acknowledgement and a shared understanding."[14] I can like you, even love you from a distance, and you can feel the same way about me, but until we both become aware of that affection, until we both agree to accept one another's affection, until some sort of reciprocity takes place, the friendship relationship does not occur. Love can be, and sometimes is, private in the sense that the beloved is unaware of the lover's affection. Friendship can never be blind in that sense.

> Finally, friendship involves mutual liking and good will. Friends are well-disposed to each other, wish each other well, and help each other in times of need. They help each other not because they think they *ought* to help their fellow humans, but because they care for each other's well-being and wish to be of mutual help. And they care for each other not because they cannot bear to see *human beings* suffer but because they cannot bear to see *their friends* suffer or feel unhappy. As friendship deepens, mutual liking generates affection and perhaps even love. Since friendship is based on mutual liking, it is an unmediated relationship between two unique individuals. Friends are friends because, for some reason, they have 'hit it off' and enjoy each other's presence. Although their common interests, temperaments, backgrounds, and so forth throw some light on why they become and remain friends, these do not determine and explain why their relationship took a specific form, acquired a specific measure of depth, and survived changes in interest and circumstances.[15]

Here, Professor Parekh focuses on what might be called the epiphenomenon that is friendship. While C.S. Lewis says that friendship always arises from, is an epiphenomenon of some activity and, that hence it is a mistake to search for friends ("those pathetic ones"), Parekh turns his attention to the epiphenomenon itself. In effect, he looks at that mysterious point where companionship turns into friendship, where two people from similar or diverse backgrounds take part in an activity, are companions, and in Parekh's phrase "hit it off."

To return to the Jackie Robinson example, there were twenty-five members of the Brooklyn Dodgers in 1947. They were companions in the activity of a baseball team that year: they tried to win games, they depended on each other to do so, they made their actions fit the actions of their teammates. In addition, willingly or not, they were part of a great social experiment which was intended to show, in part, that the races could mix and that the mixture could serve at least some utilitarian aims—if only to produce a winning baseball team.

In the course of that experiment, Robinson maintained a beneficial professional relationship with all the players. In fact, they, as companions, went on to forge a team that would be successful for the next decade. With a few of the players, such as pitchers Carl Erskine and Ralph Branca, Robinson established a relationship that, given all the criteria we have mentioned so far, would qualify as that of friends. And with one of them, the relationship had the degree of closeness that Parekh alluded to, that would qualify the two as "fast" friends.

Pee Wee Reese was the captain of the Brooklyn Dodgers. An established veteran when Robinson was brought up, Reese, a southerner who was raised in segregated Louisville, Kentucky, is the single person, with the exception of Robinson, himself, most credited with making the experiment work. A very quiet man, a very private and dignified one, not given to large public gestures, Reese signalled his acceptance of Robinson by small gestures. He talked to him on the field, ran onto the field with him, exchanged smiles and jokes. He did it for myriad reasons: he was on-field captain of the team, and was fulfilling what he took to be his obligation; he had a developed notion of social justice and even though he was a product of his time, he could see that the abuse Robinson was subjected to was unjust; and he found himself liking his teammate.

The friendship grew, lasted throughout their career, and continued when they were no longer companions on the field, when they were no longer teammates, and when they no longer lived in the same part of the country. The friendship was epiphenomenal to the activity, presumably would not have occurred without the companionship provided by being teammates, but was not dependent for its continued existence on that companionship. The friendship took on a life of its own, and while it may always have revolved around some shared activity—being involved in business ventures, being survivors of the same social experiments, being linked forever in public consciousness, it survived changes in those interests and activities and was never exhausted by those activities.

Friendship then is a nonbiological, voluntary, open-ended, informal, uninstitutionalized, and mutually acknowledged relationship between two individuals based on their goodwill and fondness for each other. Given these and its other constitutive features, it is only possible under certain conditions. Friendship presupposes a society or a culture in which human relationships are not totally structured and formalized, and leaves adequate space for informal and self-generated relationships. It also presupposes that individuals are able to rise above their socially defined roles, are willing and able to undertake the adventure of new and unpredictable relationships, and have the courage and the disposition to share their intimate thoughts, feelings, and vulnerabilities with others and mortgage their happiness to others' inherently precarious feelings. It also implies that individuals have patience, constancy of contact, and emotional energy required for a slowly maturing relationship; that they share enough experiences in common to have something to talk about; that they have the capacity to rise above their narrow self-interest and establish noncalculative relationships with others; that they have the emotional and moral maturity to understand and to adjust to each other's moods and eccentricities; and that they do not take so narrow a view of morality that it leaves no room for partiality and preference.[16]

We will return to both characteristics and conditions for friendship, but before doing that we move to Aristotle and the worth he ascribes to friendship, along with the differentiation among types of friendship that he makes. And since Aristotle makes such a late appearance in our discussion, but because he is so important to it, a brief biographical introduction may be in order.[17]

Characterized by Dante as "the master of those who know," for centuries Aristotle was called "The Philosopher." He is generally recognized as the best educated individual of his or any time, and his mastery of the world's knowledge places him on "the shortest of lists of the giants of Western thought." As Renford Bambrough explains: "All studies in formal logic until very recent times were footnote to his work. In the study of ethics, politics, and literary criticism he set standards of sanity, urbanity, and penetration of which his success two thousand years later may still be severely judged. There is no problem in any of the branches of what is still called philosophy on which his remarks do not continue to deserve the most careful attention from the modern inquirer."[18]

Born in the Macedonian town of Stagira in 384 B.C., Aristotle acquired a taste for biology and the other sciences from his father, the physician to the court of the Macedonian king. Known as the philosophical grandson of Socrates, Aristotle never gained full acceptance as a true Greek. Though honored and revered by subsequent generations, his contemporaries often referred to him, somewhat pejoratively, as "the son of the physician from Stagira" or as "the Stagirite philosopher."

Despite losing both his parents at an early age, Aristotle received an outstanding education. At age eighteen, he was sent to Athens to study at Plato's Academy. For twenty years, he studied with Plato, who described him as "the mind of the Academy." Upon Plato's death in 347 B.C., Aristotle left Athens and spent the next few years travelling in the Aegean Islands. A crucial turning point occurred in 343 B.C. with his appointment as tutor to Prince Alexander, the heir to the Macedonian throne. While the relationship between Aristotle and his soon-to-be-famous student was often strained, their association proved mutually beneficial. Alexander, the eventual conqueror of the Hellenic world, shipped back to his former teacher an enormous amount of information from those parts of the world about which the Greeks knew little or nothing. Included in this bounty were constitutions and descriptions of the culture and actions of the people encountered during those exploits. Biological and botanical specimens were also sent back, affording Aristotle and his students the opportunity to systematize and categorize the whole spectrum of human knowledge.

By this time Aristotle had established in Athens the Lyceum, a school located near a favorite meeting place of Socrates. Here, for more than a decade, Aristotle lectured to students on philosophic and scientific topics in the morning and on more general topics to a more general audience in the afternoon. A creature of habit, Aristotle often walked while he talked, with his students following close behind. Here, too, Aristotle composed his most significant works, summing up in an encyclopedic fashion the results of a life of all-embracing study and thought.

Those productive years ended as word reached Athens of Alexander's death. Longing for their cherished freedom, Athenians moved quickly to cast off the yoke of the hated Macedonians. Due, in part, to his association with the Macedonians, the Athenians charged Aristotle with crimes similar to those brought against Socrates several generations earlier. Refusing, as he put it, to allow the Athenians to sin a second time against philosophy, Aristotle withdrew to the Macedonian community of Chalcis, dying there of natural causes in 322 B.C.

It is customary to distinguish Aristotle from Plato, with the latter representing a rational, theoretical way of doing philosophy while the former is an example of a hands-on, more empirical way of approaching things. One should, remembering Dewey's advice, be careful of any such easy renderings of history—they smack of an either-or mentality. Still, there is a way of distinguishing their educational styles that is helpful for our purposes.

Plato wrote and taught by means of the dialogue—that recursive, conversational model that exists on a sea of distinct voices and perspectives. Aristotle's methodology was that of lecturing—the peripatetic philosopher walking and discussing—and writing treatises. Aristotle presents a single, dominant voice, a voice which, through the process of reasoning and the quality of its argumentation, establishes its own authority.

It is relatively easy, as we have attempted to show, to draw lines of influence from Plato and his teacher Socrates to a community of inquiry model. It is just as easy to, if not trace, influence then at least some similarity, between Aristotle's methodology and that exhibited in the traditional classroom based on a banking model of education. Aristotle tells, he instructs in much the same way as the traditional teacher does. He does not rely on an exchange with others as a source for discussing answers in the way that Plato and Socrates do. Aristotle, it can be assumed, would be able to function quite well in the traditional classroom. Plato, or more precisely Socrates, would find himself at odds with contemporary practices, would function as a gadfly once again, and either create havoc in the classroom or receive the late twentieth-century educational equivalent of hemlock—suspension, and then expulsion. To push at the image a bit more, Aristotle at home with the school women and school men, a welcome visitor, while Socrates, an unruly and unwelcome intruder. It is curious then that when Aristotle speaks of friendship, none of the school women or school men seem to hear him.

For Aristotle, friendship was important for individuals and societies. The level of that importance is shown when Aristotle talks about the relationship of friendship to law and justice within the state:

> Friendship seems to hold states together, and lawgivers to care more for it than for justice; for unanimity seems to be something like friendship, and this they aim at most of all, and expel faction as their worst enemy; and when men are friends they have no need for justice, while when they are just they need friendhip as well, and the truest form of justice is thought to be a friendly quality.[19]

Aristotle, here, is making a remarkable claim. He is giving advice to lawgivers, saying, in effect, that friendship makes a system of justice superfluous, that the latter can be safely dispersed with when the former is present and that if a system of justice is present, it will not be enough for the healthy functioning of the state without the presence of friendship. Metaphorically, friendship is the energizing principle, the soul, that gives life and vitality to the state. Without it, affairs in the state are dry and mechanical—using Dewey's distinction, one has a mere aggregate and not a live community.

Consider then two possibilities: first, that Aristotle is right about what he says regarding the crucial relationship between friendship and society, and second, that the school itself is a kind of society. By ignoring the issue of friendship, as we have throughout the modern period and especially within the contemporary American educational context, we may be ensuring that any educational reform, no matter how well intentioned and how well researched, is doomed to be hollow, to be without a soul. Again, if Aristotle is right, what we have done, in education, is to miss the elephant in the living room. We notice that the couch has been splintered, that a shade sits askew on a lamp stand, that a table has been overturned, but we do not notice the elephant who stands, most obtrusively, in the corner.

But let us return once more to Aristotle, now looking at how important friendship is for the individual. He has this to say:

> For without friends no one would choose to live, though he had all other goods; even men and those in possession of office and dominating power are thought to need friends most of all; for what is the use of such prosperity without the opportunity of beneficence, which is exercised chiefly and in most laudable form towards friends? Or how can prosperity be guarded and preserved without friends? The greater it is, the more exposed it is to risk. And in poverty and in other misfortunes men think friends are the only refuge. It helps the young, too, to keep from error; it aids older people by ministering to their needs and supplementing the activities that are failing from weakness; those in the prime of life it stimulates to noble actions—'two going together'— for with friends men are more able to think and to act.[20]

The claims here are no less remarkable. Friendship is so important that without it, regardless of social placement or wealth, no one could choose to live; it helps the young, somehow keeping them from error; and it helps people to think well and to act well.

Again, consider the implications of what Aristotle says for education: if schools are about helping people lead meaningful lives, about giving people reason to continue to be, especially when life becomes cold and hard, then by ignoring friendship, as we do, we make the achievement of that (educational) goal virtually impossible. Just as importantly, if schools are about helping the young avoid error and enabling then to think well and to act well, by ignoring friendship we are ignoring that which is most apt to help children achieve those goals.

It is clear how important friendship is for Aristotle. This is not to say, however, that Aristotle is not aware of the potential pitfalls of friendship. He is aware that some friendships can have bad consequences, both for individuals and societies. He is aware of all those commonplace dangers of friendship to which researchers allude when they speak of disruptive friendships in the classroom, and in the following he will sketch some of them. Still, he does speak of a type of friendship that arises without dangers, a "perfect" friendship:

> There are three kinds of friendship, equal in number to the things that are lovable; for with respect to each there is a mutual and recognized love, and those who love each other wish well to each other in that respect in which they love one another. Now those who love each other for their utility do not love each other for themselves, but in virtue of some good which they get from one another. So too with those who love for the sake of pleasure; it is not from their character that men love ready-witted people, but because they find them pleasant. Therefore, those who love for the sake of utility love for the sake of what is good for themselves, and those who love for the sake of pleasure do so for the sake of what is pleasant to themselves, and not in so far as the other is the person loved but in so far as he is useful or pleasant. And thus, those friendships are only incidental; for it is not as being the man that he is that the loved person is loved, but as providing some good or pleasure. Such friendships, then, are easily dissolved, if the partners do not remain like themselves; for if the same party is no longer pleasant or useful the other ceases to love him.[21]

The first two friendships, especially, as we use Ralph Waldo Emerson by way of C.S. Lewis, coupled with Parekh, to inform our discussion, are not hard to understand. Mary and James are friends-in-pleasure in the sense that they both love the same activity, let us say that it is gardening, and more than just gardening together, what they love about each other is the very delight the other takes in the activity. It is not just that James' presence helps Mary create a more productive garden, but that working with James in the production of the garden, yields more delight for Mary than working by herself would yield. The epiphenomenon that is friendship takes place in relationship to the activity, hovers over it, and is best described as pleasurable. They are, remembering Lewis's telling phrase, "side-by-side" in the garden and they look at the earth, taking their delight there, delighting in the delight the other takes.

The friends-in-utility—and here it will not hurt to remind ourselves that Aristotle is talking about ideal types; that, in effect, most friendships are mixtures of two or three of the types of friendship and, thus, when we talk about, say, friends-in-pleasure, we are really talking about a dominant, and not exclusive, characteristic of a real friendship—take part in the same activity. They work together as companions in the activity, suiting their actions to the other and to the needs of the activity. They use each other to complete successfully the activity, but what they value most about the other, what makes them hit it off, what emerges as the epiphenomenon that is their friendship, is the love that each has for the other, regarding the successful completion of the activity. It is not just that you help me achieve my ends, that you are useful in the successful completion of the activity. A companion can do that. What makes you a friend-in-utility is that I perceive you (and you perceive me) as a person who can get the job done. The shortstop who wants the ball hit to him when the game is on the line regards the pitcher who wants to be on the mound in a crucial situation. As they come to know each other and as they recognize each other's desires—each loves the same sort of thing—the probability of their becoming friends-in-utility increases.

We step back now. There is an amoral quality to friendship-in-pleasure and friendship-in-utility. We can, of course, find our pleasure in worthwhile things, but just as often that pleasure can be vicious. There are friends in gardening but there are also friends in heroin consumption. In a similar manner, while we can use each other to win a baseball game, we can also use each other to perpetrate a stock swindle. Perfect friendship, this harder-to-explain friendship, always has a moral character. As we shall see, this will lead to some interesting educational conclusions:

> Perfect friendship is that friendship of men who are good, and alike in virtue; for these wish well alike to each other *qua* good, and they are good in themselves. Now those who wish well to their friends for their sake are most truly friends; for they do this by reason of their own nature and not incidentally; therefore their friendship lasts as long as they are good—and goodness is an enduring thing. And each is good without qualification and to his friend, for the good are both good without qualification and useful to each other. So too they are pleasant; for the good are pleasant both without qualification and are pleasurable, and the actions of the good *are* the same or like. And such a friendship is as might be expected permanent, since in it are all the qualities friends should have.[22]

To attempt to paraphrase Aristotle, perfect friendship is friendship realized or actualized. It is pleasurable and useful but, using the language we have adopted in this paper, it is an epiphenomenon of a specific kind of activity, that is, virtuous activity. When the virtuous are companions in virtuous activity, they may recognize each other in the example above, and become perfect friends.

This notion of perfect friendship only makes sense within the context of an ethical system, and a very well-developed one at that. In order for the virtuous to recognize each other *in* virtuous activity, they must have a clear understanding of what virtuous activity is. Aristotle attempted to delineate the field in the *Nichomachean Ethics* and he embedded that ethical theory in a logic, a physical theory, a metaphysical one, a religious theory, a political one and rhetorical one, and a theory of poetry. It goes without saying that the system he created is an astonishing one, but it also goes without saying that there are few practitioners of what might be called an Aristotelian world view around today. Certainly, among school people the number of Aristotelians must be small. In order to rescue Aristotle's notion of perfect friendship, we must first be able to decontextualize it from its Aristotelian setting, and then find a way to relate it to a different ethical system. We will do that through the notion of community of inquiry.

The discussion, especially in the United States, about community of inquiry invariably moves to things cognitive. Community of inquiry is an alternative to the banking model of education and where the latter focuses on the transmission of information, the former sets its sights on the development of understanding. In a most significant sense, community of inquiry is about the development of thinking and the skills attendant to thinking well. And this, it should be added, is, historically, that which has attracted school administrations to the program. Here, it was thought, and is thought, is a new way to get test scores on standardized tests improved.

It should be remembered that, according to the person who formulated the concept of the banking model, Paulo Freire, in addition to its cognitive assumption—that children are in school to receive information transmitted to them by experts—the banking model has a crucial ethical-political component: by turning students into passive receptacles, it makes them more compliant and more easily manipulated by a society that oppresses them. The banking model turns students into accomplices (with their oppressors) in their own oppression.[23]

Given the fact that the banking model has this ethical component, it is not surprising that community of inquiry has a similar one. What is surprising, however, is that so little has been made of this component. Philosophy is traditionally divided into three major areas: the good, the true, and the beautiful. To do philosophy, of necessity, is to be drawn inextricably into questions of values and invariably into the specific questions of value that are said to be ethical. Every text in Philosophy for Children, starting with Matthew Lipman's *Harry*

Stottlemeier's Discovery, and continuing with texts produced through-out the world, focus, at least in part, on ethical issues. From the open-ing chapters of *Harry Stottlemeier's Discovery*, when the issue of respect for authority is raised, children, both fictional and within ex-isting communities of inquiry, are presented with important ethical issues.

In *Lisa*, the second novel in the traditional corpus, Lipman turned his attention to ethics, and devoted a novel and its teacher's manual to that task. If *Harry Stottlemeier's Discovery* can be viewed as an equivalent to a freshman level introductory philosophy course—a course where the topics are introduced without the apparatus of a technical vocabulary that accompanies the freshmen level course—then *Lisa* could be viewed as an introduction to, say, a sophomore level ethics course, again, stripped of its forbidding terminology.

Philosophy for Children, then, has always treated the ethical as fertile ground, even when conservative groups within the United States have reacted negatively to any educational program that does any-thing other than reinforce values that are endorsed by those conserva-tive groups. If philosophy is for children, *too*—remember Helmut Schreier's problem with the preposition in Philosophy for Children—if it is not just a watered-down, oversimplified version of philosophy, it must expose children to the important issues of philosophy.

Moreover, it has not just been about inquiry *into* the ethical. It has, given that which occurs throughout *Lisa*, engaged in what might be called ethical inquiry. Fields or domains color the process of inquiry and add something specific to it. Every field may require imagination but the imagination required of the aesthetician might be markedly different from that required, say, in modal logic. Every field may value precision, but the way precision is enacted in eighteenth century Brit-ish Romantic poetry is different from the way it is played out in twen-tieth century chemistry.

Laurance Splitter and Ann Margaret Sharp, in *Teaching For Bet-ter Thinking*, do a fine job of classifying this notion of ethical inquiry. In the course of that clarification they make a suggestion about a community of ethical inquiry which, we will argue, has direct applica-tions to community of inquiry in general.

> Ethical inquiry, like inquiry generally, has both procedural and substantive components. When these dimensions work in harmony with one another, the classroom community, now functioning as a classroom community of ethical

inquiry, exemplifies 'a form of moral life': a lived experience in which children think, reason, imagine, reflect, judge, decide, care, and act. The procedures of ethical inquiry are among those which are enacted and valued by the community itself, with students paying particular attention to the interconnection between what they think, feel, say, and do. We find students:

* treating one another fairly, respectfully and with care.

* valuing good thinking and reasoning (examining value assumptions, exploring criteria for making value judgements, etc.).

* exercising 'moral imagination': by contemplating different ways of proceeding and representing alternative moral positions and points of view (the 'what if. . .?' strategy, which might even involve conjuring up alternative worlds which are more reasonable, less oppressive, and so on.).

* exploring the consequences of holding certain attitudes, beliefs and values, particularly with a view to avoiding inconsistencies.

* analyzing relationships between parts and wholes, and between means and ends, in an effort to see particular actions in the context of larger goals.

* empathizing with others with a view to following their reasoning and comprehending their perspectives.

* avoiding unwanted stereotypes by learning to generalize judiciously; becoming sensitive to a wide variety of specific value-laden contexts before they act or form a judgement.

* regarding their conclusive findings as tentative resting places, rather than final solutions.

* trying to take all relevant considerations into account before coming to a decision or making a judgement.

* being provoked, by a sense that all is not well with the world, to think and to act.[24]

Inquiry is provoked "by a sense that all is not well." That sense, most simply, causes one to think, to look for a solution to that which is experienced as problematic and/or to seek membership in communities with likeminded people, with those who are provoked in a similar way.

When we have that seeking of membership, we have the beginnings of what we call community of inquiry. Again, given the language that Splitter and Sharp adopt, the community of inquiry does not begin with the first Philosophy for Children session when the teacher explains what the "subject" is and has an initial reading of *Harry Stottlemeier's Discovery*. At that point, one simply has an aggregate of children brought together by some desire on the part of the classroom teacher. The community of inquiry begins when a sufficient number of children are provoked by the same problem and begin to use one another, begin to act in consort, to try to solve the problem.

We think of the community of inquiry as a cognitive creature, as a great problem-solving beast (although in our wiser moments, we realize that this is, after all, philosophy, and the chances of solution, historically, are quite small); we are aware of the many moods—joy, elation, despair—to which the beast is prey as it goes about attempting to problem-solve; and, as teachers, we are aware that the beast must be domesticated and that it must be taught rules of manners and etiquette or it will self-destruct. We forget or perhaps we just do not remind ourselves, often enough, that the beast is a moral creature—that "community of inquiry is a form of moral life."

What are the values that drive this thing called community of inquiry? What do we discover about the nature of shared inquiry within the community? Perhaps, first and foremost, is the realization that this is serious business. When we are engaged in philosophy with children, we become aware that these people are children, that they do want to have fun, that they do want to be entertained, and that their attention span may not be of great duration—in saying this, one is reminded how like adults children are—but until members achieve the seriousness of purpose that generates hard work, that makes us continue to try and solve the problem even when we become overwhelmed or just plain tired, it is difficult to say that a community of inquiry is in existence. We may play, and we may laugh, and we may fool with one another. But if that play ultimately is not about the serious business of making of meaning or discovering truth, we have not achieved a community of inquiry. We cannot be required to succeed, but we certainly must try, and try hard.

The second thing that becomes apparent is the belief that the community is after something more or greater than itself. Here, we call that something meaning or truth, and, of course we are on dangerous grounds with those terms. Each has a long, complex history, and the latter term is a lynchpin of sorts in the battle between modernism and postmodernism. Still what becomes apparent in the course of the hard work involved with community of inquiry is the realization that we are not here simply to give our opinions and to applaud each other on the clear expression of those opinions. We listen hard to each other; we test each other's opinion in the course of the dialogue, all with the intention of ending up with an idea that is, somehow, better, that will be worthy of our effort, and that will help us come closer to that elusive thing called a solution to our problem. We are not a therapeutic community or a self-help group, although as we have suggested, therapy and self-help may indeed be outcomes of our shared inquiry. We are a community of inquiry, and it does little harm, even given the complexity of the history of the terms, to suggest that we are looking for meaningful solutions, and/or truthful ones.

The third thing that forces itself on us is that if we are to succeed in this serious business of meaning-making and/or truth-discovery, we must depend on the other members of the community. Perhaps John Donne was wrong, and there are men (and women) who are islands, but when we enter the community of inquiry what we are doing is giving up our status, at least for a time, as isolated individuals. To enter the community of inquiry is to say, implicitly, that I will work with you to try to come up with a solution to our common problems. I will fit my actions to yours and if our inquiry is a success, we will arrive at a world that is just a bit more meaningful, just a little more truthful.

The way that we achieve this fit, this working together, involves all the rules that good teachers and mature communities can come up with—we must listen to each other, respect each other's opinion, take turns in talking, monitor our own behavior (am I talking too much, am I talking not enough), but all of these rules are hollow without the exercise of what Sharp and Splitter call "moral imagination."

That faculty, moral imagination, not only allows me to extend my beliefs and actions into the future, to see how they will function there, to see what their consequences are: it enables me, as much as possible to occupy the other person's perspective. Not surprisingly my companions in the community of inquiry can serve, and will serve when things are going well, as another self. Through occupying their positions and seeing things from their perspective, I am able not only to extend my own intellectual vision but also to correct the inherent limitations of that individual perspective.

There are of course many other factors that make up the moral life of the community of inquiry. While they vary from community to community in the way that they are instantiated, and while they are always open to review and revision—that willingness to review, and when necessary revise, is a hallmark of all communities of inquiry—they seem to spring up in all existing communities of inquiry. They include a desire to state one's beliefs as cogently and coherently as possible, a reverence for evidence within the decision-making process, and a willingness to change one's beliefs as the evidence suggests. We are inquiring together; we want to be successful in this inquiry; not only must we fit our actions and beliefs to the other, but those actions and beliefs must fit the evidence.

The list, however, must be incomplete because the community of inquiry itself is never complete. It exists as much in the future as it does in the past, projecting and remembering, seeking those solutions, those temporary resting places, those perchings, that allow it to continue to inquire. Those solutions will have an impact on the moral life of the community of inquiry, but what the precise impact will be, of course, is not known.

When one spends time in a community of inquiry, one realizes that it is an ongoing, developing moral life. Certainly, it is not as elegant, as vivid with categories and sub-categories as that sketched by Aristotle in *The Nichomachean Ethics*, but it is a moral universe, and it does provide the context for the sort of perfect friendship Aristotle had in mind—a friendship that would be useful and pleasurable to the partners but which would be, at heart, a friendship of virtuous individuals valuing the virtues that make up the friend. To return to Lewis, the virtuous friend within a community of inquiry loves his/her friend because the friend loves the same truth—the friend is serious about the enterprise, the friend understands that the enterprise is about truth and meaning, the friend works cooperatively within the community, and so on.

Moreover, although we have set our focus on community of inquiry within the school, community of inquiry is at least as old as western philosophy itself, and is probably more vibrant today than that very philosophy. Look at the characteristics of community of inquiry that we have had recourse to in this chapter and throughout the book, crunch those characteristics down to a single sentence—a community of inquiry involves a group of people using agreed-upon methods and techniques to solve some problem that is of interest to them—and one can see the incredible staying power and tenacity of this moral life called community of inquiry.

Certainly, Socrates is and must be the original proponent. Explicitly, he and his students fit all of the characteristics. But any time you had a school of philosophy, any time you had a group of people who were trying to figure out what was good and what was true and what was beautiful, you had people who were forming themselves into communities of inquiry. Those communities might reflect dominant intellectual personalities, as they did with Aristotle, or they might reflect dominant ideologies, as they did with medieval thinkers, who were trying to use the tools of community of inquiry to understand and explain that which was thought to be true (the truth of religion as specified in a holy book), but to the extent that they were philosophical, they always made use of the other as an essential part of the process of inquiry.

Even when one comes to that historical period when philosophy goes into a decline of sorts, and is replaced by science as the method of inquiry *par excellence*, even when we enter that period called "modern" and the stress is placed on the formation of a methodology that any individual, regardless of caste or class, regardless of gender, race, or age, can use, it is interesting how important the notion of community is, at least for reasons of validation, if not for discovery. Philip Guin shows how important the community is for modern science in his (Guin's) explication of Karl Popper's famous Robinson Crusoe example:

> Popper asks us to imagine Robinson Crusoe on his island, replete with scientific laboratories and astronomical instruments. Regardless of his friendship, regardless of how attentive and scrupulous he is in his investigations, Crusoe fails to convince us: There is an element of scientific method missing. . . . For there is nobody but himself to check his results; nobody but himself to correct those prejudices which are the unavoidable consequence of his peculiar mental history . . . what we call 'scientific objectivity' is not a product of the individual scientist's impartiality, but a product of the public or social character of scientific method; and the individual scientist's impartiality is, so far as it exists, not the source but rather the result of the socially or institutionally organized objectivity of science.[25]

If Popper is right, and scientific practice suggests that this towering figure of modernist philosophy of science is, then even modernism with its emphasis on methodology, when it comes to validation of scientific theory is thoroughly communal. One should also point out that an unvalidated scientific theory has, for scientists, all of the force, say, of a Mesopotamian myth of creation.

Finally, the modern-postmodern dispute itself might be viewed as a split between "warring" communities of inquiry with moderns putting their faith in discovery of truth and the uncovering of meaning in a methodology that is unencumbered by factors of culture and history while postmoderns argue that truth and meaning are always a function of culture and history. To unpack the dispute that way suggests that "truth" and "meaning" would have to be defined in some way other than as objective correlation between scientific theory and extra-theoretical facts (and that, of course, is a major sticking point in the dispute), but perhaps it also suggests a way that the dispute between modernism and postmodernism might be defused of some of its explosive force.

At any rate, the claim that we are making is that community of inquiry is not an historical curiosity, not just an idea Charles Sanders Peirce thought of that Matthew Lipman developed as a means of teaching philosophy to children. Rather, it is a characteristic of the historical process, has enormous staying power, and seems to occur whenever people are troubled by a problem within their experience. Historically, when this happens, they do seem to band together and work cooperatively, to solve that problem. Historically, they seem to form themselves into communities of inquiry. And, most importantly, for our purposes, those communities are forms of moral life.

Once again, those communities will not have the elegance and the completeness of what we might call an Aristotelian one. They will not have, while they are in existence as communities of inquiry, the formalized sets of beliefs, the creed that we tend to equate with other, better known moral communities, that is, those that have a religious base. However, what they will have, as we have pointed out, is a long and diverse track record, and if modern science is an example of community of inquiry, a rich history of success in prediction, explanation, and control.

In a period of diversity, a program that has not only a respect for diversity but demands it as a condition for successful inquiry, may provide a unifying device for which all cultures strive. If culture such as the Americans are to be coherent, they need a set of beliefs, values, aspirations—Dewey's likemindedness—to hold them together. Historically, religion, a Judeo-Christian culture of belief, has provided that likemindedness within the United States. To the extent that we are serious about our respect for diversity, to the extent that America becomes more Asian and more Buddhist and more Islamic and more secular, we will have to find other candidates for providing that cohesion. A culture of inquiry presents itself as one candidate.

But perhaps we became too grandiose. What of community of inquiry in the schools? What of the benefits and weaknesses? What recommends it to school people, and what may discourage them from taking it seriously? We can take a very narrow view of Philosophy for Children and say to school people: Surely, you can grant us two hours per week. In that time, we will do *Harry Stottlemeier's Discovery* three times per week with your students. The scores of those students on standardized tests such as the Iowa Test of Basic Skills will improve, your teachers will learn a host of methods and mechanisms they can use in other situations, and, we promise to tie in, whenever possible, instruction in other curriculum areas. We will help you do better those things you do already. Philosophy for Children will be the grease that makes the educational machine run more efficiently.

An argument just like that has been used quite effectively in the American experience, 1974 to the present. School administrations have traded space in the curriculum for a promise of improvement in test scores, and the test scores have improved when Philosophy for Children has been implemented on a regular basis. And when Philosophy for Children materials have been discarded, when they have been replaced by newer innovations, the training that the teachers have received, the manuals with which they have become familiar, continue to be felt in the classroom. Here a teacher uses a difference between degree and kind learned in a Philosophy for Children session to teach a math lesson. There a kindergarten teacher uses an exercise on similarity lifted from the manual that accompanies Lipman's *Elfie*, to teach his students about grouping. And here, a high school teacher gives her students, who are preparing for the SAT's, practice with the art of analytical reasoning that she was exposed to at a workshop in Mendham, New Jersey. Philosophy for Children has a tenacity to it that makes it linger in practice long after the initial publicity and attention has subsided. It does not hurt to remind ourselves how much good Philosophy for Children, even when construed narrowly, has done for children and for the classroom. It could, however, do so much more: imagine the replacement of the banking model with a community of inquiry one.

Writing always flattens experience, turning it into something neat and manageable. We are guilty of such a flattening when we have talked throughout this book as if there are two, and only two mutually exclusive models of the classroom: the banking model vs. the community of inquiry one. Classrooms are far more complex places than theories and models would suggest, and when we talk of models we really are talking about dominant trends or procedures in existing classrooms.

Having said that, however, it is not going too far to say that the banking model dominates much of the American school. The geography of the classroom may have changed dramatically over the past century: children no longer sit in desks that are nailed to the floor, and there is far more mobility of furniture and of children than there was at the start of the century, and, with improvements in technology, the geography of the classroom has as much to do with virtual walls of cyberspace as it does with a physical ones. Still, there is so much about schooling that is just about the transmission of information from expert to novice, so much that is simply an electronic version of the banking model, so much that encourages children to passively receive that which their elders take to be important.

Imagine, now a wider view. Imagine *Harry Stottlemeier's Discovery* or, with a nod to the Germans, some other Philosophy for Children novel or novels, written over the entire curriculum, some text that would lend coherence to our endeavors, that would serve as a springboard for our inquiry, but that would not be, simply, a disguised set of essential elements that children must come to know and to master.

And then imagine groups of children working, with a skilled and committed teacher, on that same text, burrowing deeper and deeper into the text, ferreting out meaning and truth from its hiding place. Most importantly, in the course of this imagining, notice how the community is formed, and how relationships among community members emerge. Those relationships are informal, not totally structured, and change, evolve, and grow as the inquiry proceeds. Students come to the community with their persona attached—here the straight "A" student, there the star athlete—but the old persona falls away as trust levels increase and as the demands of the inquiry increase. People begin to expose what they think, believe, and desire and a new (and shared) persona appears, that of the inquirer frustrated by her/his own ignorance, that of the person of intellectual curiosity, that of the scholar.

As they talk with one another, they experience periods of friction, times when they doubt the importance of what they are about, but as they continue, in this fictional community of inquiry, they develop patience with one another, patience with their own sometimes fumbling attempts at inquiry, and they develop the constancy of effort, the sheer intellectual and moral energy required to sustain a community of inquiry. They learn how to persevere.

Those children learn in Parekh's phrase "to rise above their narrow self-interest and establish non-calculative relationships with others." Indeed our imaginary community of interests fulfills all of the conditions of friendship that Parekh lists. Of course, we cannot guarantee that this mysterious thing called friendship will occur, this mysterious hitting it off that yields mutual respect and affection, this loving of similar things, but by creating the community of inquiry in which children are companions in inquiry, we can be said to be creating a set of enabling conditions. Rather than ignoring the experience of friendship as educative tool—as the banking model does—we are recognizing the aleatory quality of the relationship and are doing that which is in our power to nurture it. Moreover, the friendship relationship we are nurturing is, if not equivalent to, then analogous with Aristotle's notion of perfect friends. We create an environment in which children can become friends in virtue. Those virtues include respect for truth, respect for evidence, respect for other persons and so on. Those are not unworthy values and it is hard to see how school systems could be faulted for encouraging them.

Those of us who are engaged in intellectual life, who work in the disciplines within university settings, are fortunate. We have friends with whom we share the pleasures and the not infrequent benefits of scholarship. Those friends understand the value of the activity in which we are engaged, know how difficult it can be and, while serving as those Edmund Wilson-like intellectual consciences, they also provide the cognitive and emotional support to help us persevere. Those friends-in-virtue, those perfect friends, are the moral life of the disciplinary community (the community of philosophers, of scientists, of artists) instantiated: They say to us, when we are doing good work, continue on. And when our work is not so good, they help us to correct.

Philosophy for Children can do many fine things for children and for schools, but perhaps the finest thing it does is that it creates the conditions of morality and friendship within the classroom that, historically, have been the province of a few fortunate adults who have developed expertise in the disciplines. For many, if not most children, the chance at perfect friendship that Philosophy for Children offers may be their only opportunity. When they finish school, or when school is finished with them, they will go on to live the lives they lead, with little thought for the life of the mind, the activity of the disciplines, or things as seemingly esoteric as the modernism-postmodernism dispute. As we have suggested, however, all of that may have an impact on their lives. It would be a good thing if they had a few perfect friends to help them lead a moral life in the context of all of that uproar. It would be good if, when the seemingly eternal, but all too transitory school life was over, a few perfect friends remained.

Notes

1. Eliot Deutsch, "On Creative Friendship" in Leroy S. Roumer (ed.), *The Changing Face of Friendship*. (Notre Dame, Indiana: University of Notre Dame Press, 1994), p. 5.

2. C.S. Lewis, "Friendship-The Least Necessary Love," in Neera Kapur Badhar (ed.), *Friendship: A Philosophical Reader*. (Ithaca, New York: Cornell University Press, 1993), p. 42.

3. *Ibid.*, pp. 42–46.

4. *Ibid.*, p. 42.

5. *Ibid.*, p. 41.

6. *Ibid.*, p. 44.

7. *Ibid.*, p. 46.

8. Bhiku Parekh, "An Indian View of Friendship," in Leroy S. Roumer (ed.), *The Changing Face of Friendship*. (Notre Dame, Indiana: University of Notre Dame Press, 1994), p. 95.

9. *Ibid.*, p. 95.

10. *Ibid.*, p. 95.

11. *Ibid.*, p. 95.

12. *Ibid.*, p. 95.

13. *Ibid.*, p. 96.

14. *Ibid.*, p. 96.

15. *Ibid.*, p. 96.

16. *Ibid.*, p. 96.

17. The Aristotle biography, in an expanded form, appears in Ronald F. Reed and Tony W. Johnson (eds.), *Philosophical Documents In Education*. (New York: Longman, 1996), pp. 18–20.

18. Renford Bambrough, *The Philosophy of Aristotle*. (New York: New American Library, 1963), p. 11.

19. Aristotle, *Nichomachean Ethics*, in Richard McKeon (ed.), *The Basic Works of Aristotle*. (New York: Random House, 1968), pp. 1058–1059.

20. *Ibid.*, p. 1058.

21. *Ibid.*, p. 1060.

22. *Ibid.*, p. 1061.

23. Paulo Freire, *The Pedagogy of the Oppressed.* (New York: Harper Collins, 1972).

24. Laurance Splitter and Ann M. Sharp, *Teaching For Better Thinking.* (Melbourne, Australia: The Australian Council for Educational Research, 1995), p. 175.

25. *Ibid.*, p. 17.

Appendix A

Abbreviated Vitae*

Matthew Lipman—born 1923

Academic Background

Stanford University; Shrivenham American University, England; School of General Studies, Columbia University (B.A.,1948); Sorbonne; University of Vienna; Columbia University (Ph.D., 1953).

Teaching Experience

Brooklyn College; Columbia University; Mannes College of Music; City College of New York; Sarah Lawrence College; Montclair State University (1972–present).

Books

What Happens in Art (New York: Appleton-Century-Crofts, 1976).

Discovering Philosophy (1st edition, New York: Appleton-Century-Crofts, 1969; 2nd edition, Englewood Cliffs; Prentice-Hall, 1977).

Contemporary Aesthetics (Boston: Allyn and Bacon, 1973).

Harry Stottlemeier's Discovery (N.J.:IAPC, 1974).

Instructional Manual to Accompany Harry Stottlemeier's Discovery, with Ann Margaret Sharp (N.J.:IAPC, 1975) Second Edition: *Philosophical Inquiry*, with Ann Margaret Sharp and Frederick S. Oscanyan (N.J.:IAPC, 1979) co-published with University Press, 1985).

Lisa, (IAPC, 1976) 2nd Edition, IAPC, 1983.

*The focus is on academic lives as they relate to Philosophy for Children.

Ethical Inquiry, with Ann Margaret Sharp and Frederick S. Oscanyan (N.J.:IAPC, 1977) 2nd ed., IAPC and UPA, 1985.

Philosophy in the Classroom, with Ann Margaret Sharp and Frederick S. Oscanyan (1st edition, N.J.:IAPC,1977, 2nd edition, Philadelphia: Temple University Press, 1980).

Growing Up with Philosophy, ed. With Ann Margaret Sharp (Philadelphia: Temple University Press, 1978).

Mark (N.J.:IAPC,1980).

Writing: How and Why (instructional manual to accompany *Suki*: N.J.:IAPC,1980).

Suki (N.J.:IAPC,1978).

Social Inquiry (instructional manual to accompany *Mark*: N.J.:IAPC,1980).

Pixie (N.J.:IAPC, 1981).

Looking for Meaning (with Ann Margaret Sharp) (N.J.:IAPC,1982) UPA,1984.

Kio and Gus (N.J.:IAPC,1982).

Wondering at the World (with Ann Margaret Sharp) (N.J.:IAPC, 1984).

Philosophy for Children (edited with Terrell Ward Bynum) (Oxford:Basil Blackwell, 1976).

Discovering Philosophy, reprint of 1st edition (Lanham, Md.: University Press of America, 1984).

Elfie (N.J.:IAPC, 1987).

Harry Prime (N.J.:IAPC, 1987).

Philosophy Goes to School (Philadelphia: Temple University Press, 1988).

Getting our Thoughts Together, with Ann Gazzard (Upper Montclair, N.J.:IAPC, 1988).

Thinking in Education (Cambridge University Press, 1991) in press.

Ann Margaret Sharp—born 1942

Academic Background

College of New Rochelle, N.Y. (A.B., 1963); Catholic University of America, Washington D.C. (M.A., 1966); Union Theological Seminary, Richmond, VA; University of New Hampshire; University of Massachusetts, Amherst (Ph.D., 1973).

Teaching Experience

Fayetteville State College, N.C.; Virginia Union University; Notre Dame's College for Women, Manchester, N.H.; Iberoamericana University (1993–present); Montclair State University (1973–present).

Books

Philosophy in the Classroom (with Matthew Lipman and Frederick Oscanyan). 2nd edition. Philadelphia: Temple University press, 1978.

Growing Up with Philosophy (with Matthew Lipman) Philadelphia: Temple University press, 1977.

Philosophical Inquiry: Manual to Accompany Harry Stottlemeier's Discovery (with Matthew Lipman) (N.J.:IAPC, 1975).

Ethical Inquiry: Manual to Accompany Lisa (with Matthew Lipman) (New Jersey: IAPC, 1976. 2nd edition. IAPC and UPA, 1985).

Looking for Meaning: Manual to Accompany Pixie, (with Matthew Lipman) (N.J.:IAPC, 1982.UPA, 1984).

Wondering at the World: Manual to Accompany Kio and Gus (with Matthew Lipman) (N.J.:IAPC and UPA, 1986).

The Doll Hospital: A philosophical novel for early childhood. In press. Institute for the Advancement of Philosophy for Children.

Making Sense of Our World: Manual to Accompany The Doll House. In press. Institute for the Advancement of Philosophy for Children.

Studies in Philosophy for Children: Harry Stottlemeier's Discovery (with Ronald F. Reed), Philadelphia: Temple University Press, 1991.

Studies in Philosophy for Children: Pixie (with Ronald F. Reed), Madrid: De La Torre Press, 1996.

Women, Feminism, and Philosophy for Children (ed.) Special Issue of *Thinking: The Journal of Philosophy for Children*, Spring, 1994.

The Classroom Community of Inquiry (with Laurance J. Splitter). Melbourne, Australia, ACER, 1995.

Accepted for Publication
Educating for Global Consciousness (with Philip C. Guin). Accepted for publication by Praeger House, Connecticut, U.S.A.

Frederick Oscanyan—1934–1990

Academic Background
University of Virginia (B.A., 1957); Yale University (Ph.D., 1969).

Teaching Background
Yale, Berea College, KY. (1977–1990).

Books
Philosophical Inquiry, with Matthew Lipman and Ann Margaret Sharp. (N.J.:IPAC, 1976).

Ethical Inquiry, with Matthew Lipman and Ann Margaret Sharp (N.J.:IAPC, 1977).

Philosophy in the Classroom, with Matthew Lipman and Ann Margaret Sharp. (Philadelphia: Temple University Press, 1990).

Gareth B. Matthews—born 1929

Academic Background
Franklin College, IN (A.B.,1951); Middlebury German School; University of Tuebingen; Free University of Berlin; Harvard University (A.M., 1952; Ph.D., 1961).

Teaching Experience
University of Virginia; University of Minnesota; University of Massachusetts (1969–present).

Books

Philosophy and the Young Child, Cambridge, MA: Harvard, 1980.

Dialogues with Children, Cambridge, MA: Harvard, 1984.

Philosophy of Childhood, Cambridge, MA: Harvard, 1994.

Appendix B

Philosophy for Children

INTERNATIONAL CENTERS AND REPRESENTATIVES*

(All satellite centers in each country not included)

ARGENTINA

The Argentine Centers for Philosophy for Children

University of Buenos Aires
Puan 4703 Piso
1406 Buenos Aires
Argentina
Director: Walter Kohan

Director: Gloria Arbones
Casilla de Correo 103
1876 Bernal
Buenos Aires
Argentina

ARMENIA

The Armenian Center for Philosophy for Children
International Institute of Argumentation
Marshal Baghramen Ave. 24
375019 Yerevan, Armenia
Director: Prof. Lilit Brutian

*compiled by I.A.P.C. and published with its permission

AUSTRALIA

The Australian Center of Philosophy for Children
Australian Council for Educational Research
Private Bag 55
Camberwell, Victoria 3124
Australia
Director: Dr. Laurance Splitter

The Sarnnambool Center of Philosophy for Children
Deakin University
Warrnambool, Victoria 3280
Australia
Director: Clive Lindop

School of Philosophy
University of New South Wales
Kensington, New South Wales 2033
Australia
Director: Dr. Phil Cam

University of New South Wales
P.O. Box 1
Kensington, New South Wales 2033
Australia
Director: San McColl
Assoc.: Sandy Yule

REPRESENTATIVES

Megan Laverty
34 Vincent St.
Glen Iris, Victoria 3146
Australia

Sarah Redshaw
5 Winbourne Rd.
Hazelbrook
New South Wales 2779
Australia

Gilbert Burgh
University of Queensland
Philosophy Department
Queensland 4072
Australia

Chris DeHaan
Macquarie University
School of Philosophy
New South Wales 2109
Australia

Dr. Lyn English
Q.U.T.
Centre for Maths & Sciences
Locked Bag No. 2
Red Hill, Queensland 4059
Australia

Dr. Christina Slade
University of Canberra
P.O. Box 1
Belconnen ACT 2616
Australia

Tim Sprod

Tasmania
Felicity Haynes
The Western Australian Philosophy for Children Assoc.
University of Western Australia
Crawley WA 6009
Australia

AUSTRIA
Osterreichische Gesellschaft fur Kinderphilosophie
Schmiedgasse 12
8010 Graz
Austria

Director: Dr. Daniela Camby
Associates: Marguerite Wenzel &
Nora Hangel

BELGIUM

PHARE A.S.B.l.
E.I.I. Universite de Mons
Avenue du Champ de Mars
7000 Mons
Belgium
Director: Prof. Marie-Pierre Doutrelepont Grosjean

Director: Richard Anthone
Lange Kongostraat 54
2060 Antwerpen 6
Belgium
Associate: Freddy Mortier

BRAZIL

Centro Brasileiro de Filosofia para Criancas
Av. 9 de Julho 3166
Jd. Paulista 01406
Sao Paulo
Brazil
Director: Ms. Melanie Wyffels
Associates: Anna Louisa,
Sylvia Mendel,
Ana Luiza Fernandes &
Marcos Lorieri

Director: Prof. Peter Buttner
Rua 41 No 182 Vila Boa Esperanca
78100 Cuiaba MT
Brazil

Director: Maria Angelica Lucas Satiro
255 Santo Antonio Belo Horizonte
Minos Gerais CEP 30350-110
Brazil

REPRESENTATIVES

Nilson Santos
Caika Postal No. 775
Porto Velho Rondonia
CEP: 78900 Brazil

BRITISH COLUMBIA

Vancouver Institute of Philosophy for Children
607 W. 53rd Ave.
Vancouver, BC V6P 1K2
Canada
Director: Susan Gardner

BULGARIA

The Bulgarian Center for Philosophy for Children: Varna
Department of Philosophy
Varna Institute of Medicine
BG-9002
Varna, Bulgaria
Director: Prof. Alexander Stoichev
Associate: Rumiana _____

The Bulgarian Center for Philosophy for Children: Sofia
Faculty of Philosophy
University of Sofia
Bul. Tzar Osvobocitel 15
Sofia, Bulgaria
Director: Prof. Alexander Andonov

CATALONIA

The Institut de Recerca per l'Ensenyament de la Filosofia
Gran Via, 608, 8e D,08007
Barcelona
Catalonia, Spain
Directors: Ms. Eulalia Bosch &
Ms. Irene de Puig
Associate: Dr. Josep Maria Terricabras
University of Girona
Department of Philosophy

REPRESENTATIVES

Virginia Ferrer-Cervero
Dept. Didactira iOrg
Escolar/Fac Pedagogi
Universitat de Barcelona
Baldiri Reixac s/u Bloc D, 46
08028 Barcelona
Spain

Manuela Gomez
c/Canig 118, Pral 2a
08031 Barcelona
Spain

Antonio Llado
Sant Evesbz 57
Barcelona 08006
Spain

CHILE

Centro de Filosofia Escolar
Huelen 85, Dpto 4
Casilla 861
Santiago 21
Chile
Co-Directors: Prof. Mario Berrios &
Robert Simon

CZECH REPUBLIC

Lannova 10
CZ 370 01 Ceske Budejovice
Rep. Tcheque
Director: Stanislava Jindrova

FINLAND

The Center for Philosophy for Children
Department of Teacher Education
University of Oulu
Oulu, Finland
Director: Prof. Hannu Juuso

FLANDERS

Flemish Center of Philosophy for Children
Lange Kongostraat 54
Antwerpen, Belgium
Director: Richard Anthone
Associates: Freddy Mortier, University of Gent &
Jan van Gils, NDO Research Center

HUNGARY

The Center for the Advancement of Children's Critical Thinking
H. 11616 Budapest Rakoczi ut 30
Hungary
Director: Prof. Gyorgyl Tamassy
Associate: Prof. E. Kiss

ICELAND

The Iceland Center for Philosophy for Children
P.O. Box 1417
121 Reykjavic
Iceland
Director: Dr. Hreinn Palsson
Associate: Hranna Baldursson

ISRAEL

The Israel Center for Philosophy for Children
School of Education and
Department of Philosophy
University of Tel-Aviv
Israel
Director: Dr. Yael Tamir
Associates: Dr. Roni Aviram,
Talya Birkham, and
Samuel Scoinicov

ITALY

Centro Ricerca Per L'Insegnamento Filosofico
Via S. Francesco
46 87022 Cetraro
Italy
Director: Prof. Antonio Cosentino

Centro Interdisciplirare di Ricerca Educative Sul Pensiero
Via Carducci n. 8
45100 Rovigo
Italy
Director: Dr. Marina Santi

JAPAN

Fukui University
College of Education
9-1 Bunkyo 3-Chome
Fukui-Shi 910
Japan
Director: Prof. Ando

KENYA

The Department of Philosophy
Kenyatta University
P.O. Box 43844
Nairobi
Kenya
Director: Prof Ben K. Wambari

KOREA

The Korean Institute of Philosophy for Children
Kilbeon Building., Room 201
1685-32 Pong-Chon Dong
Kean Ak Ku Seoul, Korea
Director: Dr. Min Kyoo Park
Associates: Ji-Aeh Lee &
Yim Pyoung Kap

LITHUANIA

The Lithuania Center of Philosophy for Children
Basanavisius St. 18-57
Vilnius 2009
Lithuania
Director: Proj. Leonarda Jekentaite-Kuzmiokiene

MALTA

The Malta Institute for Philosophy for Children

Dar 1-Armonija
28, Pjazxza Robert Samut
Floriana
Malta
Director: Karl Borg

The Program for Doing Philosophy with Children
Faculty of Education University of Malta
Msida MSD 06
Malta
Director: Joseph Giordmania

MEXICO

Centro di Filosofia Para Ninos
Department of Philosophy
Universidad Iberoamericana
Prol. Paseo de la Reforma # 880
Lomas de Santa Fe
01210 D.F.
Mexico
Director: Teresa De La Garza

CELAFIN AC
AP46 Teopisca
29410 Chiapas
Mexico
Director: Eugenio Echeverria

Centro de Filosofia para Ninos de Guadalajara
Apartado Postal 31-432
Guadalajara Jal.
Mexico
Director: Monica Velasco

Pueblo Center of Philosophy for Children
KM 3.5 Carretera Federal
72430 CP Pueblo
Mexico
Director: Enrique Paniagua-Diaz

REPRESENTATIVES

Ma. Fernanda S. Coughlan
Paseo del Campestre #14
Col. Campestre La Rosita
Torrreon, Coah CP 27250
Mexico

NETHERLANDS

Centrum voor Kinderphilosophia
Faculteit der Wijsbegeerte
Universiteit van Amsterdam
Nieuwe Doelenstraat 15
1012 CP Amsterdam
Netherlands
Director: Karel van der Leeuw
Associates: Berrie Heesen &
Helene Van Aardensweg

NEW BRUNSWICK

Universite de Moncton
Department de Philosophie
Moncton, N.B.
Canada
Director: Arsene Richard

NIGERIA

Institute of Ecumenical Education
PO Box 302
Thinkers Corner, Enuga
Anhambra State
Nigeria
Director: Dr. Stan Anih

PHILIPPINES

Department of Philosophy
University of Philippines-Diliman
Quezon City
Metro ManilaPhilippines 1101
Director: Dr. Zosimo Lee
Associate: Dr. John Holder

St. Norbert College
DePere, WI 54114

POLAND

Polish Academy of Sciences
Institute of Philosophy and Sociology
00-330 Warszawa
Nowy Swiat 72
Poland
Director: Dr. Robert Pilat
Associates: Baeta Elwich &
Anna Zagodzka

PORTUGAL

Centro Portugues de Filosofia para Criancas
Sociedade Portuguesa de Filosofia
Av. da Republica 37-4
1000 Lisboa
Portugal
Director: ZaZa Carneiro de Moura

MENON

Av. Poeta Mistral, 6,5 E
1000 Lisboa
Portugal
Director: ZaZa Carneiro de Mours

REPRESENTATIVE

Dina Mendoncza

QUEBEC

Department d'education Physique
University of Montreal
C.P. 6128, Succursale A
Montreal, Quebec
H3C 3J7
Canada
Director: Marie-France Daniel
Associate: Louise Lafortune

Association Quebecoise de Philosophie pour Enfants
University du Quebec a Montreat
CIRADE WB-220, Case Postal 8888
Succursale Centre-Ville
Montreal, Quebec
H3C 3P8
Canada
Director: Pieree LeBuis
Associate: Anita Caron

Philosophie pour les Enfants
Faculte de Philosophie
Universite Laval
Sainte-Foy, Quebec
G1K 7P4
Canada
Director: Michael Sasseville
Associate: Sophie Bouchard
Proj. Victor Thibaudeau &
Prof. Marcel Savard

Director J.A. Kyle
258 Prince Albert No. 2
Montreal, Quebec H3Z 2N6
Canada

Universite du Quebec Montreal
Department des Sciences Religieuses
Case Postale 8888
Succursale A Montreal
Quebec H3C 3P8
Canada

REPRESENTATIVE

Marie Bolduc
210 Rue Berri #4
HULL
Quebec J87 4J9
Canada

REPUBLIC OF CHINA

Caterpillar
Basement Floor #17
Ho-ping East Rd.
Sec. 2 Lane 265
Taipei
Taiwan
Director: Peter Yang
Associates: Chen Hong Min, Director of Research Center
Hong Pin Lee, Director of Teacher Education
Chow Jing Chung, Director of Publications

ROMANIA

CEDC-Central pentru Educaie si Dezvoltarea Cereativitatii
P.O. Box 2-36
78500 Bucharest
Romania
Director: Ms. Doina-Olga Stefanescu
Associates: Mihaela Miroiu &
Stefania Popp

RUSSIA

International College of Education and Psychology
Mockovaja Str. 9, "B"
Moscow 103009
Russia
Director: Arkady Margolis
Associate: Dr. Sergei Kovalev

Institute of Philosophy
Academy of Science
Volkhonka 14
Moscow 119842
Russia
Director: Proj. Nina Yulina

Ural State University
Department of Psychology and Pedagogy
620083 Ekaterinburg
Lenin Avenue 51

Russia
Director: Margarita Dudina

SINGAPORE

National Institute of Education
Nanyang Technological University
469 Bukit Timak Rd.
Singapore 1025
Director: Dr. Tock Keng Lim

SLOVAKIA

Slovenske Stredisko Filozofie pre deti
Pedagogieke Fakulta UK, Bratisiava
Comenius University
Moskovaska 3
CS-813 34 Bratislava
Slovakia
Director: Alexander Kover

SOUTH AFRICA

Program for Career Education
Faculty of Education
University of Stellenbosch
Stellenbosch 7600
(Private Bag X5018)
South Africa
Director: Prof. Willie Rautenbach

SPAIN

Centro de Filosofia para Ninos
Fernan Gonzales 23, 2-A
28009 Madrid
Spain
Director: Dr. Felix Garcia Moriyon
Associates: Juan CArlos Lago Bornstein &
Tom Lardner

Centro de Folosofia para Ninos
Ferna Gonzalez 23, 20-A
28009 Madrid, Spain
Director: Jose M. Calvo

Catedretica de Etica y Filosofia Politica
Universidad de Valencia
Facltad de Filosofia
Director: Prof. Adela Cortina

SWEDEN

Department of Philosophy
Stockholm University
S-106 91 Stockholm
Sweden
Director: Ragnar Ohlsson
Associates: Rune Jonsson &
Bosse Malmhester

UNITED KINGDOM

Dowrich House (West Wing)
Nr Sandford
Credition
Devon
EX17 4EQ
United Kingdom
Director: Will Robinson

SAPERE-Society for the Advancement of Philosophical Enquiry
and Reflection in Education
Stammerham North
Christ's Hospital
Harsham, W. Sussex RH13 7NF
England
Director: Roger Sutcliffe
Associates: Robert Fisher,
Karen Murris &
Judith Hughes

URUGUAY

Children's Philosophical Center
Hooquart 1470
C.P. 11.800 Montevideo
Uruguay
Directors: Mabel Quintela &
Ms. Marisa Bertolini

ZIMBABWE

Educational Foundations Department
P.O. Box MP 167
Mount Pleasant Harare
Zimbabwe
Director: Norman Atkinson
Associates: Proj. Josephine Zesaguli &
Ken Down

CENTERS INFORMATION

NEW ZEALAND
IRELAND
FRANCE
TURKEY

Subject Index

Name Index

Rethinking Childhood

JOE L. KINCHELOE & JANICE A. JIPSON

General Editors

A revolution is occurring regarding the study of childhood. Traditional notions of child development are under attack, as are the methods by which children are studied. At the same time, the nature of childhood itself is changing as children gain access to information once reserved for adults only. Technological innovations, media, and electronic information have narrowed the distinction between adults and children, forcing educators to rethink the world of schooling in this new context.

This series of textbooks and monographs encourages scholarship in all of these areas, eliciting critical investigations in developmental psychology, early childhood education, multicultural education and cultural studies of childhood.

Proposals and manuscripts may be sent to the general editors:

Joe L. Kincheloe
637 W. Foster Avenue
State College, PA 16801

or

Janice A. Jipson
219 Pease Court
Janesville, WI 53545